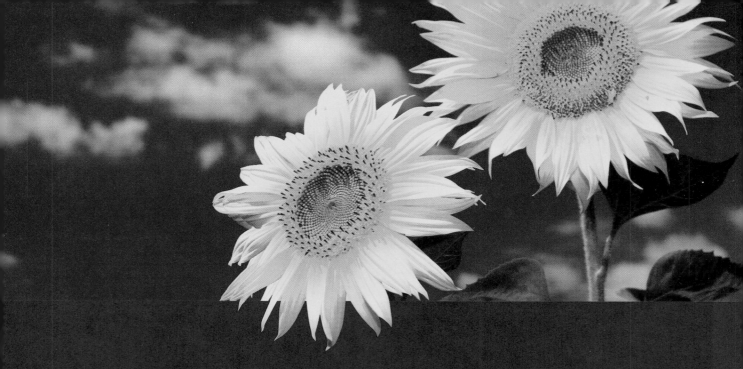

Developmental Profiles

Developmental Profiles
Pre-birth through Adolescence

7TH EDITION

Lynn R. Marotz, RN, Ph.D
University of Kansas

K. Eileen Allen
Professor Emerita
University of Kansas

WADSWORTH
CENGAGE Learning

WADSWORTH
CENGAGE Learning

Developmental Profiles: Pre-Birth through Adolescence, Seventh Edition
Lynn R. Marotz and K. Eileen Allen

Senior Publisher: Linda Schreiber-Ganster

Executive Editor: Mark Kerr

Managing Development Editor: Lisa Mafrici

Assistant Editor: Joshua Taylor

Editorial Assistant: Greta Lindquist

Media Editor: Elizabeth Momb

Marketing Manager: Kara Kindstrom Parsons

Marketing Coordinator: Klaira Markenzon

Senior Marketing Communication Manager: Heather Baxley

Manufacturing Director: Marcia Locke

Manufacturing Planner: Rebecca Cross

Content Project Management: PreMedia-Global

Senior Art Director: Jennifer Wahi

Rights Acquisitions Specialist Text & Images: Dean Dauphinais

Cover Designer: Lisa Langhoff

Cover photo credit: US Image from Shutterstock

Compositor: PreMediaGlobal

For product information and technology assistance, contact us at **Cengage Learning Customer & Sales Support, 1-800-354-9706**

For permission to use material from this text or product, submit all requests online at **cengage.com/permissions**
Further permissions questions can be emailed to **permissionrequest@cengage.com**

Library of Congress Control Number: 2011934451

ISBN-13: 978-1-111-83095-3

ISBN-10: 1-111-83095-9

Wadsworth
20 Davis Drive
Belmont, CA 94002-3098
USA

Cengage Learning is a leading provider of customized learning solutions with office locations around the globe, including Singapore, the United Kingdom, Australia, Mexico, Brazil and Japan. Locate your local office at: **www.cengage.com/global.**

Cengage Learning products are represented in Canada by Nelson Education, Ltd.

For your course and learning solutions, visit **www.cengage.com.**

Purchase any of our products at your local college store or at our preferred online store **www.cengagebrain.com.**

Printed in the United States of America
1 2 3 4 5 6 7 15 14 13 12 11

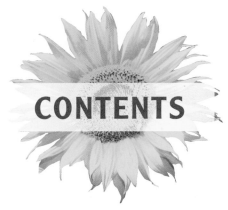

CONTENTS

CHAPTER 3   Prenatal Development   47

CHAPTER 4   Infancy: Birth to Twelve Months   69

CHAPTER 5   Toddlerhood: Twelve to Twenty-four Months   105

PREFACE

Architectural engineers know that a structurally sound building requires a strong foundation. Similarly, children require a strong foundation if they are to develop to their fullest potential. The quality of children's environments, early learning opportunities, and adult support and encouragement plays an influential role in shaping the groundwork upon which all future skill acquisition is built. When adults understand children's developmental needs, capabilities, and limitations they are able to provide effective behavioral guidance and the types of learning experiences that ultimately create a strong foundation.

Developmental Profiles: Pre-birth through Adolescence is designed to be a concise, user-friendly resource for teachers, families, caregivers, practitioners, and service providers. While the seventh edition has been revised and updated, it maintains the authors' original purpose to provide a comprehensive yet nontechnical, easy-to-follow overview of children's development. It links contemporary research, theory, and application to the guidance of children's behavior and the promotion of developmentally appropriate learning experiences.

Purpose and Philosophical Approach

The common practice of dividing infancy and childhood into age-related units of months and years can appear to distort the realities of human development. However, when describing developmental expectations, developmental progress, and delays, other systems seem to work even less well. Let it be stressed here, as it is again and again throughout the text, that age specifications are only approximate markers derived from *averages* or *norms*. In a way, they can be thought of as midpoints not intended to represent any one particular child. Rather, age expectations represent summary terms for skills that vary from child to child in form and time of acquisition. The truly important consideration in assessing a child's development is *sequence*. The essential question is not chronological age but whether the child is moving forward step by step in each developmental area. *Developmental Profiles* has long proven itself to be an invaluable resource in addressing this issue.

As in the previous editions, the early days, weeks, and months of infancy are examined in great detail. New research findings on brain and early development clearly

support the critical importance of this relatively short time span. What is now known about the infant's capacity for learning is indeed amazing given conventional wisdom, which suggests that young babies simply flounder around in a state of confusion. Far from it! With more and more infants entering programs at ever earlier ages, it is most important that teachers are knowledgeable about their development and ability to learn. It is also crucial that families and service providers hold appropriate expectations and be able to describe to teachers what they want and believe is best for infants.

The first year of life is essential for building a foundation of learning in every developmental domain. The vast array of new and complex behaviors that toddlers and preschoolers must learn in three or four short years is also monumental. At no other period in a person's lifetime will so much be expected in so short a time. With other-than-parent child care being the norm rather than the exception, it is necessary for teachers and families to have a thorough understanding of how young children grow, develop, and learn. Thus, an underlying philosophy of *Developmental Profiles* continues to be partnerships with families. No matter how many hours children spend with caregivers or teachers in school each day, families still play the most significant and influential role in their lives. They must be supported and encouraged to share their observations and concerns with teachers because this information is integral to each child's development and well-being. In turn, teachers and service providers must listen to families with focused attention and respond with genuine interest and respect.

Partnerships with families become even more critical when an infant or older child is suspected of having a developmental problem or irregularity. The Developmental Alerts identified for each age group can be especially useful to families, teachers, and service providers for initiating a discussion about their concerns. Let it be emphasized, however, that under no circumstances should this book or any other book be seen as an instrument for diagnosing a developmental problem. That is the job of professional clinicians and child development specialists.

Thus, the stated purposes of this text can be summed up as follows:

- To provide a concise overview of developmental principles.
- To provide easily accessible information about what to expect at each developmental level.
- To suggest appropriate ways for adults to facilitate learning and development.
- To pinpoint warning signs of a possible developmental problem.
- To suggest how and where to get help.
- To describe cultural and environmental diversity in terms of its impact on the developmental process.
- To emphasize the value of direct observation of children in their natural settings, whether in a classroom, early childhood program, or the child's own home.
- To help adults encourage every child to achieve his or her potential, develop a positive sense of self-esteem, and feel loved and respected.

The Intended Audience

Teachers—caregivers, families, and professionals—play an essential role in guiding children's development. For it is through their ability to foster learning and self-esteem and identify challenges that interfere with developmental progress that adults can ultimately make a difference in children's lives. Thus, *Developmental Profiles* is designed for adults who care for and work with children of all ages, including:

- Students and preservice teachers.

- Teachers in home-based settings, early childhood centers, Head Start programs, schools, before- and after-school programs, home visitors, and nonparental caregivers in the child's home.

- Allied health professionals and service providers in nursing, nutrition, audiology, social work, physical and occupational therapy, psychology, medicine, language and speech therapy, and counseling who provide services for children and their families.

- Families, the most important contributors to a child's optimum development.

Organization and Key Content

Developmental Profiles opens with a brief overview of major child development theories and principles. These chapters (1 and 2) serve as a refresher of basic concepts and provide background material on age-level expectancies for the chapters that follow. Chapter 3 is devoted to maternal practices that are essential for promoting healthy fetal development. Detailed word pictures of child and adolescent development across six developmental domains, including typical daily routines, safety alerts, developmental alerts, learning activities, and positive behavioral guidance are described in Chapters 4 through 9. When and where to seek help if there are concerns about a child's developmental progress is discussed in Chapter 10. Developmental checklists and additional resource material of interest to families, teachers, and service providers are provided in the appendixes. We believe this format encourages vigilance in identifying delays in their earliest stage and supports adults in creating developmentally appropriate learning opportunities for children of all ages.

  Developmental Profiles provides nontechnical, key information about:

- What to expect of young children and adolescents at each succeeding developmental stage.

- The ways in which all areas of development are intertwined and mutually supportive.

- The unique pathway that each child follows in a developmental process that is alike, yet different, among children of similar age.

- Sequences, not age, being the critical concept in evaluating developmental progress.

- The use of developmental norms in teaching, observing, and assessing children and in designing individualized as well as group learning experiences.

 New Content and Special Features

The seventh edition of *Developmental Profiles* continues to bring readers important content features that support understanding and practice in an easy-to-reference format:

- *New* **National Association for the Education of Young Children Professional Preparation Standards (NAEYC)** are identified at the beginning of each chapter to show readers how the content supports learning and prepares teachers for a professional role. A detailed NAEYC Standards Correlation Chart is also provided on the book's inside covers.

- **Learning Objectives** are located at the beginning of each chapter to draw the reader's attention to key points and concepts.

- *New* **chapter on** *Adolescence: Thirteen- to Nineteen-Year-Olds.* Adolescent development is addressed in a new chapter (Chapter 9) and extends the age range previously covered in *Developmental Profiles*. Adolescence has long been viewed as simply the refinement and conclusion of major developmental changes. However, recent discoveries have drawn attention to the increased importance of this developmental stage.

- *New and expanded* **information on current topics** such as brain development, children and technology, cultural awareness, gender issues, observational skills, and strategies for supporting children's transitions has been incorporated throughout the book.

- **Concise developmental profiles** highlight children's sequential progress across six developmental domains from pre-birth to age nineteen.

- **Case Studies** presented at the onset of each chapter set the stage for content that follows and encourage readers to relate what they learn to real life situations.

- *New and updated* **TeachSource Video Connections**, a technology feature, are included in each chapter to illustrate important developmental concepts. Thought-provoking questions provide opportunities for reflection, application, and professional development.

- **Developmental Alerts** are highlighted at each age level to aid in the early identification of potential delays and/or developmental problems that warrant further evaluation.

- **Daily Activities and Routines** typical at each age level are offered in each chapter to help families and teachers anticipate and respond appropriately to children's developmental needs.

- *New* **Positive Behavior Guidance sections** included in each chapter offer strategies for responding to children's behavior and promoting healthy social and emotional development.

- **Learning Activities** sections include suggestions for developmentally appropriate learning experiences that teachers and families can use to encourage children's curiosity, creativity, and problem-solving abilities.

- **Safety Alerts** reflect special safety concerns associated with each developmental stage and are designed to help adults create safe environments, maintain quality supervision, and support children's safety education.

- **Developmental Checklists** for each age group serve as an initial screening tool that teachers and parents can use to assess children's developmental progress (Appendix A).

- **Screening and Assessment Instruments** commonly utilized for evaluating infants, young children, and adolescents are identified and described in an annotated listing (Appendix B).

- **Resources** to help families and professionals locate technical assistance and additional reference information are included at the end of each chapter and in Appendix C.

Ancillaries

Education CourseMate

Cengage Learning's Education CourseMate brings course concepts to life with interactive learning, study, and test preparation tools that support the printed textbook.

- *For students*: a variety of enrichment resources and study tools such as web links, practice quizzes, chapter objectives, references, videos, and printable forms and charts can be accessed through www.cengagebrain.com.

- *For instructors*: the accompanying website offers access to password-protected resources such as an electronic version of the instructor's manual and PowerPoint® slides. Instructors can access this site by visiting http://login.cengage.com.

Instructor's Manual and Test Bank

The Instructor's Manual that accompanies the seventh edition includes answers to the developmental sketch application and review questions located in each chapter. Ideas for developing tests or guiding class discussions are provided, along with support for integrating the new TeachSource Videos with discussion questions that allow instructors to expand on important topics. For assessment support, the updated Test Bank contains an extensive collection of multiple choice, short answer, matching, and essay questions for each book chapter.

ExamView

Available for download from the instructor website, ExamView® testing software includes all items from the Test Bank, enabling you to create customized tests in print or online.

WebTutor™ for WebCT and Blackboard

Jumpstart your course with customizable, rich, text-specific content within your Course Management System. Whether you want to Web-enable your class or put an entire course online, WebTutor™ delivers. WebTutor™ offers a wide array of resources including media assets, access to the eBook, quizzes, web links, exercises, and more.

Acknowledgments

First and foremost, we wish to recognize Wadsworth Cengage Learning for their long-standing commitment to education. Their vision and dedication have contributed to an improved understanding of children and families and continue to support teachers in their efforts to help children develop to their fullest potential.

The preparation of this seventh edition reflects the collaborative efforts of many individuals. We welcome Mark Kerr, Executive Editor, on board and sincerely appreciate his foresight and support in expanding this edition to include adolescents. We are grateful to Lisa Mafrici, our development editor, who provided invaluable guidance, knowledge, and inspiration. Her exceptional feedback, suggestions, and editing were instrumental in producing an edition that we believe is much improved. There are also many behind-the-scenes individuals who we would like to personally thank for their innumerable contributions – the editorial, design, production, and marketing staff – for it is their tireless dedication that makes our books a success.

We are also grateful to our reviewers and want to express our sincere appreciation for their insightful critiques, suggestions, and ability to help us see issues from multiple perspectives. They include:

- Denise Collins, University of Texas at Arlington
- Ralph Worthing, Delta College
- Deb Farrer, California University of PA
- Genny Hay, College of Charleston
- Diane Gomez, Manhattanville College
- Jackie Allen, University of La Verne

Finally, we would like to thank our readers for their dedication and commitment to improving the quality of life for children and families everywhere.

About the Authors

Lynn R. Marotz is a member of the Department of Applied Behavioral Sciences faculty and serves as the Associate Director of the Edna A. Hill Child Development Center at the University of Kansas. She brings her nursing background, academic training, and years of experience working with children and families to the education field. Her primary interests include teacher training and administration, policy development, parent education, early identification and intervention, and the promotion of children's wellness. She teaches undergraduate and graduate courses in child development, parenting, administration, health, and nutrition. She has had extensive involvement in state policy development, health screenings, professional development training, working with families and allied health professionals, and the referral process. She has made numerous professional presentations at state, national, and international conferences and has authored many publications on children's health, environmental safety, and nutrition. In addition, she also serves on a number of state and local advisory boards.

K. Eileen Allen, professor emerita, was a member of the Early Childhood faculty at the University of Washington in Seattle and at the University of Kansas in Lawrence. For thirty-one years she taught graduate and undergraduate courses in child development, developmental disabilities in young children, parenting, early education, and an interdisciplinary approach to early intervention and inclusion. She also trained teachers and supervised research-focused classrooms at both schools and has published seven college textbooks as well as numerous research articles and position papers in major professional journals. During her retirement, she continues to write, jury research articles, consult in both the private and public sector, and actively advocate on behalf of children and families. Her most recent book is entitled, *I Like Being Old: A Guide to Making the Most of Aging.*

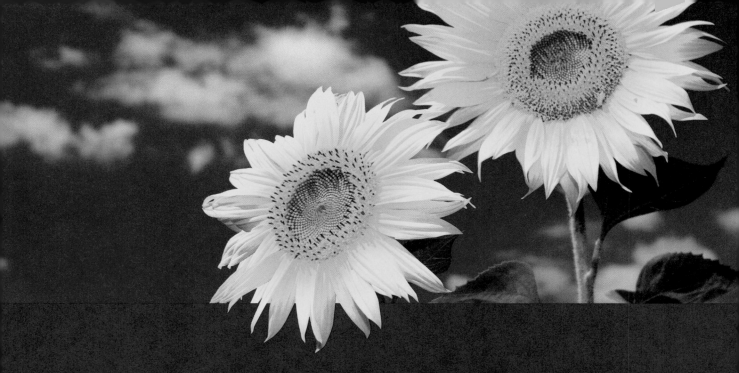

Developmental Profiles

CHAPTER 1
Child Development Theories and Data Gathering

Learning Objectives

After reading this chapter, you should be able to:

- Understand and explain each of the fundamental contemporary theories of child development.
- Understand the importance of data gathering and explain why authentic assessment is the most developmentally appropriate approach for evaluating young children.
- Describe several methods for gathering observational data about children.

naeyc Standards Chapter Links:

1a and 1b: Promoting child development and learning
2a: Building family and community relationships
3c: Observing, documenting, and assessing to support young children and families

Meet Four-Year-Old Jamal

Jamal was an undernourished and severely neglected nine-month-old when first placed in foster care. As a four-year-old, he is now in his fifth foster home, where he has been for almost a year. His foster parents, Berta and Doug Clay, have two little girls, ages four and six, of their own and three other foster children ranging in age from four to nine years. All of the children are vigorous and outgoing except for Jamal, who seems to tire easily. Berta took him in early for his well-child checkup because she was concerned. When Jamal was weighed and measured, he was only in the 30th percentile for height and weight, despite the fact that he eats far more than the other children.

continued...

Berta and Doug have also noted that Jamal rarely plays with the other children and seldom converses with anyone. However, they have overheard him holding lengthy and comprehensible conversations between himself and an imaginary friend, Honey, at times when he thinks he is alone. The talk is usually about things he fears, possibly the root of recurring bad dreams from which he often wakes up screaming. Yet, despite his problems, Jamal is a kind and lovable child. He seizes any opportunity to curl up in Berta's or Doug's lap, suck his thumb, and snuggle his free hand into one of theirs. The Clays have come to love Jamal as one of their own despite his developmental challenges, and are currently in the process of formalizing his adoption.

Ask Yourself

1. As foster parents, which essential physical needs are Berta and Doug presumably providing for Jamal?
2. What are some of Jamal's fundamental psychological needs, and how are his foster parents attempting to meet them?

Child development has been a major research focus of psychology for decades (Figure 1-1). Throughout the years, theorists have studied children and offered their viewpoints on everything from growth to behavior. In some instances, their explanations are consistent, whereas on other points there is considerable disagreement. For example, Arnold Gesell thought that all learning is determined by a biological readiness, while Jean Piaget believed that it is due to a combination of genetic and environmental factors.

At first glance, these multiple theoretical frameworks for understanding children's growth and development may appear confusing and in conflict with one another. However, it is unlikely that any one theory adequately explains the complexity of children's behavior. Each offers a somewhat different interpretation of the conditions that shape development and encourages us to consider behavior from multiple perspectives. It should also be remembered that theories reflect the ideas and conditions accepted at a given point in time. As new research is conducted, existing ideas are often revisited and modified. Thus, as societies change, so too will ideas about children's behavior and development.

Contemporary Theories

Interest in studying children's behavior peaked during the twentieth century, when many influential theories were developed. Early studies were based primarily on researchers' observations and personal interpretations. As a result, subsequent studies often contradicted or rejected previous conclusions. However, each theory has

Figure 1-1
Children's development has been the subject of study for many decades.

furthered our understanding of children's cognitive, socioemotional, and biological development.

A long-standing controversy in the field has centered on whether heredity or environment is responsible for children's development. This argument is commonly referred to as the **nature vs. nurture** controversy (Sameroff, 2010). Recent brain imaging studies have confirmed that development is no either/or process. Rather, scientists have demonstrated that learning causes actual changes in the brain's physical composition. These changes are dependent on the complex interactions of genetics (brain cells, an intact neurological system) and learning opportunities in the child's environment.

Much of our current knowledge about how children learn, grow, and mature is derived from several long-standing theories: maturational; psychoanalytic and psychosocial; cognitive-developmental; behaviorism and social learning; bioecological; and essential needs.

Maturational Theory

Maturational theory focuses on a biological or *nature* approach to human development. It explains all behavior in terms of genetics and biological changes that occur as a person ages. For example, maturational theory would argue that an infant learns to walk only when his or her neurological system has matured sufficiently to permit this activity, regardless of any other factors.

---

nature vs. nurture—refers to whether development is primarily due to biological–genetic forces (heredity–nature) or to external forces (environment–nurture).

Figure 1-2
Gesell described children's
development in terms of
biological maturation.

Arnold Gesell's historical work is still significant in this area of developmental research. He believed that all development is governed primarily by internal forces of biologic and genetic origin (Dalton, 2005; Gesell & Ilg, 1949) (Figure 1-2). This led to his notable work in which he described children's achievements by age and explained it in ways that parents could understand and use.

Few scientists would disagree that genetics exert a strong influence on human development and, in some cases, even a limiting effect. For example, a child's height, eye color, shoe size, and other distinguishing features are the direct result of genes inherited from his or her biological parents. Chromosomal abnormalities that cause Down syndrome or congenital deafness are also inherited and likely to result in lifelong learning and physical disabilities. Researchers are also looking at possible links between genetics and personality traits such as shyness, aggressiveness, and predisposition to certain mental health problems (Ebstein et al., 2010; Rueda & Rothbart, 2009). Although the genetic contribution to human development is well understood, most experts do not accept it as solely responsible for all human behavior.

Gesell's contributions continue to apply and serve a functional purpose. His observations have been translated into **norms**, or benchmarks, that have proven useful for assessing and monitoring children's developmental skills and progress. Although his original conclusions were based on observations of middle-class, Caucasian children, scientists have updated the standards to more accurately reflect today's diverse population.

---

norms—age-level expectancies associated with the achievement of developmental skills.

Psychoanalytic and Psychosocial Theory

Psychoanalytic and psychosocial theory postulates that much of human behavior is governed by unconscious processes, some of which are present at birth, while others develop over time. Sigmund Freud is the acknowledged originator of psychoanalytic theory. He believed that children's behavior is a reflection of their inner thoughts and conflicts, which vary according to stages. The way in which these emotional problems are resolved gradually forms the child's basic personality, especially during the first five years of life.

Psychosocial theory is based on the work of Erik Erikson, who expanded on Freud's ideas about personality development. He, too, believed that each developmental stage is characterized by certain conflicts that must be resolved. After a successful resolution has been achieved, a person is then motivated to undertake the next challenge.

However, unlike Freud, Erikson's theory acknowledges the influence of environment and social interactions. He coined the term *ego identity* to describe a person's conscious awareness of self (who I am in relation to others) and the lifelong changes that occur as a result of social interactions. Erikson was also the first to describe development across the life span by introducing his eight universal stages of human development (Erikson, 1950). The first four stages address the early years; the remaining four cover the span from adolescence to the later years:

- **Trust vs. mistrust (0–12 months)** Establishing a sense of trust with caregivers
- **Autonomy vs. shame and doubt (1–3 years)** Learning to gain control over some behaviors (e.g., eating, toileting, sleeping) and developing a sense of autonomy or independence
- **Initiative vs. guilt (3–5 years)** Using social interaction to gain control over one's everyday world
- **Industry vs. inferiority (6–12 years)** Developing a sense of competence and pride through successful accomplishments
- **Identity vs. confusion (13–20 years)** Learning about self in relationship to others
- **Intimacy vs. isolation (20–35 years)** Exploring and forming intimate relationships
- **Generativity vs. stagnation (35–55 years)** Focusing on family, career, and ways of contributing to society
- **Integrity vs. despair (60s–death)** Reflecting on one's life and forming a sense of satisfaction or dissatisfaction

Psychoanalytic and psychosocial theories have contributed to our understanding of personality and socioemotional skills and their influence on all aspects of children's development. They have also helped us to better understand the universal challenges children face at each stage and how to create environments that support children's social and emotional needs along a developmental continuum. Although these theories are not as popular as they once were, they continue to foster research in areas such as caregiver consistency, attachment, morality, and sibling relationships.

Figure 1-3
Piaget believed that
children learn best through
exploration.

Cognitive-Developmental Theory

Cognitive-developmental theory is attributed to Piaget, who theorized that children construct knowledge and form meaning through active exploration of their environment (Figure 1-3). The term **constructivism** is often used today in reference to this style of learning. According to Piaget, children progress through four major stages of intellectual development, beginning in infancy and continuing into the late teens (Piaget, 1954):

- **Sensorimotor (birth–2 years)** Reflexive behavior gives way to intentional behavior; children use their senses to discover the world around them. Example: The child sees an object and reaches for it.

- **Preoperational (2–7 years)** Children begin thinking in symbols about things in their immediate environment. Example: The three-year-old picks up a long stick and calls it a fishing pole. This illustration also shows a second aspect of the preoperational stage (the emergence of language), which is another form of symbolic usage.

- **Concrete operational (7–11 years)** Children are now developing the ability to comprehend and formulate ideas about their immediate world. They are learning to think logically, to anticipate outcomes, to classify objects, and to solve problems. These emerging *schema* (Piaget's term) lead to understanding such things as basic math and spatial concepts.

constructivism—a learning approach in which a child forms his or her own meaning through active participation.

- **Formal operational (11–15 years)** During these years, the child develops complex thinking skills related not only to objects and experiences but also to abstract thoughts and ideas and the ability to solve problems.

Piaget's ideas are evident today in many educational programs where developmentally appropriate learning centers and discovery learning curriculum approaches are practiced.

Lev Vygotsky offered a somewhat different perspective on children's cognitive development. Although he agreed with Piaget's notion that development follows a unique pattern, Vygotsky believed that social and cultural environments (e.g., values, beliefs, and practices) played an active and influential role in shaping the learning process (Vygotsky, 1986). For example, he explained that children initially learn how to behave through a series of adult directives: "Don't touch," "Come here," "Eat this," "Stop that." As children begin to internalize social rules and cultural expectations and to develop self-control, the nature of these directives gradually changes. Adults stop telling children what to do and instead shift to encouraging and assisting their active involvement in learning new skills. Vygotsky referred to this as the **Zone of Proximal Development**.

Vygotsky also considered children's acquisition of speech and language an important step in this process. He believed that young children spend considerable time learning new words and thinking about their meanings and uses. Vygotsky observed that some children hold conversations with themselves as a way of thinking out loud. He referred to this stage as "self-talk," or inner speech, and suggested that the process gives children an opportunity to rehearse the meanings of words and their uses as communication tools (Vygotsky, 1986). Later, children begin to internalize their ideas and are able to recall them for future use.

Marie Montessori's ideas have also contributed to our understanding of cognitive-developmental theory. Trained as a pediatrician, she later became interested in educating children who were considered ineducable. She was convinced that all children had potential but that traditional instructional methods might not always be effective. Her observations led to her belief that children learned best through a process of self-directed exploration. She designed sensory-based materials that were self-correcting and required limited adult intervention. She also developed educational programs based on a philosophy that emphasized children's natural curiosity and self-directed involvement in learning experiences.

Cognitive-developmental theorists have enhanced our understanding of how children learn and construct meaning. They have made us aware that children differ in their learning styles and that instructional approaches must be individualized to address each child's unique developmental needs. Application of these findings is evident in the National Association for the Education of Young Children's (NAEYC) position statement on Developmentally Appropriate Practice (DAP) and those of other early

---

Zone of Proximal Development—Vygotsky's term for tasks that prove too difficult for children to master by themselves, but are able to do so with guidance or assistance.

childhood organizations (NAEYC, 2009). Knowledge of cognitive-developmental theory has also influenced the concept and delivery of early intervention services. Children's cognitive development continues to intrigue researchers, particularly as it relates to curriculum, instructional methods, family involvement, the influence of culture, and social interaction, and it is likely to serve as a source of study for decades to come.

Behaviorism and Social Learning Theory

In its modern form, behaviorism and social learning theory stems from the work of B. F. Skinner and John B. Watson, who formulated a *nurture*, or environmental, approach to learning (Skinner, 1938). They argued that development, for the most part, involves a series of learned behaviors based on an individual's positive and negative interactions with his or her environment (Figure 1-4). For example, reinforcing a behavior typically causes it to be repeated. In other words, telling a child that he has done a great job on his spelling test is likely to motivate him to study even harder for the next one. However, the opposite is also true: giving in to a crying child's demands for a much-wanted toy may encourage the child to repeat the behavior the next time he or she wants something. Ignoring the child's demands will eventually extinguish the behavior because there is no reinforcement (attention).

Skinner also explained how the association between two events (stimulus-response) results in learning. For example, a toddler bumps her head (stimulus) when she stands up under the table, so she abruptly ends the activity (response). A preschooler touches

Figure 1-4
Social learning theory explains development as behavioral change that results from observation and imitation.

a hot pan (stimulus) and is careful to avoid repeating the behavior again (response). You promise to read a favorite book to your daughter (stimulus) if she picks up her toys quickly (response).

Albert Bandura modified some of these earlier ideas when he formulated his own theory of social learning (Bandura, 1977). He viewed behavior as a combination of environmental influences (nature) and cognitive abilities (nurture). He also believed that children learned both positive and negative behaviors through observation and modeling, or imitation. However, unlike Skinner, he did not agree that reinforcement was necessary to motivate or change behavior. He believed that children learned, for example, not to hit another child or not to take away a toy after observing another child being punished for the same act.

Families and teachers employ the principles of behavioral theory on a daily basis. They expect children to comply with requests and then reward or punish accordingly. They model behavior that children are likely to imitate. They provide encouragement and thus reinforce or increase the child's efforts. Behavioral procedures are also used to address serious behavior and developmental problems, such as aggression, feeding disorders, anger management, and obesity (Olin et al., 2009).

Bioecological Theory

There is little dispute today that environment exerts a direct influence on children's development (Fox, Levitt, & Nelson, 2010). Urie Bronfenbrenner, a noted psychologist, alleged that environment shaped a person's development. He proposed an ecological model that describes environment as multilayered—from the settings in which a person participates (family, school, church, teams), relationships within these groups, and experiences in other social settings (media, neighbors, social agencies) to the shared beliefs and values of one's culture (Bronfenbrenner, 1979).

Bronfenbrenner later modified his original ideas to include the influence of biological factors. His revised bioecological model offers several unique perspectives on human development. First, it recognizes environment as having multiple and often complex layers versus treating it as a single entity. It also acknowledges that a person's behavior is not determined by any one layer alone but rather by interactions that occur on multiple levels. For example, poverty by itself might not limit a child's development if effective social services, quality schools, and a nurturing family are in place. Bronfenbrenner also recognized the interactive nature of environment—that environment not only affects an individual, but that a person's behavior, age, and interactions are continually changing the nature of that environment.

The bioecological theory has had a significant impact on educational practices. It has raised awareness of diversity issues. This; in turn, has led to the development of antibias curricula, assessment procedures, play materials, and teacher education programs that reflect sensitivity and respect for individual differences. It has furthered our understanding of how environment and relationships shape a child's development and why family involvement and collaboration are essential in schools.

Essential Needs Theory

All children—those who are developing normally or typically, those who have developmental disabilities, and those who are **at risk** for developing problems—have essential physical and psychological needs in common (Maslow, 1968). These needs must be met if infants and children are to survive, thrive, and develop to their full potential. Developmental psychologists have long considered the early years to be the most critical in the entire life span (Shonkoff, 2010). Their assumptions have since been confirmed and documented by contemporary brain research studies. During these very early years, children learn all of the many behaviors that characterize the human species—walking, talking, thinking, and socializing. Never again will the child grow as rapidly, change as dramatically, or be so totally dependent on adults to satisfy life's basic needs and opportunities for learning.

Essential needs—physical, psychological, and learning—are often separated for discussion purposes. However, it must be understood that they are mutually interrelated and interdependent. Meeting a child's physical needs while neglecting his or her psychological needs may lead to serious developmental problems. The opposite also is true—a child may experience difficulty in learning and getting along with others if he or she is being abused or his or her physical needs are neglected. Only when children's essential needs are being fully met will they be able to realize their full developmental potential (Belsky et al., 2010; Sylvestre & Mérette, 2010).

Physical Needs
- Adequate shelter and protection from harm: violence, neglect, and preventable injuries
- Sufficient food that is nutritious and appropriate to the child's age
- Clothing and shoes suitable to the climate and season
- Access to preventive health and dental care; treatment of physical and mental conditions as needed; recommended immunizations
- Personal hygiene: washing hands, brushing teeth, and bathing
- Rest and activity, in balance; opportunities for indoor and outdoor play

Psychological Needs
- Affection and consistency: **nurturing** families and teachers who provide positive behavioral guidance
- Security and trust: familiar surroundings with family and teachers who are dependable and respond to the child's needs
- **Reciprocal** exchanges: beginning in earliest infancy, give-and-take interactions that promote responsiveness in the child (Lenzil et al., 2010).

---

at risk—term describing children who may be more likely to have developmental problems due to certain predisposing factors such as low birth weight (LBW), neglect, or maternal drug addiction.

essential needs—basic physical needs such as food, shelter, and safety as well as psychological needs, including love, security, and trust, which are required for survival and healthy development.

nurturing—qualities of warmth, loving, caring, and attention to physical needs.

reciprocal—exchanges between individuals or groups that are mutually beneficial (or hindering).

- Appropriate adult expectations of what the child can and cannot do at each stage of development

- Acceptance and positive attitudes toward the cultural, ethnic, language, or developmental differences that characterize the child and family

Learning Needs

- Play as an essential component of early learning. Infants and young children need unlimited opportunities to engage in play in all its many forms, with freedom to explore and safely experiment, with necessary limits clearly stated and consistently maintained (Brooker, 2010) (Figure 1-5)

- Access to **developmentally appropriate** experiences and play materials (Copple & Bredekamp, 2009; Horn & Banerjee, 2009)

- An appropriate match between a child's abilities and the learning materials and experiences presented so there is sufficient challenge without causing excessive frustration

- Treatment of errors and delays in achieving a skill as important steps in the learning process, never as reasons for criticizing or ridiculing a child

- Adults who demonstrate in their everyday lives the appropriate behaviors expected of the child, especially in language, social interactions, or ways of handling stress. Remember that adults serve as important behavior models for children; children learn far more from what adults do than from what they say

Figure 1-5
Children are continually learning through exploration and play.

developmentally appropriate—a term describing learning experiences that are individualized based on a child's level of skills, abilities, and interests.

Need for Respect and Self-Esteem

- A literacy-rich environment and inclusion in an active language "community" in which children can learn to communicate through sounds, gestures, signs, and, eventually, words and sentences (spoken, signed, or written)

- A supportive environment in which the child's efforts are encouraged and approved: "Thank you for picking up your crayons without being asked!"

- Respect for accomplishments whether small or large, for errors as well as for successes: "Look at that! You laced your shoes all by yourself" (no mention of the eyelet that was missed).

- Recognition that accomplishment and the "I can do it" attitude is the major and most essential component of a child's **self-esteem**: "You did a great job of pouring the juice without spilling!"

- Sincere attention to what the child is doing well; using **descriptive praise** to help the child recognize and respect his or her own accomplishments: "You got your shoes on the right feet all by yourself!"

- Awareness of the effort and concentration that go into acquiring basic developmental skills; providing positive responses to each small step as a child works toward mastery of a complex skill such as self-feeding with a spoon: "Right! Just a little applesauce so it stays on the spoon"

Only when children are healthy and have their basic needs satisfied can we expect them to be ready and able to learn (Marotz, 2012). Researchers continue to demonstrate the critical nature of this relationship (Casey et al., 2010). Their findings have prompted support for policy and programs that assist families in meeting children's needs for nutritious food, health care (mental, physical and oral), safe and nurturing homes, and learning opportunities. Examples include Head Start, School Breakfast,

---

▶❚❚ TeachSource Video Connections

Culturally Responsive Teaching. Children's development is shaped by an array of genetic and environmental factors. Acknowledging cultural differences is essential to recognizing and accepting children as unique individuals. Watch the Video Case entitled *Culturally Responsive Teaching: A Multicultural Lesson for Elementary Students* on the Education CourseMate website and answer the following questions:

1. How would Bronfenbrenner explain multiculturalism and its effect on children's learning?
2. Why do you think diversity should be addressed in the classroom?
3. Why is it important to remember that children are more alike than they are different?

---

self-esteem—feelings about one's self-worth.

descriptive praise—words or actions that describe to a child specifically what she or he is doing correctly or well.

Parents as Teachers, and Children's Health Insurance Program (CHIP). Educators also understand this critical connection and devote considerable time and effort to ensuring that children's needs are being addressed.

Data Gathering

What we know about children—how they grow and develop, how they learn, and how they interact with others—stems from firsthand observation. For decades, psychologists and educators have observed the daily activities of hundreds of infants and young children. They recorded what they saw and heard as children learned to walk, communicate, grasp basic science and math concepts, interact with peers, reason, and solve problems. Their observations provided the foundation for what we now know about child development, effective teaching practices, curriculum models, and the significance of family–child relationships.

Early childhood educators continue to recognize the importance of gathering information about children's behavior and development (Figure 1-6). Despite increasing pressures for standardized testing, documentation, and accountability issues in schools, teachers understand the value of observing children in their **naturalistic settings**. This approach, referred to as **authentic assessment**, is considered the most effective

Figure 1-6
Observing children in naturalistic environments yields the most reliable information about their development.

naturalistic settings—environments that are familiar and part of children's everyday experiences, such as classrooms, care arrangements, and home.
authentic assessment—a process of collecting and documenting information about children's developmental progress; data is gathered in children's naturalistic settings and from multiple sources.

and developmentally appropriate method for evaluating and supporting young children (Macy & Bagnato, 2010). Performance-based information about children's developmental progress is collected in the context of everyday settings and activities. Samples of children's products, family input, and teacher observations are collected continuously and systematically to document learning. This information provides an ongoing, well-rounded picture of the child and reduces the bias that results when decisions are based on the results of a single evaluation method. Authentic assessment also helps teachers understand children's skills, abilities, and special needs against a background of environmental factors that shape their development (Rushton, Juola-Rushton, & Larkin, 2010). Authentic assessment results can be used to design learning goals, interventions, and responsive environments that effectively meet children's individual needs.

Teachers as Classroom Observers

Regularly scheduled observations and assessments of children's developmental progress are benchmarks of high-quality schools and early childhood programs (Buysse & Hollingsworth, 2009). Watching and recording children's behavior in the classroom and during outdoor play gives teachers insight into their progress, strengths, and limitations. Information acquired through observational methods is also useful for identifying children who have special talents, developmental delays, health issues, or behavior problems. In addition, teachers can use this information to design activities, instruction, and environments that are developmentally appropriate and support effective learning.

The ability to conduct and interpret meaningful observations requires that teachers be familiar with typical child development so their expectations are both realistic and appropriate. They must also understand that family, culture, and linguistic differences can account for variations in what children know and are able to do. With time and practice, teachers become proficient at identifying specific behaviors for observation, knowing what to look for, recording observations in an objective manner, and using the results to address children's individual needs.

Families as Observers

Families should always be welcomed in their child's classroom, whether as scheduled observers or on a drop-in basis. They have a right to know what children are learning and to ask questions. When family members arrange for a scheduled observation, they can be given a clipboard for noting points of interest or questions they may want to ask about learning materials, teacher responses, or what seems to please or bother the child. Teachers should arrange a follow-up meeting to learn the family's thoughts about the classroom or program, to point out the child's positive qualities, and to share mutual concerns about the child's progress.

Figure 1-7
Family observations and information-sharing are essential to effective instruction.

Observations made by family members at home are also invaluable. Families know and understand their child better than anyone else and see him or her behaving in almost every imaginable circumstance. They are aware of the child's likes and dislikes, joys and anxieties, and positive and negative qualities. Most importantly, they often have goals they want their child to achieve and care deeply about his or her well-being. When schools create an atmosphere that encourages families to share information and any concerns, everyone—children, families, and teachers—ultimately benefits (Figure 1-7). Schools can use technology to maintain effective communication with all families. Email and a secure classroom website provide opportunities for exchanging information about children's progress, especially with families that may not be seen on a regular basis due to conflicting work schedules, younger children to care for at home, language differences, or divorce.

Observation Methods

Recorded observations take many forms: anecdotal notes, running records and logs, time and event sampling, frequency and duration counts, checklists, rating scales, audio- and video-recordings, and portfolios. Each method is described briefly in the section that follows. Additional information on screening tests is available in Chapter 10, "When and Where to Seek Help," and Appendix B, "Selected Screening and Assessment Instruments."

Anecdotal Notes

Several times each day, the teacher takes a minute or less to write down a few relevant thoughts about what they see occurring. These anecdotal notes can be recorded on a small notebook or pad (3 × 5 inches) carried in a pocket. The teacher makes brief, dated entries about the **discrete behaviors** observed for a given child: "Played in block area for 5 minutes without hitting another child," "Initiated conversation with teacher," "Seemed anxious during the test."

Anecdotal notes provide a running record, or composite picture, of the child's developmental progress in one or more **domains** over a period of time. They may also be used to document a specific concern, a need for special intervention, or a change in instructional strategies. Continued data collection can also aid teachers in determining whether a child is benefiting from a planned intervention or if a different approach is needed. When anecdotal notes are compiled chronologically by developmental domains, they also become a valuable tool for determining placements, writing progress reports, evaluating lessons plans, and/or preparing for family conferences.

Time or Event Sampling

Sampling techniques enable a teacher to collect behavioral data on one or more children simultaneously during a given time frame or activity. For example, a teacher may be interested in learning which behaviors children use to resolve conflicts during free play: physical aggression (pa), verbal aggression (va), or cooperative problem solving (cps) skills. A simple score sheet can be developed for recording purposes with children's names listed along one axis and the times and behavioral codes or categories identified across the other (Figure 1-8). A new sheet is dated and used for recording each day's observations.

A sampling approach is often used to obtain information about children's language development. Counts can be obtained during a live observation or from prerecorded audio- or videotaped sessions. An observer writes down every utterance exactly as the child says it. One purpose of the samplings, which are usually recorded for ten to fifteen minutes at a time over a month-long period or so, is to track the child's speech and language progress. Another purpose is to see whether the child's language works. Is the child communicating effectively? Does the child get what he or she needs and wants by using language? No other behavior (except communicative gestures or facial grimaces) is recorded, although brief notations may be made, for example, that other children rarely respond to the child's verbal overtures. Language samples are invaluable for monitoring developmental progress and planning individualized programs. They also are effective for recalling humorous quips or insightful statements the child has made.

---

discrete behaviors—behaviors that can clearly be observed and described: hitting, pulling hair, spitting.

domains—a term describing an area of development such as physical, motor, socioemotional, or speech and language.

Figure 1-8
Time sampling form.

_____ date									Activity: Free Play			

Code:
  pa – physical aggression
  va – verbal aggression
  cps – cooperative play/problem solving

Child	8:30			8:40			8:50			9:00		
	pa	va	cps	pa	va	cps	pa	va	cps	pa	va	cps
LaShauna												
Jose												
Markie												
Winston												

Total: pa ____ va ____ cps ____

Figure 1-9
Sample frequency and
duration counts.

Child's name: Nicholas J.
Week of: June 4–9, 2010
Observer: Juanita M.
Behavior observed: Not attending/distracting other children

Activity:	Mon	Tues	Wed	Thurs	Fri	Comments
Morning circle	II	0	II	I	III	
Afternoon circle	III	II	IIII	0	III	

Frequency and Duration Counts

When concerns about a specific aspect of a child's behavior arise, teachers must first determine how often the behavior actually occurs (frequency) or how long it continues (duration) (Figure 1-9). Observations are made and data recorded while teachers go about their daily tasks. One form of frequency count simply requires the teacher to make a tally mark every time the child engages in the specified behavior. A count might

reveal that a two-year-old who was said to cry or hit "all the time" was actually doing so only once or twice per morning and some mornings not at all. For behaviors that occur at a high rate, teachers sometimes use a golf stroke or handheld counter. Frequency counts yield objective information that can help teachers decide whether a "problem" is indeed a problem.

A duration count measures the amount of time a child engages in particular behavior. For example, a teacher might simply jot down the time when a child enters and leaves an area or activity. Another example would be penciling (unobtrusively) on a corner of a painting or collage the time the child started and finished the project. Or, the teacher might note when a child's tantrum began and ended. Duration counts are helpful for deciding whether interventions are needed to increase or decrease a specific behavior.

Checklists and Rating Scales

Checklists permit a teacher or other observer to record quickly the occurrence of certain skills or behaviors. For example, in infant centers, many firsts can be checked off: the day Josie first smiled, rolled over, or walked alone. In preschools, a checklist can be an effective method for monitoring children's skill acquisition. The date can be inserted as teachers check off when, for example, Carmella correctly identified and matched her primary colors; when Jayson built a tower of eight one-inch cubes; or, when Sophia zipped up her own jacket. Teachers may wish to construct their own checklists to reflect unique program objectives. The lists, whether teacher-made or commercial, can be simple or detailed, depending on the need (see Appendix A, "Developmental Checklists").

Rating scales, like checklists, are usually designed to target specific behaviors (Figure 1-10). They provide an efficient method for recording teacher observations and later retrieving information in a meaningful way.

Figure 1-10
Sample rating scale form.

Child's name: <u>Nicholas J.</u>
Date: _____

Task:	Not Yet	Attempts/ Not always accurate	Usually accurate	Proficient	Comments (observer/date):
Identifies numbers 1–10					
Arranges numbers 1–10 in correct order					
Counts from 1–10 with prompting					
Counts from 1–10 without prompting					
Writes numbers 1–10					

Portfolios

Representative examples of a child's work—drawings, digital photographs of a special block structure or science project, notes describing manipulative activities completed, audiotapes of conversations and language samples, digital movies of a class play or attempts at learning a new skill—offer another effective method for tracking children's developmental progress (Harris, 2009). Teachers select materials that reflect a child's learning across all developmental domains and assemble them in a child's individual portfolio. Children should also be given opportunities to choose items for inclusion. Information obtained from teacher observations and family conferences should also be a part of this collection as they provide additional insight and meaning to the child's products.

Materials in a child's portfolio should be reviewed periodically to monitor changing interests, mastery of specific skills, and need for additional instruction. Teachers can also use these items when preparing for parent conferences, to illustrate discussion points, and to share with families. In addition, children's portfolios often reveal important information about the effectiveness of a curriculum or teaching methods and can thus be beneficial for program improvement.

 TeachSource Video Connections

Assessing Children's Development. Adults are able to support and guide children's development when they have appropriate information about a child's progress and expected achievements. Watch the Video Case entitled *Portfolio Assessment: Elementary Classroom* on the Education CourseMate website and answer the following questions:

1. What does portfolio assessment involve?
2. What information does it provide that may not be obtainable from other assessment methods?
3. In what ways can teachers and families use portfolio assessment results to support learning?

SUMMARY

Today's knowledge of child development is a composite of human development theories: maturational, psychoanalytic, psychosocial, cognitive-developmental, behaviorism and social learning, bioecological, and essential needs. All theories concur that meeting children's basic physical and psychological needs is a powerful determinant of optimum development. For the first time, changes within the brain's physical structure have been documented as the result of satisfying children's essential needs. Paramount among these are providing adequate physical care, responsive nurturing, abundant learning experiences, and opportunities for developing positive self-esteem.

Current explanations about how children grow and develop rarely rest on any one theory exclusively. Each approach has made major contributions to our understanding of children's behavior. The majority of today's researchers dismiss the nature vs. nurture question as an improbable either/or proposition; human development is not that simplistic. Instead, it is generally viewed as a complex series of interactions involving environmental and biological characteristics.

Teachers and families continue to play an important role in gathering information about children's growth and development. Their observations contribute to a better understanding of children's unique interests, abilities, talents, and needs. The process of documenting children's behavior enables teachers to make necessary adjustments in curriculum and instructional methods to improve and support learning.

Key Terms

nature vs. nurture **p. 3**

norms **p. 4**

constructivism **p. 6**

Zone of Proximal Development **p. 7**

at risk **p. 10**

essential needs **p. 10**

nurturing **p. 10**

reciprocal **p. 10**

developmentally appropriate **p. 11**

self-esteem **p. 12**

descriptive praise **p. 12**

naturalistic settings **p. 13**

authentic assessment **p. 13**

discrete behaviors **p. 16**

domains **p. 16**

Apply What You Know

A. Apply What You Have Learned

Reread the developmental sketch about Jamal at the beginning of the chapter and answer the following questions.

1. Could Jamal's early months of living in an impoverished environment have any effect on his current development? Explain your answer based on the theories described in this chapter.
2. Although Jamal's motor skill development may be delayed, he has learned to sit up, crawl, stand, walk, and eventually run. Which is more important to consider in his case, the fact that he was older than is typical when he learned these skills or that he has developed them in this particular order? Explain.
3. Based on the brief description of Jamal and his family, what reciprocal effect might you anticipate when Jamal crawls up onto his father's lap? How would Skinner and Bandura explain this response?

B. Review Questions

1. What is the nature vs. nature controversy, and how does it contribute to our understanding of children's development?

2. What behaviors would children be likely to exhibit during each of the first five stages of Erikson's developmental theory (infancy–adolescence)?
3. In what ways does the maturational theory differ from the cognitive-developmental theory?
4. What is behaviorism, and how does it explain why a child might continue to refuse eating despite repeated warnings from her mother?
5. What data and collection method(s) would you use to confirm or disprove your suspicions about a child's ability to complete a specific task?

Helpful Websites

Early Childhood Knowledge & Learning Center
http://eclkc.ohs.acf.hhs.gov

Children's Defense Fund
http://www.childrensdefense.org

National Institute of Child Health & Human Development
http://www.nichd.nih.gov

References

Bandura, A. (1977). *Social learning theory*. New York: General Learning Press.

Belsky, D., Moffitt, T., Arseneault, L., Melchior, M., & Caspi, A. (2010). Context and sequelae of food insecurity in children's development, *American Journal of Epidemiology, 172*(7), 809–818.

Bronfenbrenner, U. (1979). *The ecology of human development: Experiments by nature and design*. Cambridge, MA: Harvard University Press.

Brooker, L. (2010). Learning to play in a cultural context. In P. Broadhead, J. Howard, & E. Wood (Eds.), *Playing & learning in the early years: From research to practice*. Thousand Oaks, CA: Sage.

Buysse, V., & Hollingsworth, H. (2009). Program quality and early childhood inclusion, *Topics in Early Childhood Special Education, 29*(2), 119–128.

Casey, P., Ettinger de Cuba, S., Cook, J., & Frank, D. (2010). Child hunger, food insecurity, and social policy, *Archives of Pediatrics & Adolescent Medicine, 164*(8), 774–775.

Copple, C., & Bredekamp, S. (2009). Developmentally appropriate practice in early childhood programs serving children from birth through age 8 (3rd ed.). Washington, DC: NAEYC.

Dalton, T. (2005). Arnold Gesell and the maturation controversy, *Integrative Psychological & Behavioral Science, 40*(4), 182–204.

Ebstein, R., Israel, S., Chew, S., Zhong, S., & Knafo, A. (2010). Genetics of human social behavior, *Neuron, 65*(6), 831–844.

Erikson, E. (1950). *Childhood and society*. New York: Vintage.

Fox, S., Levitt, P., & Nelson, C. (2010). How timing and quality of early experiences influence the development of brain architecture, *Child Development, 81*(1), 28–40.

Gesell, A., & Ilg, F. (1949). *Child development*. New York: Harper.

Harris, M. (2009). Implementing portfolio assessment, *Young Children, 64*(3), 82–85.

Horn, E., & Bannerjee, R. (2009). Understanding curriculum modifications and embedded learning opportunities in the context of supporting all children's success, *Language, Speech, & Hearing Services in Schools, 40*, 406–415.

Lenzil, D., Trentini, C., Pantanol, P., Macaluso, E., Iacoboni, M., Lenzil, G., & Ammanitit, M. (2010). Neural basis of maternal communication and emotional expression processing during infant preverbal stage, *Cerebral Cortex, 19*(5), 1124–1133.

Macy, M., & Bagnato, S. (2010). Keeping It "R-E-A-L" with authentic assessment, *NHSA Dialog: A Research-to-Practice Journal for the Early Intervention Field, 13*(1), 1–20.

Marotz, L. (2012). *Health, safety, & nutrition for the young child* (8th ed.). Belmont, CA: Wadsworth Cengage.

Maslow, A. (1968). *Toward a psychology of being* (2nd ed.). New York: Van Nostrand Reinhold.

NAEYC (2009). Position statement: Developmentally appropriate practice in early childhood programs serving children from birth through age 8. Accessed on October 29, 2010 from http://www.naeyc.org/files/naeyc/file/positions/position%20statement%20Web.pdf.

Olin, S., Hoagwood, K., Rodriquez, J., Ramos, B., Burton, G., Penn, M., Crowe, M., Radigan, M., & Jensen, P. (2009). The application of behavior change theory to family-based services: Improving parent empowerment in children's mental health, *Journal of Child & Family Studies, 19*(4), 462–470.

Piaget, J. (1954). *The construction of reality in the child.* New York: Basic Books.

Rueda, M., & Rothbart, M. (2009). The influence of temperament on the development of coping: The role of maturation and experience, *New Directions for Child & Adolescent Development, 124*(2009), 19–31.

Rushton, S., Juola-Rushton, A., & Larkin, E. (2010). Neuroscience, play and early childhood education: Connections, implications and assessment, *Early Childhood Education Journal, 37*(5), 351–361.

Sameroff, A. (2010). A unified theory of development: A dialectic integration of nature and nurture, *Child Development, 81*(1), 6–22.

Shonkoff, J. (2010). Building a new biodevelopmental framework to guide the future of early childhood policy, *Child Development, 81*(1), 357–367.

Skinner, B. F. (1938). *The behavior of organisms: An experimental analysis.* New York: Appleton-Century.

Sylvestre, A., & Mérette, C. (2010). Language delay in severely neglected children: A cumulative or specific effect of risk factors?, *Child Abuse & Neglect, 34*(6), 414–428.

Vygotsky, L. (1986). *Thought and language* (2nd ed.). Cambridge, MA: MIT Press.

Principles of Growth and Development

Learning Objectives

After reading this chapter, you should be able to:

- Define growth and development as separate concepts and provide at least two examples of each.
- Defend this statement: "Sequence, not age, is the important factor in evaluating a child's progress."
- Identify the six major developmental domains that are the focus of this text.

naeyc Standards Chapter Links:

1a and 1b: Promoting child development and learning
2a and 2c: Building family and community relationships
4a: Using developmentally effective approaches

Meet the Twins Emma and Ethan

The identical twins, Emma and Ethan, soon to be three years old, weighed in at a little over four pounds each at birth. Despite having being born two months early and considered to be low-birth-weight babies, they are now strong and healthy. They look similar, with dark brown eyes, thick eyelashes, and high cheekbones. Although they behave alike in many ways, there are also marked differences. Since early infancy, Emma has been more physically active. She slept less, ate more, sat up, crawled, and walked alone weeks before Ethan or other babies her age. She also has been more adventuresome in trying out new experiences such as going down

continued…

a slide and climbing on playground equipment. Ethan, however, was the first to smile, play peek-a-boo, and say recognizable words. He now uses complete sentences and has considerable letter, word, and number recognition skills. He likes to "read" to Emma and acts as her interpreter when she can't make herself understood. In turn, Emma is first to comfort Ethan when he is hurt or frightened. Recently, the two were enrolled in an early childhood program to which they adjusted easily but still needed to stay close to one another throughout the day.

Ask Yourself

1. From the brief descriptions of Emma and Ethan, which developmental characteristics can be attributed solely to genetic makeup?
2. How might environment help to explain the children's developmental differences?
3. In what ways do Emma's and Ethan's motor skills differ?

Basic Patterns and Concepts

Groups of children of approximately the same age appear to be remarkably similar in size, shape, and abilities. However, closer observation reveals a wide range of individual differences (Figure 2-1). Both similarities and differences depend on a child's unique patterns of growth and development. What defines this complementary process of *growth and development*? Why do children experience this progression differently? Many terms are used, sometimes interchangeably, to explain these concepts, but they are not describing identical concepts.

Growth

Growth refers to specific physical changes and increases in the child's actual size. Additional numbers of cells, as well as enlargement of existing cells, are responsible for the observable gains in a child's height, weight, **head circumference**, shoe size, length of arms and legs, and body shape. Changes in growth also lend themselves to direct and fairly reliable measurement.

The growth process continues throughout the life span, although the rate varies by age. For example, growth occurs rapidly during infancy and adolescence but is typically much slower and less dramatic in the school-age child. Even into old age, the body continues to repair and replace its cells, although much less vigorously.

---

growth—physical changes leading to an increase in size.

head circumference—measurement of the head taken at its largest point (across the forehead, around the back of head, returning to the starting point).

Figure 2-1
Children's development
includes a wide range of
individual differences.

Development

Development refers to an increase in complexity—a change from the relatively simple to the more complex and advanced. The process involves an orderly progression along a continuum, or pathway. Little by little, knowledge, behaviors, and skills are learned and refined. Although the sequence is basically the same for all children, the rate of acquisition can vary greatly from child to child. The physiological maturity of children's neurological, muscular, and skeletal systems determines when they are capable of learning. Environmental conditions, culture, and family values influence what they are likely to learn (Figure 2-2). Collectively these factors account for the wide range of individual variations observed in children's developmental progress. For example, families in many cultures encourage their children to begin crawling and walking at an early age, whereas in other cultures the early acquisition of motor skills is not highly valued or supported.

Developmental
Milestones

Major markers or points of accomplishment are referred to as developmental milestones and are useful for tracking the emergence of motor, social, cognitive, and language skills. They represent behaviors that appear in somewhat orderly steps and within fairly predictable age ranges for typically developing children. For example, almost every child begins to smile socially by ten to twelve weeks and to speak a first word or two at around twelve months. These achievements (social smile, first words) are but two of the many significant behavioral indications that a child's developmental progress is on track. When children do not achieve one or more developmental milestones within a reasonable time frame, they should be monitored carefully and systematically by a child development specialist or health care provider.

---

development—refers to an increase in complexity, from simple to more complicated and detailed.

Figure 2-2
Many factors play a collective role in fostering children's development.

Sitting, walking, and talking are examples of developmental milestones that depend on biological maturation, yet these skills do not develop independently of the environment. For example, learning to walk requires muscle strength and coordination. It also requires an environment that encourages practice, not only of walking as it emerges, but also of the behaviors and skills that precede walking such as rolling over, sitting, and standing.

Sequences of Development

A sequence of development is composed of predictable steps along a developmental pathway common to the majority of children. This process is sometimes referred to as **continuity**. Children must be able to roll over before they can sit and sit before they can stand. *The critical consideration is the order in which children acquire these developmental skills, not their age in months and years.* The appropriate sequence in each area of development is an important indication that the child is moving steadily forward along a sound developmental continuum (Figure 2-3). For example, in language development, it does not matter how many words a child speaks by two years of age. What is important is that the child has progressed from cooing and babbling to jabbering (inflected **jargon**) to syllable production. The two- or three-year-old who has progressed through these stages usually produces words and sentences within a reasonable period of time.

Developmental progress is rarely smooth and even. Irregularities, such as periods of **stammering** or the onset of a **food jag**, often characterize children's development.

---

continuity—developmental progress that gradually becomes increasingly refined and complex.
jargon—unintelligible speech; in young children, it usually includes sounds and inflections of the native language.
stammering—to speak in an interrupted or repetitive pattern; not to be confused with stuttering.
food jag—a period when only certain foods are preferred or accepted.

Figure 2-3
Typical sequence of motor development.

Regression, or taking a step or two backward now and then, is perfectly normal. For example, a child who has been toilet trained for some time might begin to have "accidents" when under stress or starting school; an older child might resort to hitting or become verbally aggressive following a family move.

Age-Level Expectancies or Norms

Age-level expectancies can be thought of as **chronological**, or age-related, levels of development. Psychologists, including Gesell, Piaget, and Erikson, conducted hundreds of systematic observations of infants and children of various ages. Analyses of their findings represent the average or typical age at which many specifically described developmental skills are acquired by most children in a given culture (Gesell & Ilg, 1949;

---

chronological—events or dates in sequence in the passage of time.

Piaget, 1954). This average age is often referred to as the norm. Thus, a child's development may be described as at the norm, above the norm, or below the norm. For example, a child who begins walking at eight months is ahead of the norm (twelve to fifteen months), while a child who does not walk until twenty months is considered to be below the norm.

Age-level expectancies *always represent a range and never an exact point in time* when specific skills are most likely to be achieved. Profiles in this text (age expectancies for specific skills) should always be interpreted as approximate midpoints on a range of months (as in the example on walking, from eight to twenty months with the midpoint at fourteen months). Once again, a reminder: It is *sequence* and *not age* that is the important factor in evaluating a child's progress (Knight & Zerr, 2010; Blaga et al., 2009). In real life, there is probably no child who is truly typical in every way. The range of skills and the age at which skills are acquired show great individual variation. Relevant again is the example of walking—one infant may begin at eight months and another not until twenty months (many months apart on either side of the norm). No two children grow and develop at exactly the same rate, nor do they perform in exactly the same way. For example, there are a half dozen ways of creeping and crawling. Most children, however, use what is referred to as *contralateral locomotion*, an opposite knee–hand method of getting about prior to walking. Yet, some normally walking two-year-olds never crawl, indicating a distinct variation in typical development.

Organization and Reorganization

Development can be thought of as a series of phases. Spurts of rapid growth and development often are followed by periods of disorganization. The child then seems to recover and move into a period of reorganization. It is not uncommon for children to demonstrate behavior problems or even regression during these phases. The reasons vary. Perhaps a new baby has become an active and engaging older infant who is now the center of family attention. Three-year-old brother might revert to babyish ways about the same time. He begins to have tantrums over minor frustrations and might, for the time being, lose his hard-won bladder control. Usually, these periods are short-lived. The three-year-old will almost always learn more age-appropriate ways of getting attention if given adequate adult support and understanding.

Brain Growth and Development

Brain maturation lays the foundation for all other aspects of a child's development. Growth and development of the fetal brain is rapid, exceedingly complex, and influenced by a combination of maternal environment (see Chapter 3, "Prenatal Development") and genetics. Infants are born with an excess of brain cells (neurons)—more than adults have or will ever need! However, these neurons must first be organized into functional networks before they can be used for purposeful activity.

Children's brains increase in size and complexity as neural connections, or networks, are formed as a direct result of new and repetitive learning experiences (Giedd & Rapoport, 2010). Once established, these neural connections allow brain cells to communicate with one another in order to perform specific tasks. Active cells and neural connections are gradually strengthened through a natural process called **pruning** that eliminates those that are seldom used. This explains, for example, why a child learns to speak in his or her own native language but not in one that is different; or why one child becomes an outstanding pianist while another child may excel at playing sports or chess. Thus, it is important to remember that both genetic factors and learning experiences play a significant role in fostering brain growth and development (Figure 2-4).

Research has revealed amazing information about the relationship between the brain and language development (Fox, Levitt, & Nelson, 2010). For example, infants not only take in the sounds of the language they are hearing, but they replicate them complete with a dialect. Furthermore, the dialect is maintained without change for years to come. It is as if, in the case of language development, the brain will not easily sever connections made in the earliest months and years of life, regardless of subsequent changes in language environments.

It has long been thought that the child's brain simply continued to develop complexity in response to ongoing experiences. However, recent discoveries have determined that a new layer of grey matter forms on the brain's frontal lobes during

Figure 2-4
Growth and development are shaped by a combination of genetics and learning experiences.

---

pruning—elimination of neurons and neural connections that are not being used; this process strengthens developing connections the child is using.

adolescence. This particular region is responsible for regulating emotion, impulsivity, and decision-making processes (Romer, 2010). Once again, new neural connections must be established through repeated experience, refinement, and pruning before they are able to perform with any degree of consistency and adult-like sophistication. These findings may help to explain why adolescents engage in behaviors and make irrational decisions that adults often find puzzling.

 TeachSource Video Connections

Brain Development in Infancy. Early brain development sets the stage for future learning and success. Adults play a critical role in fostering this early development by providing young children with enrichment opportunities, positive support, and consistent nurturing and care. Watch the learning video entitled *Infancy: Brain Development* on the Education CourseMate website and answer the following questions:

1. What causes neural connections to form?
2. What type of learning experiences can adults provide to promote children's brain development?
3. What are "sensitive periods"?

Typical Growth and Development

The terms **typical** and *normal* development are often used interchangeably to describe the acquisition of certain skills and behaviors according to a predictable rate and sequence. However, as previously stated, the range of typical behaviors within each developmental domain is broad and includes mild variations and simple irregularities such as the three-year-old who stutters or the twelve-month-old who learns to walk without having crawled. The use of these terms also oversimplifies the concept. Normal or typical development implies:

- An integrated process governing change in size, **neurological** structure, and behavioral complexity
- A cumulative or building-block process in which each new aspect of growth or development includes and builds on earlier changes; each accomplishment is necessary to acquisition of the next set of skills
- A continuous process of give and take (reciprocity) between the child and the environment, each changing the other in a variety of ways. For example, the three-year-old drops a cup and breaks it, and the parent scolds the child. Both events—the broken cup and the adult's displeasure—are environmental changes

---

typical—achievement of certain skills according to a fairly predictable sequence, although with many individual variations.
neurological—refers to the brain and nervous system.

that the child triggered. From this experience, the child might learn to hold on more firmly next time, and this constitutes a change in both the child's and the adult's behavior—fewer broken cups, thus less adult displeasure.

Interrelatedness of Developmental Domains

Discussions about development usually focus on several major domains: physical, motor, perceptual, cognitive, social-emotional, and language. However, no single area develops independently of the others. Every skill, whether simple or complex, requires a mix of developmental abilities. Social skills are a prime example. Why are some young children said to have good social skills? Often the answer is because they play well with other children and are sought out as playmates. To be a preferred playmate, a child must have many skills, all of them interrelated and interdependent. For example, a four-year-old should be able to:

- Run, jump, climb, and build with blocks (good motor skills).
- Ask for, explain, and describe what is going on (good language skills).
- Recognize likenesses and differences among play materials and so select appropriate materials in a joint building project (good perceptual skills).
- Problem-solve, conceptualize, and plan ahead in cooperative play ventures (good cognitive skills).

Every developmental area is well represented in the preceding example, even though social development was the primary area under consideration.

Temperament

The term *temperament* refers to the genetic component of an individual's personality (Neppl et al., 2010; Bornstein & Cote, 2009). It describes the characteristic nature of a person's emotional responses such as the intensity, disposition or mood, focus, and ability to adjust. It accounts for differences in children's behavior such as activity level, alertness, irritability, soothability, restlessness, and/or willingness to cuddle. Such qualities often lead to labels—the "easy" child, the "difficult" child, and the "slow-to-warm" child— which tend to influence adult expectations and responses to the child (Todd & Dixon, 2010). In turn, the nature of adult responses is likely to reinforce the child's behavior (Figure 2-5). For example, a slow-to-warm child may evoke few displays of affection from others and so perceive this as rejection, making it even more difficult for the child to act warm and outgoing.

Gender Roles

Early in life, young children learn gender roles appropriate to their culture (Martin & Ruble, 2010). Each boy and girl develops a set of behaviors, attitudes, and commitments that are defined, directly or indirectly, as acceptable male or female attributes (Denham, Bassett, & Wyatt, 2010). In addition, each child plays out gender roles according

Figure 2-5
A child's temperament can affect the nature of caregiver responses.

to everyday experiences. Genetics, playmates and play opportunities, toys, media exposure, cultural expectations, and, especially, adult role models (families, neighbors, teachers) collectively influence the child's sense of maleness or femaleness.

Ecological Factors

Beginning at conception, **ecology**—the environmental influence of family and home, community, and society—affects all aspects of a child's development (Conger, Conger, & Martin, 2010). The following are examples of powerful ecological factors.

- Financial resources; adequacy and availability of food and shelter (Duncan, Ziol-Guest, & Kalil, 2010)

---

ecology—in terms of children's development, refers to interactive effects between children and their family, child care situation, school, and everything in the wider community that affects their lives.

- Cultural values and practices
- General health and nutrition; access to prenatal and postnatal care for mother and child
- Families' education level (mother's level of education is a major predictor of a child's school achievement) (Pettit, Davis-Kearn, & Magnuson, 2009)
- Families' understanding of obligations and responsibilities before and after the infant's birth
- Family communication and child-rearing practices (loving or punitive, nurturing or neglectful); family stress (Son & Morrison, 2010)
- Family structure—single- or two-parent, blended, or extended family; grandparent with primary parenting role; nontraditional household; foster homes

Differences in the way each of these factors are experienced ultimately results in a child being unlike any other child. For example, the child born to a single, fifteen-year-old mother living in poverty will have life experiences significantly different from those of a child born and reared in a two-parent professional family.

Transactional Patterns of Development

From birth, children influence the behavior of their adult caretakers (e.g., families, teachers). In turn, these same adults exert a strong influence on children's behavior and development. For example, a calm, cuddly baby expresses his or her needs in a clear and predictable fashion. This infant begins life with personal–social experiences that are quite different from those of a tense, colicky infant whose sleeping and eating patterns are highly irregular and often stressful to parents. This complex **transactional process** of give and take between children and their families and daily events is ongoing, continually changing, and results in developmental experiences that shape each child's unique qualities.

Infants and young children thrive when adults respond promptly and positively, at least a fair share of the time, to appropriate things a child says and does. Research indicates that children develop healthier self-concepts as well as earlier and better language, cognitive, and social skills when raised by responsive adults (Glascoe & Leew, 2010).

Children at Risk

Some children are born into situations that may be harmful to their development or interfere with its typical progress. These children are often described as being *at risk*. Premature birth and low birth weight are examples of two conditions that increase a child's vulnerability and chances of developing physical problems, learning disabilities, behavioral problems, or all three (Davis, Harris, & Burns, 2010). They are typically

---

transactional process—the give-and-take relationship between children, their primary caregivers, and daily events that influences behavior and developmental outcomes.

associated with poor maternal health, inadequate prenatal care, substance abuse during pregnancy, poverty, or maternal age outside the "normal" range (very young teenagers and women in their forties). Children who live in poverty or are exposed to abusive or neglectful treatment are also considered to be at higher risk for behavioral and/or developmental problems (Denham, Bassett, & Wyatt, 2010). Harsh physical punishment such as repeated spanking has been shown to interfere with learning and lower a child's IQ (Scarborough & McCrae, 2010).

Atypical Growth and Development

The term *atypical* describes children with developmental differences, deviations, or marked delays—children whose development appears to be incomplete or inconsistent with typical patterns and sequences. There are many causes of atypical development, including genetic errors, poor health, inadequate nutrition, injury, and too few or poor-quality opportunities for learning.

Abnormal development in one area may or may not interfere with development in other areas. However, the child with developmental delays might perform in one or more areas of development like a much younger child. For example, the three-year-old who is still babbling with no recognizable words is an example of a child with delayed development. This condition need not be disabling unless the child never develops **functional language**. The term *developmental deviation* describes an aspect of development that is different from what is expected in typical development (Figure 2-6). For example, the child born with a missing finger or a profound hearing loss has a developmental deviation. The child with a missing finger is not likely to be disabled. In contrast, the child who is deaf will experience a significant developmental disability unless early and intensive intervention is obtained.

In any event, the concepts and principles described in this chapter apply to the child with developmental differences as well as to the child who is said to be developing typically. However, one must always be cautious not to make judgments about a child's development without first being sensitive to cultural, ethnic, socioeconomic, language, and gender variations that might indeed account for any differences (Trawick-Smith, 2009). It must also be remembered that a child who experiences any type of developmental problem is, most importantly, a child with the same basic needs as all other children.

Developmental Domains

A framework is needed to describe and accurately assess children's developmental progress. In this book, we focus on six major domains, or developmental areas: physical, motor, perceptual, cognitive, speech and language, and social-emotional. Each

---

functional language—language that allows children to get what they need or want.

Figure 2-6
A vision impairment is an
example of a developmental
deviation.

domain includes the many skills and behaviors that will be discussed in the developmental profiles that are the major focus of this book (Chapters 4 through 9). Although these developmental areas are separated for the purpose of discussion, they cannot be separated from one another in reality. Each is integrally related to, and **interdependent** with, each of the others in the overall developmental process.

Developmental profiles, or word pictures, are useful for assessing both the immediate and ongoing status of children's skills and behavior. It is important to remember that the rate of development is uneven and occasionally unpredictable across areas. For example, the language and social skills of infants and toddlers are typically less well developed than is their ability to move about. Also, children's individual achievements can vary across developmental areas: a child might walk late but talk early. Again, an important reminder: Development in any of the domains is dependent in a large part on children having appropriate stimulation and adequately supported opportunities to learn. Additionally, the types of learning experiences individual children encounter are highly variable and reflect cultural, socioeconomic, and family values.

---

interdependent—affecting or influencing development in other domains.

Physical Development and Growth

This domain governs the major tasks of infancy and childhood. Understanding the patterns and sequences of physical development is essential to being effective parents, teachers, and caregivers. It is healthy growth and development, not adult pressure or coaching, that makes new learning and behavior possible. Adult pressure cannot hurry the process and, in fact, is more likely to be counterproductive. A seven-month-old infant cannot be toilet trained; the **sphincter** muscles are not yet developed sufficiently to exert such control. Nor can the majority of kindergartners catch or kick a ball skillfully; such coordination is impossible given a five- or six-year-old's stage of physical development, yet most of us have seen a coach or family reduce a child to tears for missing a catch or a kick.

Governed by heredity and greatly influenced by environmental conditions, physical development and growth is a highly individualized process (Leve et al., 2010). It is responsible for changes in body shape and proportion as well as for overall body size. Growth, especially of the brain, occurs more rapidly during prenatal development and the first year than at any other time. Growth is also intricately related to progress in other developmental areas. It is responsible for increasing muscle strength necessary for movement, coordinating vision and motor control, and synchronizing neurological and muscular activity in gaining bladder and bowel control. A child's growth is also closely linked to nutritional status and ethnicity (Stang & Bayerl, 2010). Thus, the state of a child's physical development serves as a reliable index of his or her general health and well-being. Physical growth and development also exert a direct influence on determining whether children are likely to achieve their full cognitive and academic potential.

Motor Development

The child's ability to move about and control various body parts are major functions of this domain. Refinements in motor development depend on maturation of the brain, input from the *sensory system*, increased bulk and number of muscle fibers, a healthy nervous system, and opportunities for practice. This holistic approach contrasts markedly with the way early developmentalists such as Gesell viewed the emergence of motor skills. They described a purely maturational process, governed almost entirely by instructions on the individual's genetic code (nature). Today's psychologists consider such an explanation misleading and incomplete. Their research suggests that when young children show an interest, for example, in using a spoon to feed themselves, it is always accompanied by improved eye–hand coordination (to direct the spoon to the mouth), motivation (*liking* and *wanting* to eat what is in the bowl), and the drive to imitate what others are doing. In other words, the environment, that is, experience, plays a major role in the emergence of new motor skills (nurture).

---

sphincter—the muscles necessary to accomplish bowel and bladder control.

Motor activity during very early infancy is purely **reflexive** and gradually disappears as the child develops **voluntary** control over his or her movements. If these earliest reflexes do not phase out at appropriate times in the **developmental sequence**, it may be an indication of neurological problems (see Chapter 4, "Infancy"). In such cases, medical evaluation should be sought. Three principles govern motor development:

1. **Cephalocaudal** Bone and muscular development that proceeds from head to toe (Figure 2-7). The infant first learns to control muscles that support the head and neck, then the trunk, and later, those that allow reaching. Muscles for walking develop last.

Figure 2-7
Cephalocaudal development proceeds from head to toe.

reflexive—movements resulting from impulses of the nervous system that cannot be controlled by the individual.

voluntary—movements that can be willed and purposively controlled and initiated by the individual.

developmental sequence—a continuum of predictable steps along a developmental pathway of skill achievement.

cephalocaudal—bone and muscular development that proceeds from head to toe.

Figure 2-8
Proximodistal development
proceeds outward from the
trunk.

2. **Proximodistal** Bone and muscular development that begins with improved control of muscles closest to the central portion of the body, gradually extending outward and away from the midpoint to the extremities (arms and legs) (Figure 2-8). For example, control of the head and neck is achieved before the child is able to pick up an object with thumb and forefinger (pincer grasp or finger–thumb opposition).

3. **Refinement** Muscular development that progresses from the general to the specific in both **gross motor** and **fine motor** activities. In the refinement of a gross motor skill, for example, a two-year-old might attempt to throw a ball but achieves little distance or control. The same child, within a few short years, might pitch a ball over home plate with speed and accuracy. As for a fine motor skill, compare the self-feeding efforts of a toddler with those of an eight-year-old who is motivated (for whatever reason) to display good table manners.

---

proximodistal—bone and muscular development that begins closest to the trunk, gradually moving outward to the extremities.

refinement—progressive improvement in ability to perform fine and gross motor skills.

gross motor—large muscle movements such as locomotor skills (walking, skipping, swimming) and nonlocomotive movements (sitting, pushing and pulling, squatting).

fine motor—also referred to as manipulative skills; includes stacking blocks, buttoning and zipping, and toothbrushing.

Perceptual Development

The increasingly complex way a child uses information received through the senses—sight, hearing, touch, smell, taste, and body position—forms the basis of perceptual development (Santrock, 2009). It might be said that perception is a significant factor which determines and orchestrates the functioning of the various senses, singly or in combination. The perceptual process also enables the individual to focus on what is relevant at a particular moment and to screen out whatever is irrelevant: Which details are important? Which differences should be noted? Which should be ignored? Perceptual development involves three important functions:

1. **Multisensory** Information is generally received through more than one sensory system at a time. For example, when listening to a speaker, we use sight (watching facial expressions and gestures) and sound (listening to the words) (Frank et al., 2009).

2. **Habituation** This term refers to a person's ability to concentrate on a specific task while ignoring everything else. For example, a child may be focused on reading a book of interest and be completely unaware of classmates' conversation or music playing in the background. In other words, the child is able to tune out things around him or her and devote full attention to what is most immediately important (Casasola & Bhagwat, 2007).

3. **Sensory integration** This process involves translating **sensory information** into functional behavior. For example, the five-year-old sees and hears a car coming and waits for it to pass before crossing the street.

The basic perceptual system is in place at birth. Through experience, learning, and maturation, it develops into a smoothly coordinated operation for processing complex information from multiple senses. As a result, children can sort shapes according to size and color and make fine discriminations or hear and distinguish the difference among initial sounds in rhyming words such as *rake, cake,* and *lake.* The sensory system also enables each of us to respond appropriately to different messages and signals, such as smiling in response to a smile or keeping quiet in response to a frown.

Cognitive Development

This domain addresses the expansion of a child's intellect or mental abilities. Cognition involves recognizing, processing, and organizing information and then using it appropriately (Charlesworth, 2011). The cognitive process includes such mental activities as discovering, interpreting, sorting, classifying, and remembering. For preschool- and school-aged children it means evaluating ideas, making judgments, solving

sensory information—information received through the senses: eyes, ears, nose, mouth, touch.

complex problems, understanding rules and concepts, anticipating, and visualizing possibilities or consequences.

Cognitive development is an ongoing process of interaction between the child and his or her perceptual view of objects or events in the environment (Piaget, 1954). It is probably safe to say that neither cognitive nor perceptual development can proceed independently of each other. Cognitive skills always overlap with both perceptual and motor development. Early in the second year, the emergence of speech and language adds yet another dimension.

 TeachSource Video Connections

Temperament and Personality Development. Temperament is considered one component of an individual's personality. It influences a person's feelings and behavior. It explains, in part, why infants and toddlers differ in their emotional perceptions and responses to caregivers and the environment. Watch the learning video entitled *0–2 Years: Temperament in Infants and Toddlers* on the Education CourseMate website and answer the following questions:

1. What determines a child's temperament?
2. Which terms did parents in the video use to describe their child's temperament?
3. How does a child's temperament influence the transactional process of parenting?
4. How would you describe your own temperament?
5. Do you think there are cultural differences in temperament? Explain.

The development of cognition begins with the primitive or reflexive behaviors that support survival and early learning in the healthy newborn. One example of very early learning is when a mother playfully sticks out her tongue several times and the baby begins to imitate her. This and other early behaviors led developmental psychologists to ponder the many striking similarities in how infants and children learn. During the 1950s, repeated observations of such similarities led the Swiss psychologist Jean Piaget to formulate his four stages of cognitive development: sensorimotor, preoperational, concrete operations, and formal operations (see Chapter 1, "Child Development Theories and Data Gathering").

Language Development

Language is often defined as a system of symbols, spoken, written, and gestural (waving, smiling, scowling, cowering) that enables us to communicate with one another. Normal language development is regular and sequential and depends on maturation as well as on learning opportunities (Hammer, Farkas, & Maczuga, 2010). The first year of life is called the prelinguistic or prelanguage phase. The child is totally dependent on body movements and sounds such as crying and laughing to convey needs and feelings. This is followed during the second year by the linguistic or language stage, in which speech becomes the primary mode for communicating. Over the next three or four years, the

Figure 2-9
Most five-year-olds are able to express their thoughts clearly and with correct grammar.

child learns to put words together to form simple and then compound sentences that make sense to others because the child has learned the appropriate grammatical constructions. Between five and seven years of age, most children have become skilled at conveying their thoughts and ideas verbally (Figure 2-9). Many children at this age have a vocabulary of fourteen thousand words or more, which can double or triple during middle childhood, depending on a child's literacy environment.

Most children seem to understand a variety of words, concepts, and relationships long before they have the words to describe them. This ability is referred to as **receptive language**, which precedes **expressive language** (the ability to speak words to describe and explain). Speech and language development is closely related to the child's general cognitive, social, perceptual, and neuromuscular development. Language development and the rules that address how it is to be used are also influenced by the type of language children hear in their homes, schools, and community (Pungello et al., 2009).

Social and Emotional Development

This is a broad area that covers how children feel about themselves and their relationships with others (Stack et al., 2010). It refers to children's behaviors, the way they respond to play and work activities, and their attachments to family members, caregivers,

---

receptive language—understanding words that are heard.
expressive language—words used to verbalize thoughts and feelings.

teachers, and friends. Gender roles, temperament, independence, morality, trust, acceptance of rules, and social and cultural expectations are also important components of this developmental area (Denham, Bassett, & Wyatt, 2010).

In describing personal and social development, it must also be remembered that children develop at different rates. Individual differences in genetic and cultural backgrounds, health status, living arrangements, family interactions, and daily experiences within the larger community continuously shape and reshape children's development. Consequently, no two children can ever be exactly alike, not in social and emotional development or in any other developmental area.

Age Divisions

The following age divisions, used throughout this book, are commonly referred to by many child development specialists when describing significant changes within developmental areas:

Infancy	birth to 1 month
	1–4 months
	4–8 months
	8–12 months
Toddlerhood	12–24 months
	24–36 months
Early Childhood	3–5 years
	6–8 years
Middle Childhood	9–12 years
Adolescence	13–14 years
	15–16 years
	17–19 years

Age divisions are to be used with extreme caution and great flexibility when dealing with children. They are based on the average achievements, abilities, and behaviors of large numbers of children at various stages in development. As stated again and again, there is great variation from one child to another.

The step-by-step development we detail in Chapters 4 through 9 speaks to the importance of understanding that it is the sequential acquisition, *not age*, that indicates developmental progress in each domain and in each child's overall development.

SUMMARY

Growth and development are influenced by a child's unique genetic makeup and the quality of the everyday environment, which includes nurturing, health care, nutrition, and opportunities to learn the vast range of skills that are evidence of developmental progress. Each child's well-being depends on acquiring the necessary skills across six developmental domains: physical, motor, perceptual, cognitive, language, and social-emotional. Although the six domains are separated for discussion purposes, they are interwoven and interdependent during the developmental years and throughout life.

Although age-level expectations (*norms*) are useful in assessing an individual child's developmental status, they must be used cautiously. The accepted range of normalcy is broad and recognizes that each child is unique. Thus, the more important factor is not age but sequence—is the child progressing through each step in each developmental area even though it might be somewhat later (or earlier) than most children of similar age? Atypical development is characterized by marked delays or characteristics not seen in typical development. Nevertheless, it must be remembered that all children have the same basic needs regardless of their special abilities, limitations, or challenges.

Key Terms

growth **p. 24**

head circumference **p. 24**

development **p. 25**

continuity **p. 26**

jargon **p. 26**

stammering **p. 26**

food jag **p. 26**

chronological **p. 27**

pruning **p. 29**

typical **p. 30**

neurological **p. 30**

ecology **p. 32**

transactional process **p. 33**

functional language **p. 34**

interdependent **p. 35**

sphincter **p. 36**

reflexive **p. 37**

voluntary **p. 37**

developmental sequence **p. 37**

cephalocaudal **p. 37**

proximodistal **p. 38**

refinement **p. 38**

gross motor **p. 38**

fine motor **p. 38**

sensory information **p. 39**

receptive language **p. 41**

expressive language **p. 41**

A. Apply What You Have Learned

Reread the brief developmental sketch about Emma and Ethan at the beginning of the chapter and answer the following questions.

1. How do Emma and Ethan differ in terms of their personal-social development? Given that they are twins, what factors might explain these differences?
2. According to Piaget, which stage of cognitive development are the twins, who are almost three, currently experiencing? Give an example of this concept from the descriptions of Emma and Ethan.
3. Just because Emma and Ethan are twins, should you expect them to grow and develop in exactly the same way and at exactly the same rate? How would developmental theorists account for these differences (see Chapter 1)?

B. Review Questions

1. Explain how the concepts of growth and development differ.
2. Identify and discuss three factors that might contribute to atypical development.
3. What role does environment play in children's brain development?
4. What is meant by the term *perceptual information*? Give three examples to illustrate this concept.
5. Why would you not be concerned about a toddler who was learning to walk but now insists on crawling instead? Explain.
6. What are developmental milestones and what purpose do they serve?

Centers for Disease Control & Prevention
http://www.cdc.gov/ncbddd/child

National Association for Child Development
http://www.nacd.org

National Institute of Child Health & Human
http://www.nichd.gov

Development National Association for the Education of Young Children
http://www.naeyc.org

References

Blaga, O., Shaddy, D., Anderson, C., Kannass, K., Little, T., & Colombo, J. (2009). Structure and continuity of intellectual development in early childhood, *Intelligence, 37*(1), 106–113.

Bornstein, M., & Cote, L. (2009). Child temperament in three U.S. cultural groups, *Infant Mental Health Journal, 30*(5), 433–451.

Casasola, M., & Bhagwat, J. (2007). Do novel words facilitate 18-month-olds' spatial categorization?, *Child Development, 78*(6), 1818–1829.

Charlesworth, R. (2011). *Understanding child development* (8th ed.). Belmont, CA: Wadsworth Cengage Learning.

Conger, R., Conger, K., & Martin, M. (2010). Socioeconomic status, family processes, and individual development, *Journal of Marriage & Family, 72*(3), 685–704.

Davis, D., Harris, R., & Burns, B. (2010). Attention regulation in low-risk very low birth weight preschoolers: The influence of child temperament and parental sensitivity, *Early Child Development & Care, 180*(8), 1019–1040.

Denham, S., Bassett, H., & Wyatt, T. (2010). Gender differences in the socialization of preschoolers' emotional competence, *New Directions for Child and Adolescent Development, 2010*(128), 29–49.

Duncan, G., Ziol-Guest, K., & Kalil, A. (2010). Early childhood poverty and adult attainment, behavior, and health, *Child Development, 81*(1), 306–325.

Fox, S., Levitt, P., & Nelson, C. (2010). How the timing and quality of early experiences influence the development of brain architecture, *Child Development, 81*(1), 28–40.

Frank, M., Slemmer, J., Marcus, G., & Johnson, S. (2009). Information from multiple modalities helps 5-month-olds learn abstract rules, *Developmental Science, 12*(4), 504–509.

Gesell, A., & Ilg, F. (1949). *Child development.* New York: Harper.

Giedd, J., & Rapoport, J. (2010). Structural MRI of pediatric brain development: What have we learned and where are we going?, *Neuron, 67*(5), 728–734.

Glascoe, F., & Leew, S. (2010). Parenting behaviors, perceptions, and psychosocial risk: Impacts on young children's development, *Pediatrics, 125*(2), 313–319.

Hammer, C., Farkas, G., & Maczuga, S. (2010). The language and literacy development of Head Start children: A study using the Family and Child Experiences Survey database, *Language, Speech, and Hearing Services in Schools, 41*, 70–83.

Knight, G., & Zerr, A. (2010). Informed theory and measurement equivalence in child development research, *Child Development Perspectives, 4*(1), 25–30.

Leve, L., Neiderhiser, J., Scaramella, L., & Reiss, D. (2010). The Early Growth and Development Study: Using the prospective adoption design to examine genotype-environment interplay, *Behavior Genetics, 40*(3), 306–314.

Martin, C., & Ruble, D. (2010). Patterns of gender development, *Annual Review of Psychology, 61*(1), 353–381.

Neppl, T., Donnellan, M., Scaramella, L., Widaman, K., Spilman, S., Ontai, L., & Conger, R. (2010). Differential stability of temperament and personality from toddlerhood to middle childhood, *Journal of Research in Personality, 44*(3), 386–396.

Pettit, G., Davis-Kean, P., & Magnuson, K. (2009). Educational attainment in developmental perspective: Longitudinal analyses of continuity, change, and process, *Merrill-Palmer Quarterly, 55*(3), 217–123.

Piaget, J. (1954). *The construction of reality in the child.* New York: Basic Books.

Pungello, E., Iruka, I., Dotterer, A., Mills-Koonce, R., & Reznick, J. (2009). The effects of socioeconomic status, race, and parenting on language development in early childhood, *Developmental Psychology, 45*(2), 544–557.

Romer, D. (2010). Adolescent risk taking, impulsivity, and brain development: Implications for prevention, *Developmental Psychobiology, 52*(3), 263–276.

Santrock, J. (2009). *Children* (10th ed.). New York: McGraw-Hill.

Scarborough, A., & McCrae, J. (2010). School-age special education outcomes of infants and toddlers investigated for maltreatment, *Children & Youth Services, 32*(1), 80–88.

Son, S., & Morrison, F. (2010). The nature and impact of changes in home learning environment on development of language and academic skills in preschool children, *Developmental Psychology, 46*(5), 1103–1118.

Stack, D., Serbin, L., Enns, L., Ruttle, P., & Barrieau, L. (2010). Parental effects on children's emotional development over time and across generations, *Infants & Young Children, 23*(1), 52–69.

Stang, J., & Bayerl, C. (2010). Position of the American Dietetic Association: Child and adolescent nutrition assistant programs, *Journal of the American Dietetic Association, 110*(5), 791–799.

Todd, J., & Dixon, W. (2010). Temperament moderates responsiveness to joint attention in 11-month-old infants, *Infant Behavior & Development, 33*(3), 297–308.

Trawick-Smith, J. (2009). *Early childhood development: A multicultural approach.* Upper Saddle River, NJ: Merrill/Prentice Hall.

You are just a click away from a variety of interactive study tools and resources. Access the text's Education CourseMate website at **www.cengagebrain.com**, where you'll find a variety of enrichment materials, including videos, glossary flashcards, activities, tutorial quizzes, web links, and more.

CHAPTER 3
Prenatal Development

Learning Objectives

After reading this chapter, you should be able to:

- Discuss the functional roles performed by the placenta.
- Describe several practices a mother should follow throughout pregnancy to improve her chances of giving birth to a healthy infant.
- Name five teratogens and describe their preventive measures.
- Explain several changes that signal the onset of active labor.
- Discuss maternal depression and its potential effect on infant development.

naeyc Standards Chapter Links:

1b: Promoting child development and learning
2a: Building family and community relationships
6e: Becoming a professional

Meet Anna and Miguel

Anna and Miguel were elated when they learned that she was seven weeks pregnant. Six months earlier, Anna had experienced a miscarriage during her third month of pregnancy. At the time, Anna's doctor advised her to stop smoking before attempting future pregnancies. Although she was not able to quit, she did significantly reduce the number of cigarettes she was smoking each day. Anna also made an effort to improve her diet by eating more fruits and vegetables and eliminating alcohol consumption.

When Anna and Miguel shared their exciting news with family members, everyone had advice for preventing another miscarriage. Her mother insisted that Anna rest

continued…

and avoid any type of activity, including cleaning the house and cooking. Miguel's aunt advised Anna not to drink milk and to eat all she could "because she was now eating for two." Her sister discouraged Anna from continuing to work at the bank because she had heard that stress could cause miscarriage. However, Anna's job was the only way she and Miguel could maintain their health insurance coverage. Anna appreciated her family's suggestions, but she was convinced that everything would be okay this time around.

Ask Yourself

1. What lifestyle changes did Anna make to improve her chances of having a healthy infant? Are there other things she might also try?
2. Do you think Anna should follow the advice offered by her friends and family? Why or why not?

Each of the approximately 266 days of prenatal development (from **conception** to birth) is critical to producing a healthy newborn. **Genes** inherited from the baby's biological mother and father determine all physical characteristics as well as many abnormalities. Studies have suggested that **temperament** may also have a biological basis (Aron et al., 2010). However, because it is the mother who provides everything physically essential (as well as harmful) to the growing fetus, she plays a major role in promoting its healthy development. Her personal health, nutritional status, and lifestyle before and during pregnancy strongly influence the birth of a healthy baby. Researchers have recently determined that a father's health, personal habits, and his caring support for the mother throughout the pregnancy also contribute to the unborn infant's development (Haber et al., 2010). Thus, it is important for every potential parent to be familiar with the patterns of normal prenatal development as well as with practices that support and interfere with this process (Figure 3-1).

The Developmental Process

The prenatal period is commonly divided into stages. In obstetrical practice, pregnancy is described in terms of trimesters, each consisting of three calendar months:

- First trimester—conception through the third month
- Second trimester—fourth through the sixth month
- Third trimester—seventh through the ninth month

---

conception—the joining of a single egg or ovum from the female and a single sperm from the male.

genes—genetic material that carries codes, or information, for all inherited characteristics.

temperament—an individual's characteristic manner or style of response to everyday events, including degree of interest, activity level, and regulation of behavior.

Figure 3-1
A mother's and father's lifestyles have a direct effect on their baby's development.

Pregnancy can also be discussed in terms of fetal development (Table 3-1). This approach emphasizes the critical changes that occur week by week and encompasses three stages as well:

* Germinal

* Embryonic

* Fetal

The *germinal stage* refers to the first fourteen days of pregnancy. The union of an ovum and sperm produces a **zygote**. Cell division begins within twenty-four hours and gradually forms a pinhead-size mass of specialized cells called a *blastocyst*. Around the fourteenth day, this small mass attaches itself to the wall of the mother's uterus. Successful attachment (**implantation**) marks the beginning of the **embryo** and the embryonic stage. Approximately two-thirds of zygotes will survive this phase and continue to develop.

The *embryonic stage* includes the third through the eighth week of a pregnancy and is a critical period for the developing fetus. Cell division continues and forms specialized cell layers that are responsible for all major organs and systems, such as the heart, lungs, digestive system, and brain. Many of these structures will be functional near the end of this period. For example, embryonic blood begins to flow through the fetus's primitive cardiovascular system (heart and blood vessels) in the fourth to the fifth weeks.

During this time, other important changes are also taking place. When implantation is completed, a **placenta** begins to form. This organ serves four major functions, including:

* Supplying nutrients and hormones to the fetus.

* Removing fetal waste products throughout the pregnancy.

zygote—the cell formed as a result of conception; called a zygote for the first fourteen days.

implantation—the attachment of the blastocyst to the wall of the mother's uterus; occurs around the twelfth day.

embryo—the cell mass from the time of implantation through the eighth week of pregnancy.

placenta—a specialized lining that forms inside the uterus during pregnancy to support and nourish the developing fetus.

Table 3-1 Characteristics of Fetal Development

2 weeks	• Cell division results in an embryo consisting of 16 cells.
3–8 weeks	• Structures necessary to support the developing embryo have formed: placenta, chorionic sac, amniotic fluid, and umbilical cord.
	• Embryonic cell layers begin to specialize, developing into major internal organs and systems as well as external structures.
	• First bone cells appear.
	• Less than 1 inch (2.54 cm) in length at eight weeks.
12 weeks	• Weighs approximately 1 to 2 ounces (0.029–0.006 kg) and is nearly 3 inches (7.6 cm) in length.
	• Sex organs develop; baby's gender can be determined.
	• Kidneys begin to function.
	• Arms, legs, fingers, and toes are well defined and movable.
	• Forms facial expressions (e.g., smiling, looking around) and is able to suck and swallow.
16 weeks	• Weighs about 5 ounces (0.14 kg) and is 6 inches (15.2 cm) in length.
	• Sucks thumb.
	• Moves about actively; mother may begin to feel baby's movement (called "quickening").
	• Has strong heartbeat that can be heard.
20 weeks	• Weighs nearly 1 pound (0.46 kg) and has grown to approximately 11 to 12 inches (27.9–30.5 cm) in length (approximately half of baby's birth length).
	• Experiences occasional hiccups.
	• Eyelashes, eyebrows, and hair forming; eyes remain closed.
24 weeks	• Weight doubles to about 1.5 to 2 pounds (0.68–0.90 kg) and length increases to 12 to 14 inches (30.5–35.6 cm).
	• Eyes are well formed, often open; responds to light and sound.
	• Grasp reflex develops.
	• Skin is wrinkled, thin, and covered with soft hair called *lanugo* and a white, greasy, protective substance called *vernix caseosa*.
28 weeks	• Weighs about 3 to 3.5 pounds (1.4–1.6 kg); grows to approximately 16 to 17 inches (40.6–43 cm) in length.
	• Develops a sleep/wake pattern.
	• Remains very active; kicks and pokes mother's ribs and abdomen.
	• Able to survive if born prematurely, although lungs are not yet fully developed.
32 weeks	• Weighs approximately 5 to 6 pounds (2.3–2.7 kg) and is 17 to 18 inches in length (43–45.7 cm).
	• Baby takes iron and calcium from mother's diet to build up reserve stores.
	• Becomes less active due to larger size and less room for moving about.
36–38 weeks	• Weighs an average of 7 to 8 pounds (3.2–3.6 kg) at birth; length is approximately 19 to 21 inches (48–53.3 cm).
	• Moves into final position (usually head down) in preparation for birth.
	• Loses most of lanugo (body hair); skin still somewhat wrinkled and red.
	• Is much less active (has little room in which to move about).
	• Body systems are more mature (especially the lungs and heart), thus increasing baby's chances of survival at birth.

- Filtering out many harmful substances as well as some viruses and other disease-causing organisms. (Unfortunately, many drugs can get through the placenta's filtering system.)
- Acting as a temporary immune system by supplying the fetus with the same antibodies the mother produces against certain infectious diseases. (In most instances, the infant is protected for approximately six months following birth.)

An umbilical cord, containing two arteries and one vein, develops as the placenta forms and establishes a linkage between the fetus, its mother, and the outside world. From this point on, the fetus is affected by the mother's health and lifestyle and begins to share everything the mother experiences and takes into her body via the placenta. During this early stage, the fetus is especially vulnerable if exposed to certain chemical substances such as alcohol, cigarette smoke, medications (see Table 3-2, p. 60), or infectious illnesses (see Table 3-3, p. 61) that enter the mother's body. Exposure to any of these substances can potentially damage developing fetal organs and systems and increase the risk of irreversible birth defects.

The *fetal stage* refers to the period between the ninth week and the onset of labor and delivery (around the thirty-eighth week). Most fetal systems and structures are now formed, and this final and longest period is devoted to continued growth and maturity. By seven months, a fetus is capable of surviving birth. During the final two months, few developmental changes occur. Instead, the fetus undergoes rapid and important increases in weight and size by adding layers of fat. For example, a seven-month-old fetus who weighs 2 to 3 pounds (0.9–1.4 kg) will gain approximately 1/2 pound (0.23 kg) per week until birth. Body systems are also maturing and growing stronger, thus improving the fetus's chances of surviving outside of the mother's body.

Promoting Healthy Fetal Development

Critical aspects of fetal development are taking place during the earliest days of pregnancy. Because the mother may not yet know that she is pregnant, it is important that both parents follow healthy lifestyle practices throughout their reproductive years. Researchers have identified many practices that can improve a mother's chances of having a healthy infant, including:

- The importance of obtaining early prenatal care
- Consuming a nutritious diet
- Maintaining a moderate weight gain
- Obtaining sufficient rest
- Avoiding excessive stress
- Having a positive emotional state
- Planning pregnancies when a mother is in her twenties to thirties and in good health
- Participating in daily physical activity

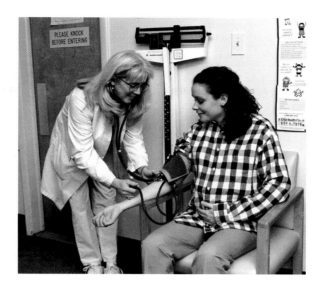

- Limiting exposure to teratogens such as drugs, alcohol, tobacco, and environmental chemicals
- Adequate spacing between pregnancies.

Prenatal Care

Medically supervised prenatal care is critical for ensuring the development of a healthy infant (Figure 3-2). Arrangements for this care should be made as soon as a woman suspects that she is pregnant. Women should not rely solely on home pregnancy tests before seeking medical care because the results are not always accurate, especially during the early days and weeks. During the initial visit to a health care provider, pregnancy can be confirmed (or refuted), and any medical problems the mother may have can be evaluated and treated. The parents-to-be can also be counseled on practices that influence fetal development. For example, mothers can be encouraged to participate in a program of regular noncontact exercise. (As long as there are no complications, regular exercise can improve weight control, circulation, muscle tone, and elimination, and is believed to contribute to an easier labor and delivery.)

Although nearly 80 percent of pregnant women in the United States currently receive prenatal care during the first trimester of pregnancy, this figure still leaves considerable room for improvement (CDC, 2009). A lack of prenatal care is often associated with an increased rate of medical complications, preterm births, **low birth weight (LBW)** infants, fetal death, and disabilities (Figure 3-3). Poverty may limit a mother's access to medical care as well as to her understanding about its importance (Buckner-Brown et al., 2011). Language barriers, differences in cultural beliefs, being a teen mother, and ethnicity have

---

low birth weight (LBW)—an infant who weighs less than 5.5 pounds (2500 grams) at birth, regardless of age.

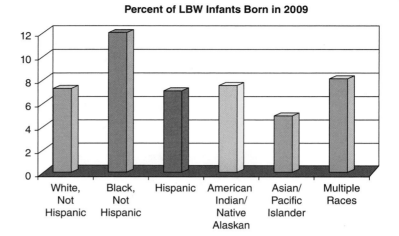

Figure 3-3
Percent of low birth weight infants in the United States for 2009.

(*Source:* National Vital Statistics Reports, Vol. 59, No. 3, December 21, 2010).

also been identified as inhibiting factors (Debiec et al., 2010). Consequently, continued efforts must be made to improve mothers' awareness of government-sponsored nutrition programs such as the national WIC program (Supplemental Food for Women, Infants, and Children), low-cost medical insurance, and community-sponsored health clinics.

Nutrition

A mother's nutritional status, determined by what she eats before and during pregnancy, has a significant effect on her own health as well as on that of the developing fetus. Consuming a healthy diet lessens the risk of having a low birth weight or **premature infant**, two conditions commonly associated with serious developmental problems (Khanani et al., 2010).

It is important that pregnant women continue to follow national nutrition recommendations to ensure an adequate intake of essential nutrients and calories (www.choosemyplate.gov) (Figure 3-4). Pregnancy increases a woman's dietary need for calories (energy); proteins; fluids; certain vitamins such as folacin (folic acid), B_6, B_{12}, C, and D; and minerals such as iron and calcium. Breast-feeding further increases a mother's need for calories and these same nutrients. Studies have established a critical link between folic acid intake (consumed before and during pregnancy: 400 micrograms daily for nonpregnant women, 600 micrograms daily for pregnant women) and the reduced incidence of neural tube defects (i.e., **spina bifida**, **anencephaly**) and **cleft lip/cleft palate** deformities (Amarin & Obeidat, 2010; Wehby & Murray, 2010). Folic acid is a

---

premature infant—an infant born before thirty-seven weeks following conception.

spina bifida—a birth defect caused by a malformation of the baby's spinal column.

anencephaly—a birth defect resulting in malformation of the skull and brain; portions of these structures might be missing at birth.

cleft lip/cleft palate—incomplete closure of the lip, palate (roof of the mouth), or both, resulting in a disfiguring deformity.

Figure 3-4
Explore the interactive tools to find daily food plans for pregnant and breast-feeding mothers. (www.choosemyplate.gov)

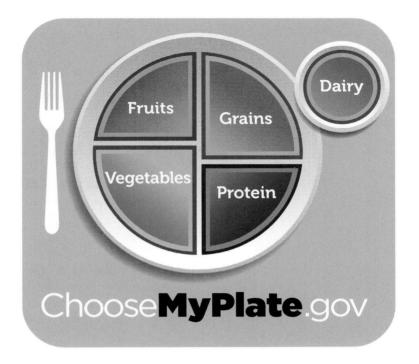

B vitamin found abundantly in many foods, especially raw leafy green vegetables, dried beans, lentils, orange juice, and fortified whole grain products such as pastas, breads, and breakfast cereals.

Although vitamin supplements are generally prescribed, they must not be considered a substitute for a nutritious diet. They lack essential proteins, calories, and other important nutrients found in most foods that are required for healthy fetal development and that aid the body in using the vitamins and minerals taken in tablet form. Herbal preparations are usually not recommended due to a lack of sufficient information about their safety during pregnancy (Broussard et al., 2010).

Several groups, including the U.S. Environmental Protection Agency (EPA), have advised women contemplating pregnancy, pregnant women, nursing mothers, and young children to limit their intake of certain fish and seafood due to potential mercury and pesticide contamination (Kuntz et al., 2010). However, because fish are low in calories and a rich source of high-quality protein and essential fats, researchers suggest that the benefits of including them in one's diet can outweigh the potential risks. Thus, women and young children are encouraged to limit their consumption to no more than 12 ounces of seafood such as shrimp, salmon, pollock, catfish, and canned light tuna (not albacore tuna, which has a higher mercury content) per week. Fish such as shark, swordfish, tilefish, and mackerel should be avoided. Consumers are also encouraged to check with authorities before eating fish that are caught in local rivers and lakes to determine whether mercury contamination is a concern.

Weight

What is the optimum weight gain during pregnancy? Most medical practitioners agree that a woman of normal weight (BMI) should ideally gain between 25 and 35 pounds (10–14 kg) over the nine-month period (ACOG, 2010). Gains considerably under or over this range can pose increased risks for both the mother and child during pregnancy and at birth.

Following a diet that is nutritionally adequate helps ensure optimum weight gain. Including the recommended servings of a wide variety of fruits and vegetables also supplies vitamins essential for fetal growth (vitamins A and C) and fiber to decrease constipation. Choosing low-fat dairy products and lean meats and plant proteins (e.g., dried beans, legumes, whole grains) aids in moderating caloric intake while providing key minerals (e.g., iron and calcium) required for the infant's and mother's health. Consuming too many empty calories, such as those found in junk foods, sweets, and alcohol, can lead to excessive weight gain and deprive the mother and fetus of critical nutrients found in a balanced diet.

Rest and Stress

Pregnancy places added strain on the mother's body and often increases her sense of fatigue. Adequate nighttime sleep and occasional daytime rest periods can help ease these problems. Pregnancy can also induce or increase emotional stress. Prolonged or excessive stress can adversely affect the mother's health, contributing to sleep and eating disorders, high blood pressure, depression, headaches, lowered resistance to infections, and backaches (Woods et al., 2010). It has also been shown to have negative effects on the fetus by reducing weight, breathing rate, heartbeat, and brain development (Davis & Sandman, 2010). Although it might not be possible for a pregnant woman to avoid all stress, strain, and fatigue, the ill effects can be lessened with proper rest, nutrition, and physical activity.

Age and General Health

A woman's age at the time of conception is an important factor in fetal development. Numerous studies conclude that the mid-twenties to early thirties are the optimum years for childbearing (Partington et al., 2009). Teenage mothers experience a rate of premature births, low birth weight babies, infant deaths, and infants born with developmental disabilities that is nearly double that for all mothers. These problems are often the result of inadequate prenatal care, poor nutrition and housing, substance abuse, or all three. In addition, the immaturity of a teen mother's reproductive system and her lack of basic lack knowledge about how best to care for her own personal needs often place these infants at increased risk.

Pregnancy in older women (late thirties and beyond) presents a different set of concerns (Ghosh et al., 2010). Genetic material contained in the ova gradually deteriorates as a woman ages, thus increasing the probability of certain birth defects such as Down

Figure 3-5
Mother's age at the time
of birth.

(*Source:* www.cdc.gov/
nchs/data/nvsr/nvsr59/
nvsr59_03.pdf).

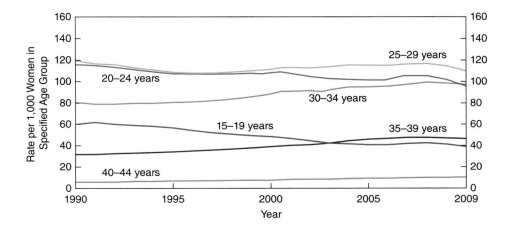

syndrome. It has also been determined that male sperm deteriorates with age and exposure to environmental contaminants and may increase the risk of autism and other birth defects (Grether et al., 2010). Older women are also more likely to experience medical problems during pregnancy. However, greater awareness of nutrition, physical activity, and medical supervision has improved an older mother's chances of giving birth to a healthy infant (Figure 3-5).

Increased knowledge and improved technology are also contributing to a reduction in fetal risk for mothers of all ages. Genetic counseling, ultrasound scanning (**sonogram**), **CVS** (chorionic villus sampling), **amniocentesis**, and new maternal blood tests enable medical personnel to monitor fetal growth closely and detect specific genetic disorders earlier. These procedures are especially beneficial for women who are electing to delay childbearing until their late thirties and early forties (Franz & Husslein, 2010).

Although the risks of pregnancy are undeniably greater for older women and teenagers, the problems often have as much to do with limited knowledge and poverty as with age. (Exceptions are the chromosomal abnormalities such as Down syndrome.) Regardless of maternal age, a significant number of fetal problems are closely associated with a lack of medical care, unhealthy diet, substandard housing, substance abuse, and limited education, all often closely associated with poverty. Allowing a two-year interval between pregnancies also improves the mother's health and ability to carry another pregnancy to full-term (Nabukera et al., 2009).

---

sonogram—visual image of the developing fetus, created by directing high-frequency sound waves.

CVS—chorionic villus sampling; a genetics-screening procedure in which a needle is inserted and cells removed from the outer layer of the placenta; performed between the eighth and twelfth weeks to detect some genetic disorders such as Down syndrome.

amniocentesis—genetics-screening procedure in which a needle is inserted through the mother's abdomen into the sac of fluids surrounding the fetus to detect abnormalities such as Down syndrome or spina bifida; usually performed between the twelfth and sixteenth weeks.

TeachSource Video Connections

Prenatal Assessment. Several procedures can be used during pregnancy to detect some genetic abnormalities. Each test has its advantages and disadvantages and may present the family with a difficult decision if genetic conditions are detected. Watch the learning video entitled *0-2 Years: Prenatal Assessment* on the Education CourseMate website and answer the following question:

1. How is a sonogram performed and for what purpose is it used?
2. What is an amniocentesis and what risks are associated with this procedure?
3. How common are genetic abnormalities?
4. For a period of time, businesses offered on-the-spot sonograms in local shopping malls. Do you think this is a good idea? Why or why not?

 # Threats to Optimum Fetal Development

Much is known about lifestyle practices that improve a mother's chances of having a healthy infant. However, there is also evidence to suggest that a number of environmental substances called **teratogens** can have negative consequences on the unborn child (Gilbert-Barness, 2010). Several are especially damaging during the earliest weeks, often before a woman realizes that she is pregnant. It is during these sensitive or critical periods that various fetal structures and major organ systems are rapidly forming and, thus, are most vulnerable to the effects of any harmful substance. The length of these critical periods varies. For example, the heart is most vulnerable from the third to sixth weeks; the palate, from the sixth to eighth weeks. Extensive research has identified a number of major teratogens, including:

- Alcohol consumption
- Maternal smoking
- Addictive drugs (e.g., cocaine, heroin, amphetamines)
- Hazardous chemicals (e.g., mercury, lead, carbon monoxide, polychlorinated biphenols [PCBs], paint solvents)
- Pesticides and insecticides
- Some medications (Table 3-2, p. 60)
- Maternal infections (Table 3-3, p. 61)
- Radiation such as x-rays

---

teratogens—harmful agents that can cause fetal damage (e.g., malformations, neurological, behavioral problems) during the prenatal period.

Researchers continue to study other potential links between environmental factors and birth defects. To date, many findings are still considered to be inconclusive, controversial, or both. Some of the factors being investigated include:

- Prolonged exposure to high temperatures (hot baths, saunas, hot tubs)
- Secondary smoke
- Herbal supplements and over-the-counter medications
- Electromagnetic fields such as those created by heating pads and electric blankets
- Caffeine (Peck, Leviton, & Cowan, 2010)
- Hazardous waste sites

The relationship between teratogen exposure and fetal damage is not always clear or direct. Several factors can influence a teratogen's harmful effect on fetal development, including the amount of exposure (dose), fetal age (timing), and genetic makeup of the mother and fetus. Thus, women who are contemplating pregnancy should avoid unnecessary contact with known teratogens that are capable of crossing the placental barrier. As noted earlier, fetal organs and body systems are especially vulnerable to these agents during the early weeks following conception. This is not to suggest that there is ever a completely safe time period. Even during the later months, fetal growth can be seriously affected by maternal exposure to or use of substances mentioned here and in the following sections. There is also evidence to suggest that teratogens can have a lifelong effect on an individual's health (Visser, Mulder, & Ververs, 2010).

Alcohol

Alcohol consumption during pregnancy can have serious consequences for both the mother and the developing fetus (O'Leary et al., 2010). Warnings to this effect appear on the labels of all alcoholic products. Mothers who consume alcohol during pregnancy have a greater risk of miscarriages, stillbirths, premature infants, and low-birth-weight infants. The incidence of fetal death is also significantly higher. Because alcoholic beverages contain only calories and no nutrients, consuming them on a regular or binge basis limits the mother's dietary intake of essential proteins, vitamins, and minerals necessary for her well-being and that of her infant.

Alcohol is also a potentially toxic teratogen that can have a wide range of irreversible effects on fetal development. Because mother and infant share a common circulatory system (through the placenta and umbilical cord), both are affected by any alcohol that is consumed. However, alcohol remains in the fetal circulatory system twice as long as in that of the mother. It is especially damaging to the fetus during the critical first trimester of pregnancy when most body structures and organs, especially the brain, heart, and nervous system, are forming.

Prenatal exposure to alcohol can result in conditions commonly referred to as fetal alcohol spectrum disorders (FASDs). Heavy or binge drinking is associated with a preventable condition known as fetal alcohol syndrome (FAS), which causes mental and growth retardation, behavior and learning problems (hyperactivity), poor motor coordination,

heart defects, characteristic facial deformities (eyes set wide apart, shortened eye lids, flattened nose), and speech impairments (Ismail et al., 2010). Moderate alcohol consumption is associated with a milder form of this condition known as fetal alcohol effect (FAE). These children often exhibit a range of learning and behavior disorders. When alcohol is consumed later in the pregnancy, it typically interferes with proper fetal growth.

Precisely how much alcohol might be damaging to an unborn child is difficult to determine. Most likely, the relationship between alcohol and fetal damage is more complex than it might initially appear. *Thus, no amount of alcohol is considered safe to consume during pregnancy.*

Smoking

Many pregnant women continue to smoke despite warnings issued by the U.S. Surgeon General and those printed on all tobacco products (Figure 3-6). Maternal smoking has been linked to a variety of fetal malformations and birth complications (Ashford et al., 2010). Cigarette smoke contains substances, including nicotine, tars, and carbon monoxide, that cross the placental barrier and interfere with normal fetal development. Carbon monoxide reduces the amount of oxygen available to the fetus. This early oxygen deprivation seems to correlate with learning and behavior problems, especially as exposed children reach school age. Mothers who smoke during pregnancy are more likely to experience miscarriage, premature births, stillborn infants, and low-birth-weight infants. Their babies are also at higher risk for developing sudden infant death syndrome (SIDS) and a range of acute and chronic respiratory problems (e.g., allergies, asthma, colds). Studies have also shown that attention deficit disorders are more common among children whose mothers smoked during their pregnancy (Nomura, Marks, & Halperin, 2010).

Chemicals and Drugs

Numerous chemicals and drugs are also known to have an adverse effect on the developing fetus. These substances range from prescription and nonprescription medications to pesticides, fertilizers, and street drugs (Mattison, 2010) (Table 3-2). Some

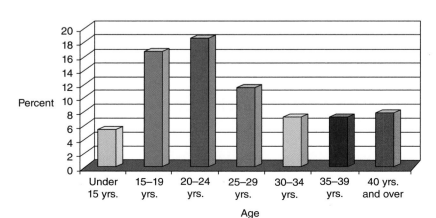

Figure 3-6
Percentage of mothers who smoke during pregnancy.
(*Source:* National Vital Statistics Reports, Vol. 56, No. 6, December 5, 2007).

Table 3-2 Examples of Potentially Teratogenic Drugs

- Analgesics (more than an occasional dose of aspirin or ibuprofen)
- Antibiotics (particularly tetracyclines and streptomycin)
- Anticonvulsants (such as Dilantin)
- Anticoagulants (used to thin the blood, such as Coumadin)
- Antidepressants
- Antihistamines
- Antihypertensives (used to treat high blood pressure)
- Antineoplastic drugs (used to treat cancers and some forms of arthritis, such as Methotrexate)
- Antiviral agents
- Hormones (such as diethylstilbesterol [DES] and progesterin)
- Large doses of vitamin A (in excess of 10,000 IU; includes some acne treatments such as Accutane and Retin-A)
- Thyroid and antithyroid drugs
- Diet pills
- Nicotine
- Cocaine, heroin, marijuana, methadone

cause severe malformations such as missing or malformed limbs or facial features. Others can lead to fetal death (spontaneous abortion), premature birth, or lifelong behavior and learning disabilities. Not all exposed fetuses will be affected in the same manner or to the same degree. The nature and severity of an infant's abnormalities seem to be influenced by the timing of exposure during fetal development, the amount and type of substance, the mother's general state of health, and maternal and fetal genetics. Research has not yet provided a definitive answer about which drugs and chemicals (if any) have absolutely no harmful effects on the developing fetus. Thus, women who are or may become pregnant are encouraged to check with their medical provider before using any chemical substance or medication (prescription or nonprescription). Exposure to previously discussed environmental hazards, such as high doses of radiation and x-rays, particularly in the early stages of pregnancy, should also be avoided.

Maternal Infections

Although the placenta effectively filters out many infectious organisms, it cannot prevent all disease-causing agents from reaching the unborn child. Some are known to cause fetal abnormalities (Table 3-3). Whether a fetus will be affected and, if so, the resulting abnormality, depends on the particular disease and stage of pregnancy when the infection occurs. For example, a pregnant woman who develops rubella (German

Table 3-3 Examples of Potentially Teratogenic Maternal Conditions and Infections

- Chickenpox
- Cytomegalovirus (CMV)
- Diabetes
- Fifth disease
- Herpes
- HIV
- Mumps
- Rubella (German measles)
- Syphilis
- Toxoplasmosis

Note: Information about any of these infectious diseases can be found on the Centers for Disease Control's website (*www.cdc.gov*).

measles) during the first four to eight weeks following conception is at high risk for giving birth to an infant who may have heart problems, be deaf, and/or blind (an example of the extreme vulnerability of the fetus during its earliest weeks). *Note*: Rubella can be controlled if women who do not have natural immunity are immunized following a pregnancy or not less than three to four months prior to becoming pregnant.

Fortunately, only a small percentage of infants exposed to infectious agents will experience abnormalities. It is still unknown why some fetuses are affected, whereas others are not. What is reasonably certain is that pregnant women who are well nourished, have regular prenatal care, are generally healthy, and are free of addictive substances have a higher probability of giving birth to a strong and healthy infant.

An Infant's Arrival: Labor and Delivery

For most women, childbirth is a natural process that follows months of anticipation and preparation. Several birthing options are available to families today, including birthing centers, hospitals, and home deliveries with physicians or certified nurse midwives in attendance. Although the fundamental labor and delivery process is similar for most mothers-to-be, the actual experience is often unique. Labor and delivery can occur prematurely, on time, or beyond one's expected due date, be long or short in duration, be considered relatively easy or difficult, and occur with or without complications.

The onset of labor is usually signaled by a number of changes. Approximately two weeks before labor begins, the mother might observe that she is carrying the baby lower in her abdomen. This occurs as the baby's head drops into the birth canal in preparation for delivery and is commonly referred to as *lightening*. The mother may also notice that her contractions are becoming stronger and more regular as they prepare the birth

---

canal for delivery. When active labor begins, she may experience a small amount of bloody discharge as the mucus plug that has protected the birth canal opening for nine months becomes dislodged. Some mothers also have a leaking of amniotic fluid if the sac surrounding the fetus tears or breaks.

The normal birthing process is divided into three stages. The first and longest stage lasts approximately fourteen to seventeen hours for first-time mothers and six to eight hours for subsequent births. During this stage, contractions slowly cause the diameter of the **cervix** to expand (dilate) in preparation for delivery. Stage two begins when the cervix is completely dilated and lasts until the infant is delivered, a period of approximately thirty to ninety minutes. Contractions become more intense and painful throughout this stage. When the baby is born, the umbilical cord is clamped, and the infant begins to function independently. The third and final stage begins after the baby arrives and ends when the placenta is delivered; this stage usually lasts only a few minutes.

The majority of births proceed normally and without complications. However, a small percentage of deliveries might require some form of medical intervention. In less than 5 percent of live births, the infant decides to descend feet or buttocks first (rather than head first) into the birth canal. This situation usually requires a **cesarean section** (C-section) to be performed (Peterson, 2010). A C-section may also be necessary when labor does not progress, the mother's birth canal is too small, the umbilical cord prolapses, or a medical problem such as fetal distress develops. Medical intervention is sometimes used to assist the baby out of the birth canal. Forceps (a salad tong–like device) are placed around the infant's head and used to gently pull the baby out during contractions. Temporary bruises may be left on the baby's face or head, but these will fade within several days. Vacuum-assisted births are replacing the use of forceps in many hospitals today. A large plastic or rubber cap is fitted on the baby's head and suction is applied, creating a gentle traction to aid the baby in exiting the birth canal.

Throughout the birth process, the infant is monitored closely for signs of distress. Heart rate is checked by using a stethoscope or ultrasound device (Doppler) or by placing a tiny electrode on the infant's head. Immediately following birth, the newborn's condition is assessed at one minute and five minutes, using the Apgar scale (Figure 3-7). The infant receives a score between zero and two in each of five areas: appearance, pulse, grimace, activity, and respirations; a score of eight or better is considered normal (Apgar, 1953). The Apgar scale provides a reliable measure of how well the infant is doing at the time but is not a predictor of future health or developmental problems.

Healthy mothers and infants are typically released from the hospital within one to two days after the birth. Mothers who have had a C-section or health complications may remain in the hospital for several days longer. Infants born prematurely or of low birth weight will remain hospitalized until they are healthy enough to go home.

Cultural differences can influence how a mother and her family perceive pregnancy and an infant's birth (Maternowska et al., 2010). Some groups view pregnancy and

cervix—the lower portion of the uterus that opens into the vagina.
cesarean section—the delivery of a baby through an incision in the mother's abdomen and uterus.

Figure 3-7
Apgar scale for evaluating newborns.
Source: Adapted from
V. Apgar (1953).

	0	1	2
Appearance (skin color)	Bluish or pale	Pink, except extremities	Pink all over
Pulse	None	Fewer than 100 beats/minute	Greater than 100 beats/minute
Grimace (reflex response)	None	Makes some facial response	Strong response: cries, coughs, or sneezes
Activity (muscle tone)	Limp	Weak flexion of extremities	Active movement
Respiration (breathing)	None	Slow and/or irregular	Regular; strong cry

delivery as normal events that require little special attention or recognition. Others consider a child's birth an experience to be shared by extended family members. Myths and ideas about everything from the mother's diet to how she responds to physical discomforts, sexuality, and daily living routines are also unique to various cultural groups (Carolan, Steele, & Margetts, 2010). Although these views may differ from your own, it is important to show respect and support for the family's beliefs and values.

 TeachSource Video Connections

Newborn Assessment. For nine months, the newborn relies on its mother for all essential needs—nutrients, oxygen, warmth, and protection. At birth, the infant arrives into an unfamiliar world and must immediately take over many of these functions. Careful monitoring of the newborn's vital signs (heart rate, breathing) provides valuable information about how well he or she is making this transition. Watch the learning video entitled *0-2 Years: Birth* on the Education CourseMate website and answer the following questions:

1. How would you describe the newborn's appearance immediately following birth?
2. What is the Apgar scale and how is the test administered?
3. What information does the Apgar provide?
4. What does a low score indicate?

 ## Maternal Depression

New mothers often undergo a range of mixed emotions following an infant's birth. Feelings of exhilaration, uncertainty, anxiety, and overwhelming fatigue may come and go at a moment's notice. A majority of new mothers experience these mood swings, commonly referred to as the *baby blues* (Figure 3-8), several days following delivery.

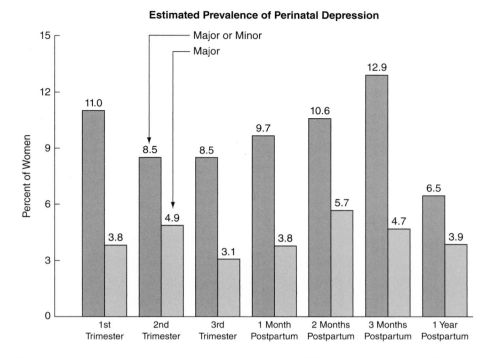

Figure 3-8
Estimated incidence of
maternal depression.

Source: U.S. Department
of Health and Human
Services, Health Resources
and Services Administration,
*Women's Health USA
2005.* Rockville, MD: U.S.
Department of Health and
Human Services, 2005.

Symptoms can include weepiness, sadness, anxiety, difficulty sleeping, lack of energy, appetite loss, irritability, or any or all of these. Hormonal changes, lack of sleep, and added responsibilities are thought to trigger these feelings, which typically improve within several weeks. Compassionate support from family members and friends, moderate exercise, adequate rest, and a healthy diet can help to ease this temporary discomfort. However, a doctor should be consulted if symptoms are severe or persist because this could be a sign of postpartum depression.

Fewer than 10 to 12 percent of new mothers experience signs of postpartum depression, which typically develops within six months of delivery (Wood, Middleton, & Leonard, 2010). Although the symptoms are similar to the baby blues, they are more serious and can include hallucinations, thoughts of harming the infant, hopelessness, and/or suicide. Postpartum depression can last three to twelve months and has been shown to interfere with the quality of maternal care and emotional attachment with the infant (Bagner et al., 2010). It has also been shown to affect an infant's language and social-emotional development (Conroy et al., 2010; Pemberton et al., 2010).

SUMMARY

A human pregnancy requires approximately 266 days (nine months) from conception until an infant is fully developed. The mother's general health, age, quality of diet, emotional state, and physical fitness influence healthy fetal development. Exposure to environmental factors (teratogens) such as certain infectious illnesses, alcohol, addictive drugs, smoking, and some medications (prescription and over-the-counter)

are known to have a harmful effect on fetal development. Mothers can take steps to improve their chances of having a healthy pregnancy and infant by obtaining routine prenatal care, maintaining good health, following a nutritious diet, gaining an appropriate amount of weight (not too much or too little), participating in daily physical activity, and maintaining a positive state of mental health.

Most mothers experience a normal labor and delivery, although a C-section may be performed if complications develop. Infants who are born prematurely or at a low birth weight will remain in the hospital until they are healthy and have gained sufficient weight. Although baby blues are fairly common among new mothers, a small percentage will develop maternal depression which interferes with infant development and requires medical treatment

Key Terms

conception **p. 48**	spina bifida **p. 53**
genes **p. 48**	anencephaly **p. 53**
temperament **p. 48**	cleft lip/cleft palate **p. 53**
zygote **p. 49**	sonogram **p. 56**
implantation **p. 49**	CVS **p. 56**
embryo **p. 49**	amniocentesis **p. 56**
placenta **p. 49**	teratogens **p. 57**
low birth weight (LBW) **p. 52**	cervix **p. 62**
premature infant **p. 53**	cesarean section **p. 62**

Apply What You Know

A. Apply What You Have Learned

Reread the developmental sketch about Anna and Miguel at the beginning of the chapter and answer the following questions.

1. At what point is Anna likely to begin feeling the baby move?
2. What practices should Anna avoid during pregnancy to improve her chances of having a healthy baby?
3. What negative effects might Anna's smoking have on her pregnancy?
4. Which nutrients are especially important for Anna to include in her daily diet?

B. Review Questions

1. Discuss three practices that promote a healthy pregnancy.
2. Describe three factors that appear to be hazardous to fetal development.
3. Identify one characteristic or change in fetal development that occurs during each month of pregnancy.
4. What role(s) does the placenta perform during pregnancy?
5. What characteristics would you expect to observe in a child who has Fetal Alcohol Syndrome (FAS)? Explain how this condition can be prevented.

Helpful Websites

March of Dimes
http://www.modimes.org

Medline Plus
http://www.nlm.nih.gov/medlineplus/
pregnancy.html

The National Women's Health Information Center
http://www.womenshealth.gov/pregnancy/index.cfm

References

Amarin, Z., & Obeidat, A. (2010). Effect of folic acid fortification on the incidence of neural tube defects, *Paediatric & Perinatal Epidemiology, 24*(4), 349–351.

American Congress of Obstetricians & Gynecologists (ACOG). (2010). *Nutrition during pregnancy.* Accessed on October 22, 2010, from http://www.acog.org/publications/patient_education/bp001.cfm.

Apgar, V. (1953). Proposal for a new method of evaluation of the newborn infant. *Current Researches in Anesthesia & Analgesia, 32*(4), 260–267.

Aron, A., Ketay, S., Hedden, T., Aron, E., Markus, H., & Gabrieli, J. (2010). Temperament trait of sensory processing sensitivity moderates cultural differences in neural response, *Social Cognitive & Affective Neuroscience, 5*(2–3), 219–226.

Ashford, K., Hahn, E., Hall, L., Rayens, M., Noland, M., & Ferguson, J. (2010). The effects of prenatal secondhand smoke exposure on preterm birth and neonatal outcomes, *Journal of Obstetric, Gynecologic, and Neonatal Nursing, 39*(5), 525–535.

Bagner, D., Pettit, J., Lewinsohn, P., & Seeley, J. (2010). Effect of maternal depresssion on child behavior: A sensitive period?, *Journal of the American Academy of Child & Adolescent Psychiatry, 49*(7), 699–707.

Broussard, C., Louik, C., & Honein, M., & Mitchell, A. (2010). Herbal use before and during pregnancy, *American Journal of Obstetrics & Gynecology, 202*(5), 443.e1–443.e6.

Buckner-Brown, J., Tucker, P., Rivera, M., Cosgrove, S., Coleman, J., Penson, A., & Bang, D. (2011). Racial and ethnic approaches to community health: Reducing health disparities by addressing social determinants of health, *Family & Community Health, 34*(1), S12–S22.

Carolan, M., Steele, C., & Margetts, H. (2010). Attitudes towards gestational diabetes among a multiethnic cohort in Australia, *Journal of Clinical Nursing, 19*(17–18), 2446–2453.

Centers for Disease Control & Prevention (CDC). (2009). Pediatric and Pregnancy: Nutrition Surveillance System. Accessed on October 22, 2010, from http://www.cdc.gov/pednss/pnss_tables/tables_analysis.htm.

Conroy, S., Marks, M., Schacht, R., Davies, H., & Moran, P. (2010). The impact of maternal depression and personality disorder on early infant care, *Social Psychiatry & Psychiatric Epidemiology, 45*(3), 285–292.

Davis, E., & Sandman, C. (2010). The timing of prenatal exposure to maternal cortisol and psychosocial stress is associated with human infant cognitive development, *Child Development, 81*(1), 131–148.

Debiec, K., Paul, K., Mitchell, C., & Hitti, J. (2010). Inadequate prenatal care and risk of preterm delivery among adolescents: A retrospective study over 10 years, *American Journal of Obstetrics & Gynecology, 203*(2), 122.e1–122.e6.

Franz, M., & Husslein, P. (2010). Obstetrical management of the older gravida, *Women's Health, 6*(3), 463–468.

Ghosh, S., Feingold, E., Chakraborty, S., & Dey, S. (2010). Telomere length is associated with types of chromosome 21 nondisjunction: A new insight into the maternal age effect on Down syndrome birth, *Human Genetics, 127*(4), 403–409.

Gilbert-Barness, E. (2010). Teratogenic causes of malformations, *Annals of Clinical & Laboratory Science, 40*(2), 99–114.

Grether, J., Anderson, M., Croen, L., Smith, & Windham, G. (2010). Risk of autism and increasing maternal and paternal age in a large North American population, *American Journal of Epidemiology, 170*(9), 1118–1126.

Haber, J., Bucholz, K., Jacob, T., Grant, J., Scherrer, J., Sartor, C., Duncan, A., & Heath, A. (2010). Effect of paternal alcohol and drug dependence on offspring conduct disorder: Gene-environment interplay, *Journal of Studies on Alcohol & Drugs, 71*(5), 652–663.

Ismail, S., Buckley, S., Budacki, R., Jabbar, A, & Gallicano, G. (2010). Screening, diagnosing, and prevention of fetal alcohol syndrome: Is this syndrome treatable?, *Developmental Neuroscience, 32*, 91–100.

Khanani, I., Elam, J., Hearn, R., Jones, C., & Maseru, N. (2010). The impact of prenatal WIC participation on infant mortality and racial disparities, *American Journal of Public Health, 100*(S1), S204–S209.

Kuntz, S., Ricco, J., Hill, W., & Anderko, L. (2010). Communicating methylmercury risks and fish consumption benefits to vulnerable childbearing populations, *Journal of Obstetric, Gynecologic, & Neonatal Nursing, 39*(1), 118–126.

Maternowska, C., Estrada, F., Campero, L., Herrera, C., Brindis, C., & Vostrejs, M. (2010). Gender, culture and reproductive decision-making among recent Mexican immigrants in California, *Culture, Health & Sexuality, 12*(1), 29–43.

Mattison, D. (2010). Environmental exposures and development, *Current Opinion in Pediatrics, 22*(2), 208–218.

Nabukera, S., Wingate, M., Owen, J., Salihu, H., Swaminathan, S., Alexander, G., & Kirby, R. (2009). Racial disparities in perinatal outcomes and pregnancy spacing among women delaying initiation of childbearing, *Maternal & Child Health Journal, 13*(1), 81–89.

Nomura, Y., Marks, D., & Halperin, J. (2010). Prenatal exposure to maternal and paternal smoking on attention deficit hyperactivity disorders symptoms and diagnosis in offspring, *Journal of Nervous & Mental Disease, 198*(9), 672–678.

O'Leary, C., Nassar, N., Kurinczuk, J., de Klerk, N., Geelhoed, E., Elliott, E., & Bower, C. (2010). Prenatal alcohol exposure and risk of birth defects, *Pediatrics, 126*(4), e843–e850.

Partington, S., Steber, D., Blair, K., & Cisler, R. (2009). Second births to teenage mothers: Risk factors for low birth weight and preterm birth, *Perspectives on Sexual & Reproductive Health, 41*(2), 101–109.

Peck, J., Leviton, A., Cowan, L. (2010). A review of the epidemiologic evidence concerning the reproductive health effects of caffeine consumption: A 2000-2009 update, *Food & Chemical Toxicology, 48*(10), 2549–2576.

Pemberton, C., Neiderhiser, J., Leve, L., Natsuaki, M., Shaw, D., Reiss, D., & Ge, X. (2010). Influence of parental depressive symptoms on adopted toddler behaviors: An emerging developmental cascade of genetic and environmental effects, *Developmental Psychopathology, 22*(4), 803–818.

Peterson, C. (2010). Are race and ethnicity risk factors for breech presentation? *Journal of Obstetric, Gynecologic, & Neonatal Nursing, 39*(3), 277–291.

Visser, G., Mulder, E., & Ververs, F. (2010). Fetal behavioral teratology, *Journal of Maternal-Fetal and Neonatal Medicine, 23*(S3), 14–16.

Wehby, G., & Murray, J. (2010). Folic acid and orofacial clefts: A review of the evidence, *Oral Diseases, 16*(1), 11–19.

Wood, A., Middleton, S., & Leonard, D. (2010). When it's more than the blues: A collaborative response to postpartum depression, *Public Health Nursing, 27*(3), 248–254.

Woods, S., Melville, J., Guo, Y., Fan, M., & Gavin, A. (2010). Psychosocial stress during pregnancy, *American Journal of Obstetrics & Gynecology, 202*(1), 61.e1– 61.e7.

You are just a click away from a variety of interactive study tools and resources. Access the text's Education CourseMate website at **www.cengagebrain.com**, where you'll find a variety of enrichment materials, including videos, glossary flashcards, activities, tutorial quizzes, web links, and more.

CHAPTER 4
Infancy: Birth to Twelve Months

Learning Objectives

After reading this chapter, you should be able to:

- Define the term *reflexive motor activity* and identify examples that are characteristic of newborns.
- React to the statement, "babies can't learn," and describe activities that promote infants' cognitive development.
- Discuss ways in which infants communicate with adults.
- Explain the phenomenon known as "stranger anxiety."

naeyc Standards Chapter Links:

1a, 1b, and 1c: Promoting child development and learning
2a and 2c: Building family and community relationships
3c and 3d: Observing, documenting, and assessing to support young children and families
4a, 4b, 4c and 4d: Using developmentally effective approaches
5c: Using content knowledge to build meaningful curriculum

Meet Juan

Anna and Miguel beamed as they watched their infant son Juan sleep. Anna is thankful that her pregnancy went smoothly and that Juan is healthy despite being born almost two weeks early. Their family and friends tell them what a "good baby" Juan seems to be. He sleeps three to four hours between feedings, follows their every movement, is discovering his fingers and toes, and often falls asleep peacefully in his father's arms.

Juan's parents cannot believe their son will already be two months old next week. When placed on his stomach, he tries to pick up

continued...

his head to study the brightly colored geometric pictures his mother has fastened to the sides of the crib. He is also beginning to reach and grasp the small stuffed toys his parents offer to him. Anna is fascinated by how much Juan seems to be learning each day. Their pediatrician is also pleased with Juan's rate of growth and development.

Anna's maternity leave will soon end, and it is difficult for her to think about leaving Juan and returning to her job at the bank. However, she finds some comfort in the fact that Miguel's mother, having raised four children of her own, has offered to care for Juan until they are able to locate space in a nearby child care center. Juan's parents have visited several neighborhood programs and placed his name on waiting lists, but none have openings for an infant at this time.

Ask Yourself

1. In what ways are Juan and his parents communicating with one another to form a strong emotional bond?
2. What activities can Anna and Miguel begin doing now to encourage Juan's future language development?

The Newborn (Birth to One Month)

The healthy newborn infant is truly amazing. Within moments of birth, he or she begins to adapt to an outside world that is radically different from the one experienced **in utero**. The newborn's systems for breathing, eating, eliminating, and regulating body temperature are functional and ready to take over at the time of birth. However, because these systems are still quite immature the infant remains completely dependent on adults for survival.

Motor development (movement) is both reflexive and protective. There is no voluntary control of the body during the early weeks. Although newborn infants sleep most of the time, they do not lack awareness. They are sensitive to their environment and have unique methods of responding to it. Crying is their primary method for communicating needs and emotions. Perceptual and cognitive abilities are present, but they are primitive and relatively difficult to distinguish from one another during the initial weeks following birth (Robinson & Sloutsky, 2010).

in utero—Latin term for "in the mother's uterus."

DEVELOPMENTAL PROFILES AND GROWTH PATTERNS

Growth and Physical Characteristics

The newborn's physical characteristics are distinct from those of a slightly older infant. At birth, the skin usually appears wrinkled. Within the first few days, it will become dry and likely to peel. All infants have relatively light-colored skin that gradually darkens to a shade characteristic of their genetic makeup. The head may have an unusual shape as the result of the birth process, but it regains a normal shape within the first weeks. Hair color and amount vary. Additional physical characteristics include:

- Weight at birth averages 6.5–9 pounds (3.0–4.1 kg); females weigh approximately 7 pounds (3.2 kg), and males weigh approximately 7.5 pounds (3.4 kg).

- From 5–7 percent of birth weight is lost in the days immediately following birth.

- Weight increases an average of 5–6 ounces (0.14–0.17 kg) per week during the first month.

- Length at birth ranges between 18–21 inches (45.7–53.3 cm).

- Respiration rate is approximately 30–50 breaths per minute; breathing can be somewhat irregular in rhythm and rate.

- Chest appears small, cylindrical, and nearly the same size as the head.

Figure 4-1
Measuring head circumference.

- Normal body temperature ranges from 96°F–99°F (35.6°C–37.2°C); fluctuations are normal during the early weeks and then stabilize as the system matures and a fat layer develops beneath the skin.

- Skin is sensitive, especially on the infant's hands and around the mouth.

- Head is large in relation to body and accounts for nearly one quarter of the total body length.

- Head circumference averages 12.5–14.5 inches (31.7–36.8 cm) at birth (Figure 4-1).

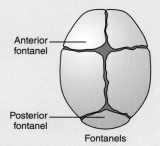

Figure 4-2
Location of fontanels.

- "Soft" spots (**fontanels**) are located on the top (anterior) and back (posterior) of the head (Figure 4-2).

- Tongue appears large in proportion to the mouth.

---

fontanels—small openings (sometimes called "soft spots") in the infant's skull bones; covered with soft tissue; eventually, they grow closed.

Birth to 1 month

DEVELOPMENTAL PROFILES AND GROWTH PATTERNS *(continued)*

- Cries without tears.
- Eyes are extremely sensitive to light.
- Sees only outlines and shapes; is unable to focus on distant objects.

Motor Development

The newborn's motor skills are purely reflexive movements that are designed primarily for protection and survival. During the first month, the infant gains some control over several of these early reflexes. Gradually, many of these reflexes disappear as the infant's central nervous system matures and begins to take over control of purposeful behavior. The failure of reflexes to fade according to schedule can be an early indicator of possible neurological problems (Yasuyuki & Yasuhiro, 2010). During the first month, the infant:

- Engages in motor activity that is primarily reflexive (Figure 4-3):
  - Swallowing, sucking, gagging, coughing, yawning, blinking, and elimination reflexes are present at birth.
  - Rooting reflex is triggered by gently touching the sensitive skin around the cheek and mouth; the infant turns toward the cheek being stroked.
  - Moro (startle) reflex is set off by a sudden loud noise or touch, such as bumping of the crib or quick lowering of the infant's position downward (as if dropping); both arms are thrown open and away from the body, then quickly brought back together over the chest.
  - Grasping reflex occurs when the infant tightly curls its fingers around an object placed in its hand.
  - Stepping reflex involves the infant moving the feet up and down in walking-like movements when held upright with feet touching a firm surface (Figure 4-4).

Appears	swallow,* gag,* cough,* yawn,* blink suck rooting Moro (startle) grasp stepping plantar elimination tonic neck reflex (TNR)	Landau tear* (cries with tears)	parachute palmar grasp pincer grasp				
(Age)	(birth)	(1–4 mos)	(4–8 mos)	(8–12 mos)	(12–18 mos)	(18–24 mos)	(3–4 years)
Disappears		grasp suck (becomes voluntary) step root tonic neck reflex (TNR)	Moro (startle)	palmar grasp plantar reflex	Landau	parachute	elimination (becomes voluntary)

* Permanent; present throughout person's lifetime.

Figure 4-3
Summary of reflexes.

- Tonic neck reflex (TNR) occurs when the infant, in supine (face up) position, extends arm and leg on the same side toward which the head is turned; the opposite arm and leg are flexed (pulled in toward the body). This is sometimes called the "fencing position" (Figure 4-5).
- Plantar reflex is initiated when pressure is placed against the ball of the infant's foot, causing the toes to curl.

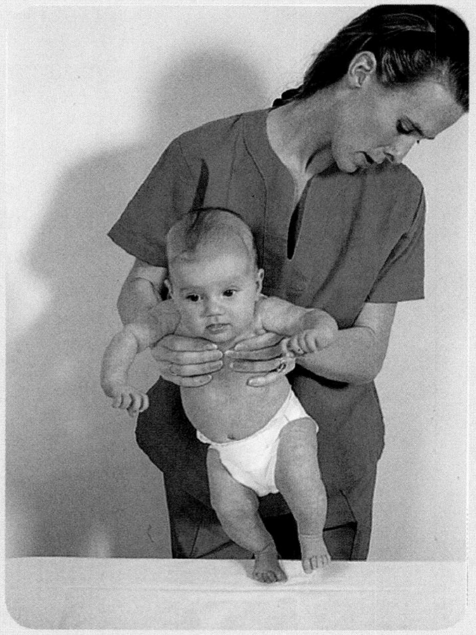

- Maintains "fetal" position (back flexed or rounded, extremities held close to the body, knees drawn up), especially when asleep.
- Holds hands in a fist; does not reach for objects.
- When held in a prone (face down) position, infant's head falls lower than the horizontal line of the body with hips flexed and arms and legs hanging downward (Figure 4-6).

Figure 4-4
Stepping reflex.

- Has good muscle tone in the upper body when supported under the arms.
- Turns head from side to side when placed in a prone position.
  - **Pupils** dilate (enlarge) and constrict (become smaller) in response to light.
  - Eyes do not always work together and may appear crossed at times.
  - Attempts to track (follow) objects that are out of direct line of vision; unable to coordinate eye and hand movements.

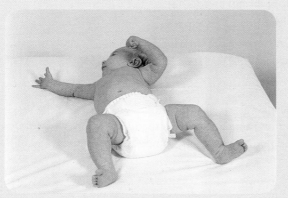

Figure 4-5
Tonic neck reflex (TNR).

Figure 4-6
Prone suspension.

---

pupil—the small, dark, central portion of the eye.

DEVELOPMENTAL PROFILES AND GROWTH PATTERNS *(continued)*

Perceptual-Cognitive Development

The newborn's perceptual-cognitive skills are designed to capture and hold the attention of family and caregivers and to gain some sense of the environment. Hearing is the most well developed of the skills. Newborns can hear and respond to differences among certain sounds and are especially responsive to their mother's voice (Vouloumanos et al., 2010). They can often be soothed with quiet sounds (cooing, humming) and movements (rocking, swaying). Newborns also are responsive to touch, with the skin around the mouth and hands being especially sensitive. Vision is present, although limited. However, newborns are especially attracted to highly contrasting (black-and-white) geometric designs. They are able to briefly focus both eyes on objects (especially faces) that are close and moving slowly (Balas, 2009).

From the earliest days of life, newborns are absorbing information through all of their senses and learning from what they see, hear, touch, taste, and smell. Thus, the newborn's cognitive behaviors can be characterized as purely reflexive. They take the form of sucking, startle responses, grimacing, flailing of arms and legs, and uncontrolled eye movements, all of which overlap with perceptual responses. During the first month, the infant:

- Blinks eyes in response to a fast-approaching object.
- Follows a slowly moving object through a complete 180° arc.
- Follows objects moved vertically if object is close to infant's face (10–15 inches [25.4–38.1 cm]).
- Continues looking about, even in the dark.
- Begins to study own hand when lying in TNR position.
- Hears as well (with the exception of quiet sounds) at birth as do most adults; hearing is more acute than vision.
- Prefers to listen to mother's voice rather than a stranger's; opens eyes and looks toward mother.
- Often synchronizes body movements to speech patterns of parent or caregiver.
- Distinguishes some tastes; shows preference for sweet liquids.
- Has a keen sense of smell at birth; turns toward preferred (sweet) odors, away from strong or unpleasant odors (Lagercrantz & Changeux, 2009).

Speech and Language Development

The beginnings of speech and language development can be identified in several of the newborn's reflexes. These include the bite–release action that occurs when the infant's gums are rubbed, the rooting reflex, and the sucking reflex. In addition, the newborn communicates directly and indirectly in a number of other ways.

- Crying and fussing are major forms of communication at this stage.
- Reacts to loud noises by blinking, moving, stopping a movement, shifting eyes about, or exhibiting a startle response.
- Shows a preference for certain sounds, such as music and human voices, by calming down or quieting.

- Turns head in an effort to locate voices and other sounds.
- Makes occasional sounds other than crying.

Social-Emotional Development

Newborns possess a variety of built-in social skills. They indicate needs and distress and respond to adults' reactions (Hari & Kujala, 2009). The infant thrives on feelings of security and soon displays a sense of attachment to primary caregivers. The newborn:

- Experiences a brief period of calm alertness immediately following birth; gazes at parents and listens to their voices.
- Sleeps 17–19 hours per day; is gradually awake and responsive for longer periods (Figure 4-7).
- Likes to be held close and cuddled when awake; opens eyes and looks toward mother.
- Shows qualities of individuality; each infant varies in ways of responding or not responding to similar situations.
- Begins to establish an emotional attachment, or a **bonding** relationship, with parents and caregivers; opens eyes; relaxes body tension.
- Develops a gradual sense of security or trust with parents and caregivers. Is able to sense caregiver differences and responds accordingly. For example, an infant may become tense with an adult who is unfamiliar or uncomfortable with the infant.

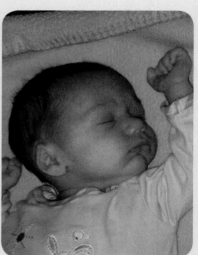

Figure 4-7
Young infants spend most of their time sleeping.

▶️❚❚ TeachSource Video Connections

Newborn Reflex Development. Newborns are not capable of purposeful movement. However, this does not suggest they are passive individuals. Reflexes serve important protective functions and gradually give way to increasingly complex motor development. As you watch the learning video entitled *0–2 Years: The Newborn and Reflex Development* on the Education CourseMate website, answer the following questions:

1. Which involuntary reflexes are considered to be critical for the infant's survival?
2. What does it indicate when one or more of the infant's reflexes are absent, do not fade at the correct time, or reappear later on?
3. How does the infant's reflex system affect early cognitive development?

---

bonding—the establishment of a close, loving relationship between an infant and adult, usually the mother and father; sometimes called *attachment*.

DAILY ROUTINES

Eating

- Takes 6–10 feedings, totaling approximately 22 ounces (660 ml) per 24 hours at the beginning of this period; later, the number will decrease to 5–6 feedings as the amount consumed increases.
- Drinks 2–4 ounces of breast milk or formula per feeding; takes 25–30 minutes to complete a feeding; may fall asleep toward the end.
- Expresses the need for food by crying.
- Benefits from being fed in an upright position; this practice reduces the risk of choking and of developing ear infections (Ladomenou et al., 2010).

Toileting, Bathing, and Dressing

- Signals the need for a diaper change by crying. (If crying does not stop when diaper has been changed, another cause should be sought.)
- Enjoys bath; keeps eyes open, coos, and relaxes body tension when placed in warm water.
- Expresses displeasure (fusses, cries) when clothes are pulled over head (best to avoid over-the-head clothes).
- Prefers to be wrapped firmly (swaddled) in a blanket; coos, stops crying, and relaxes muscles; swaddling seems to foster a sense of security and comfort.
- Has 1–4 bowel movements per day.

Sleeping

- Begins to sleep 4–6 periods per 24 hours after the first few days following birth; one of these might be 5–7 hours in length.
- Cries sometimes before falling asleep (usually stops if held and rocked briefly).
- *Placing baby on his or her back only and on a firm mattress to sleep reduces the risk of sudden infant death syndrome (SIDS).* Remove all pillows, fluffy blankets, bumper pads, toys, and other soft items from crib or sleeping area. Dress infant lightly to avoid overheating.

Play and Social Activities

- Prefers light and brightness; may fuss if turned away from a light source.
- Stares at faces in close visual range (10–12 inches [25.4–30.5 cm]).
- Signals the need for social stimulation by crying; stops when picked up or put in infant seat close to voices and movement.
- Is content to lie on back much of the time.
- Needs to be forewarned (e.g., touched, talked to) before being picked up to avoid being startled.
- Enjoys lots of touching and holding; however, may become fussy with too much handling or overstimulation.
- Enjoys en face (face-to-face) position (Frank, Vul, & Johnson, 2009).

Learning Activities

Developmental applications for families and teachers:

- Respond with gentle and dependable attention to infant's cries so he or she feels secure and learns to trust. (Infants always cry for a reason; crying signals a need.) Stroking the skin gently may help soothe and relax the infant.

- Make eye-to-eye contact when infant is in an alert state; make faces or stick out your tongue, which are activities that new babies often imitate. (Imitation is an important avenue for early learning.)

- Talk and sing to the infant in a normal voice during feeding, diapering, and bathing; vary voice tone and rhythm of speech.

- Show delight in baby's responsiveness: smile, laugh, comment. (Mutual responsiveness and social turn-taking are the bases for all teaching and learning in the months and years ahead.)

- Show baby simple pictures (young infants are attracted to black-and-white geometric designs and faces); gently move a stuffed animal or toy in baby's visual pathway approximately 10–15 inches (25–37.5 cm) from the infant's face to encourage visual tracking; hang toys or mobile within baby's visual range (change often—novelty increases interest).

- Take cues from the infant; too much stimulation can be as distressing as too little attention; stop activities temporarily if baby begins to cry, becomes fussy, or loses interest.

Developmental Alerts

Check with a health care provider or early childhood specialist if, by one month of age, the infant *does not*:

- Show alarm or startle responses to loud noise.
- Suck and swallow with ease.
- Gain in height, weight, and head circumference.
- Grasp with equal strength in both hands.
- Make eye-to-eye contact when awake and being held.
- Roll head from side to side when placed on stomach.
- Express needs and emotions with distinctive cries and patterns of vocalizations that can be distinguished from one another.
- Stop crying or become soothed (relaxed) most times when picked up and held.

1 to 4 months

Safety Concerns

Before the baby arrives, be sure to complete first aid and cardiopulmonary resuscitation (CPR) courses. Always be aware of new safety issues as the infant continues to grow and develop.

Burns

- Never heat bottles in a microwave oven; hot spots can form and burn the infant's mouth.
- Set temperature of hot water heater so that it is no higher than 120°F (49°C).
- Always check temperature of water before bathing an infant.

Choking

- Learn CPR.
- Always hold infant in an upright position while feeding; do not prop bottles.

Suffocation

- Provide a firm mattress that fits crib snugly to prevent the infant from becoming wedged in open cracks.

- *Always put infants to sleep on their back;* this practice reduces the risk of sudden infant death syndrome (SIDS). Tuck bottom edges of a light blanket under bottom end of the mattress. Remove all soft items from baby's crib (e.g., fluffy blankets, bumper pads, stuffed animals, pillows).
- Do not use infant sleep positioners or sling carriers.
- Install smoke and carbon monoxide detectors near the infant's room.

Transportation

- Always use an approved, rear-facing carrier when transporting the infant in a vehicle; check for proper installation.

One to Four Months

During these early months, the wonders of infancy continue to unfold. Growth proceeds at a rapid pace. Body systems are fairly well stabilized, with temperature, breathing patterns, and heart rate becoming more regular. Motor skills improve as strength and voluntary muscle control increase. Longer periods of wakefulness encourage the infant's socioemotional development. Social responsiveness begins to appear as infants practice and enjoy using their eyes to explore the environment (Mundy & Jarrold, 2010). As social awareness develops, the infant continues to establish a sense of trust and emotional attachment to parents and caregivers.

Although crying remains a primary way of communicating and of gaining adult attention, more complex communication skills are beginning to emerge. Infants soon find great pleasure in imitating the speech sounds and gestures of others (Vouloumanos et al., 2010). Cooing often begins around two months of age and represents an important step in the acquisition of language and give-and-take interaction with others.

Learning takes place continuously throughout the infant's waking hours as newly acquired skills are used for exploring and gathering information about a still new and unfamiliar environment. However, differences in cultural expectations and environmental conditions can influence the rate and acquisition of these skills. Critical brain development is fostered by providing infants with numerous opportunities for learning

(see Learning Activities). It is important to note once again that perceptual, cognitive, and motor developments are closely interrelated and nearly impossible to differentiate during these early months.

DEVELOPMENTAL PROFILES AND GROWTH PATTERNS

1 to 4 months

Growth and Physical Characteristics

- Averages 20–27 inches (50.8–68.6 cm) in length; grows approximately 1 inch (2.54 cm) per month (measured with infant lying on back, from top of the head to bottom of heel, knees straight and foot flexed).
- Weighs an average of 8–16 pounds (3.6–7.3 kg); females weigh slightly less than males.
- Gains approximately 1/4–1/2 pound (0.11–0.22 kg) per week.
- Breathes at a rate of approximately 30–40 breaths per minute; rate increases significantly during periods of crying or activity.
- Normal body temperature ranges from 96.4°F–99.6°F (35.7°C–37.5°C).
- Head and chest circumference are nearly equal.
- Head circumference increases approximately 3/4 inch (1.9 cm) during the first and second months and 5/8 inch (1.6 cm) during months three and four. Increases are an important indication of continued brain growth.
- Continues to breathe using abdominal muscles.
- Posterior fontanel closes by the second month; anterior fontanel closes to approximately 1/2 inch (1.3 cm).
- Skin remains sensitive and easily irritated.
- Arms and legs are of equal length, size, and shape; easily flexed and extended.
- Legs may appear slightly bowed; feet appear flat with no arch.
- Cries with tears.
- Begins moving eyes together in unison (binocular vision).
- Detects color (color vision is now present) (Franklin et al., 2010).

Motor Development

- Reflexive motor behaviors are changing (Figure 4-3):
  - Tonic neck and stepping reflexes disappear.
  - Rooting and sucking reflexes are well developed.
  - Swallowing reflex and tongue movements are still immature; continues to drool; is not able to move food (other than milk) to the back of the mouth.

DEVELOPMENTAL PROFILES AND GROWTH PATTERNS *(continued)*

1 to 4 months

- Grasp reflex gradually disappears.
- Landau reflex appears near the middle of this period: when baby is held in a prone (face down) position, the head is held upright and legs are fully extended (Figure 4-8).
- Grabs onto objects using entire hand (palmar grasp); however, strength is insufficient to hold onto items at the beginning of this period.
- Holds hands in an open or semi-open position much of the time.

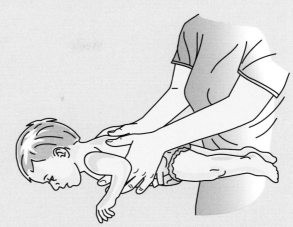

Figure 4-8
Landau reflex

- Muscle tone and development are equal for boys and girls.
- Movements tend to be large and jerky, gradually becoming smoother and more purposeful as muscle strength and control improve.
- Raises head and upper body on arms when in a prone position.
- Turns head side to side when in a supine (face up) position; near the end of this period, can hold head up and in line with the body.
- Shows greater activity level in upper body parts: clasps hands above face, waves arms about, reaches for objects.
- Begins rolling from front to back by turning head to one side and allowing trunk to follow. Near the end of this period, infant can roll from front to back to side at will.
- Can be pulled to a sitting position, with considerable head lag and rounded back at the beginning of this period. Later, can be positioned to sit with minimal head support (Figure 4-9). By four months, most infants can sit with support, holding their head steady and back fairly erect; enjoys sitting in an infant seat or being held on an adult's lap.

Figure 4-9
Can be pulled to a sitting position.

Perceptual-Cognitive Development

- Fixates on a moving object held at a distance of 12 inches (30.5 cm); smoother visual tracking of objects across 180° pathway, vertically, and horizontally.

- Continues to gaze in direction of moving objects that have disappeared.

- Exhibits some sense of size, color, and shape recognition of objects in the immediate environment—for example, recognizes own bottle even when bottle is turned about, thus presenting a different shape (Figure 4-10).

- Ignores (does not search for) a bottle that falls out of a crib or a toy hidden under a blanket: "out of sight, out of mind." (The infant has not yet developed what Piaget refers to as **object permanence** [Piaget, 1954]).

- Moves eyes from one object to another.

- Focuses on small object and reaches for it; watches own hand movements intently.

1 to 4 months

Figure 4-10
Recognizes familiar objects.

- Alternates looking at an object, at one or both hands, and then back at the object.

- Imitates gestures that are modeled: bye-bye, patting head.

- Hits at object closest to right or left hand with some degree of accuracy.

- Looks in the direction of a sound source (sound localization).

- Connects sound and rhythms with movement by moving or jiggling in time to music, singing, or chanting.

- Distinguishes parent's face from stranger's face when other cues, such as voice, touch, or smell are also available (Parsons et al., 2010).

- Attempts to keep toy in motion by repeating arm or leg movements that started the toy moving in the first place.

- Begins to mouth objects (Figure 4-11).

Figure 4-11
Most objects end up in the infant's mouth.

---

object permanence—Piaget's sensorimotor stage when infants understand that an object exists even when it is not in sight.

DEVELOPMENTAL PROFILES AND GROWTH PATTERNS *(continued)*

1 to 4 months

Speech and Language Development

- Reacts (stops whimpering, startles) to sounds, such as a voice, rattle, or doorbell. Later, will search for source by turning head and looking in the direction of sound.
- Coordinates vocalizing, looking, and body movements in face-to-face exchanges with parent or caregiver; can follow and lead in keeping communication going.
- Babbles or coos when spoken to or smiled at; even infants who are deaf will begin to babble (McGowan, Nittrouer, & Chenausky, 2008).
- Coos, using single vowel sounds (*ah, eh, uh*); also imitates his or her own sounds and vowel sounds produced by others.
- Laughs out loud.

Social-Emotional Development

- Imitates, maintains, terminates, and avoids interactions—for example, infants can turn at will toward or away from a person or situation.
- Reacts differently to variations in adult voices; for example, might frown or appear anxious if voices are loud, angry, or unfamiliar.
- Enjoys being held and cuddled at times other than feeding and bedtime.
- Coos, gurgles, and squeals when awake.
- Smiles in response to a friendly face or voice; smiles occurring during sleep are thought to be reflexive (Kawakami et al., 2009).
- Entertains self for brief periods by playing with fingers, hands, and toes.
- Enjoys familiar routines such as being bathed and having diaper changed (Figure 4-12).
- Delights (squeals, laughs) in play that involves gentle tickling, laughing, and jiggling.
- Spends much less time crying; stops crying when parent or caregiver comes near.
- Recognizes and reaches out to familiar faces and objects, such as father or bottle; reacts by waving arms and squealing with excitement.

Figure 4-12
Recognizes and reacts to familiar routines.

> **▶ ‖ TeachSource Video Connections**
>
> *Early Infant Learning.* It is probably true that we will never again learn as much as infants do during their first year of life! Every experience creates an opportunity for infants to learn something new about the world around them. As you watch the learning video entitled *0–2 Years: Early Learning in Infants and Toddlers* on the Education CourseMate website, answer the following questions:
>
> 1. What sensory systems does the infant use to gather information for learning?
> 2. What behavior does the term *habituation* describe?
> 3. Why is it important to provide infants with a variety of different toys and activities from time to time?

1 to 4 months

DAILY ROUTINES

Eating

- Takes 5–8 feedings (5–6 ounces each) per day.
- Begins fussing before anticipated feeding times; does not always cry to signal the need to eat.
- Needs only a little assistance in getting nipple to mouth; may begin to help caregiver by using own hands to guide nipple or to hold onto the bottle.
- Sucks vigorously; may choke on occasion because of the vigor and enthusiasm of sucking.
- Becomes impatient if bottle or breast continues to be offered once hunger is satisfied.
- Requires only breast milk or formula to meet all nutrient needs; not ready to eat solid foods.

Toileting, Bathing, and Dressing

- Enjoys bath time on most occasions; kicks, laughs, and splashes.
- Has one or two bowel movements per day; may skip a day.
- Begins to establish a regular time or pattern for bowel movements.

Sleeping

- Averages 14–17 hours of sleep per day; often awake for two or three periods during the daytime.
- Falls asleep for the night soon after the evening feeding.
- Begins to sleep through the night; many infants do not sleep more than six hours at a stretch for several more months.
- May begin thumb sucking during this period.
- Begins to entertain self before falling asleep: "talks," plays with hands, jiggles crib.

DAILY ROUTINES *(continued)*

Play and Social Activity

1 to 4 months

- Spends waking periods engaged in physical activity: kicking, turning head from side to side, clasping hands together, grasping objects.
- Vocalizes with delight; becomes more "talkative."
- Smiles and coos when being talked and sung to; might cry when the social interaction ends.
- Appears content when awake and alone (for short periods of time).

Learning Activities

Developmental applications for families and teachers:

- Imitate baby's vocalizations and faces (grunting, smacking, yawning, squinting, frowning). When baby begins to smile, smile back and sometimes remark, "You are smiling! Happy baby!"
- Sing songs and read to baby out of magazines, books, or whatever interests you; it is the sound of your voice and your closeness that matter.
- Play simplified peek-a-boo (hold cloth in front of your own face, drop it, and say "peek-a-boo"); repeat if baby shows interest.
- Gently stretch and bend baby's arms and legs while making up an accompanying song; later, start a gentle "bicycling" or arm-swaying activity.
- Touch baby's hand with a small toy* (soft rattles or other quiet noisemakers are especially good); encourage baby to grasp toy.
- Walk around with baby, touching and naming objects. Stand with baby in front of a mirror, touching and naming facial features: "Baby's mouth, Daddy's mouth. Baby's eye, Mommy's eye."
- Position an unbreakable mirror near the crib so baby can look and talk to himself or herself.
- Hang brightly colored or geometric pictures (black and white) or objects near baby's crib; change often to maintain baby's interest and attention.
- Fasten (*securely*) small bells to baby's booties; this helps baby localize sounds and learn at the same time that he or she has power and can make things happen simply by moving about.

__Rule of Fist:__ Toys and other objects given to an infant should be no smaller than the baby's fist (1.5 inches; 3.8 cm) to prevent choking or swallowing.

Developmental Alerts

Check with a health care provider or early childhood specialist if, by four months of age, the infant *does not*:

- Continue to show steady increases in height, weight, and head circumference.
- Smile in response to the smiles of others. (The social smile is a significant developmental milestone.)
- Gaze at and follow a moving object with eyes focusing together.
- Bring hands together over mid-chest.
- Turn head to locate sounds.
- Begin to raise head and upper body when placed on stomach.
- Reach for objects or familiar persons.

4 to 8 months

Safety Concerns

Continue to implement safety practices described for the previous stages. Always be aware of new safety issues as the baby continues to grow and develop.

Burns

- Do not bring hot beverages or appliances near the infant.
- Check temperature of bottles (if warming formula or breast milk) before offering them to an infant.

Choking

- Check rattles and stuffed toys for small parts that could become loose. Purchase only toys larger than 1.5 inches (3.75 cm) in diameter.
- Remove all small items within baby's reach.

Falls

- Attend to the infant at all times when on an elevated surface (changing table, sofa, counter, bed); baby may turn over or roll unexpectedly.
- Always place infant carrier on the floor (not on table or countertop) and fasten safety strap.

Sharp Objects

- Keep pins and other sharp objects out of baby's reach.
- Check nursery furniture for sharp or protruding edges; only purchase furnishings and toys that comply with federal safety standards (see Helpful Websites).

Four to Eight Months

Between four and eight months, infants are developing a wide range of skills and greater ability to use their bodies for purposeful activity. Infants seem to be busy every waking moment, manipulating and mouthing toys and other objects. They "talk" all the time with more variety and complexity of vowel and consonant sounds. They initiate social

Figure 4-13
Is becoming more verbal and
outgoing.

4 to 8 months

interactions and respond to all types of cues (facial expressions, gestures) and the comings and goings of everyone in their world. Infants at this age are both self-occupied and sociable (Goldstein & Schwade, 2009) (Figure 4-13). They move easily from spontaneous, self-initiated activity to social activities initiated by others.

DEVELOPMENTAL PROFILES AND GROWTH PATTERNS

Growth and Physical Characteristics

- Gains approximately 1 pound (2.2 kg) per month in weight; doubles original birth weight by eight months.
- Increases length by approximately 1/2 inch (1.3 cm) per month; average length is 27.5–29 inches (69.8–73.7 cm).
- Head circumference increases by an average of 3/8 inch (0.95 cm) per month until six to seven months of age then slows to approximately 3/16 inch (0.47 cm) per month. Continued increases are a sign of healthy brain growth and development.
- Takes approximately 25–50 breaths per minute, depending on activity; rate and patterns vary from infant to infant; breathing is abdominal.
- Begins to develop teeth, with upper and lower incisors coming in first.
- Gums may become red and swollen, accompanied by increased drooling, chewing, biting, and mouthing of objects.
- Legs often appear bowed; bowing gradually disappears as infant grows older.
- True eye color is established.

Motor Development

- Reflexive behaviors are changing (Figure 4-3).
  - Blinking reflex is well established.
  - Sucking reflex becomes voluntary.
  - Moro reflex disappears.
  - Parachute reflex appears toward the end of this stage: when held in a prone, horizontal position and lowered suddenly, infant throws out arms as a protective measure (Figure 4-14).
  - Swallowing reflex appears (a more complex form of swallowing that involves tongue movement against the roof of mouth); this allows the infant to move solid foods from front of mouth to the back for swallowing.

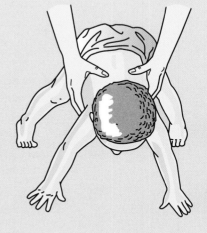

Figure 4-14
Parachute reflex.

- Reaches for objects with both arms simultaneously; later reaches with one hand or the other.
- Transfers objects from one hand to the other; still grasps objects using entire hand (palmar grasp).
- Handles, shakes, and pounds objects; puts everything in mouth.
- Helps to hold onto own bottle during feedings.
- Sits alone without support, holding head erect, back straightened, and arms propped forward for support (Figure 4-15).

Figure 4-15
Sits alone with support.

- Pulls self into a crawling position by rising up on arms and drawing knees up beneath the body; rocks back and forth but generally does not move forward.
- Rolls over from front to back and back to front.
- Begins scooting backward, sometimes accidentally, when placed on stomach; soon will learn to crawl forward.
- Enjoys being placed in standing position, especially on someone's lap; jumps in place.
- Begins to pick up objects using finger and thumb (pincer grip) near the end of this period (Figure 4-16).

Pincer grip

Figure 4-16
Pincer grip.

4 to 8 months

DEVELOPMENTAL PROFILES AND GROWTH PATTERNS *(continued)*

Perceptual-Cognitive Development

- Turns toward and locates familiar voices and sounds; this behavior can be used for informal testing of an infant's hearing.
- Focuses eyes on small objects and reaches for them accurately with either hand.
- Uses hand, mouth, and eyes in coordination to explore own body, toys, and surroundings.
- Imitates actions, such as pat-a-cake, waving bye-bye, and playing peek-a-boo.
- Shows evidence of **depth perception**; tenses, pulls back, and becomes fearful of falling from high places such as changing tables and stairs.
- Looks over side of crib or high chair for objects dropped; delights in repeatedly throwing objects overboard for adult to retrieve.
- Searches for toy or food that has been partially hidden under cloth or behind screen; beginning to understand that objects continue to exist even when they cannot be seen. (Piaget refers to this as *object permanence*.)
- Handles and explores objects in a variety of ways: visually, turning them around, feeling all surfaces, banging, and shaking.
- Picks up inverted object (for instance, recognizes a cup even when it is positioned differently).
- Ignores second toy or drops toy in one hand when presented with a new toy; unable to deal with more than one toy at a time.
- Plays actively with small toys such as rattle or block.
- Bangs objects together playfully; bangs spoon or toy on table.
- Continues to put everything into mouth.
- Establishes full attachment to mother or primary caregiver: seeks out and prefers to be held by this adult, which coincides with a growing understanding of object permanence.

4 to 8 months

▶❚❚ TeachSource Video Connections

Attachment. Attachment is a special emotional bond formed between parent and infant through a process of give-and-take interactions. It develops as infants and parents begin to synchronize their response patterns. Studies have shown that attachment helps the infant build a sense of trust and is essential for future social-emotional development. As you watch the learning video entitled *0–2 Years: Attachment in Infants and Toddlers* on the Education CourseMate website, answer the following questions:

1. What can parents do to foster the attachment process?
2. What is a reciprocal relationship and what purpose does it serve?
3. Why do infants develop "stranger anxiety"?
4. How can families and teachers help infants get through this phase (stranger anxiety)?

---

depth perception—ability to determine the relative distance of objects from the observer.

4 to 8
months

Speech and Language Development

- Responds appropriately to own name and simple requests such as "come," "eat," and "wave bye-bye."
- Imitates some nonspeech sounds such as cough, tongue click, and lip smacking.
- Produces a full range of vowels and some consonants: *r, s, z, th,* and *w.*
- Responds to variations in the tone of voice of others—anger, playfulness, sadness.
- Expresses emotions, such as pleasure, satisfaction, and anger, by making different sounds.
- "Talks" to toys.
- Babbles by repeating same syllable in a series: *ba, ba, ba.*
- Reacts differently to noises, such as a vacuum cleaner, phone ringing, or dog barking; might cry, whimper, or look for reassurance from parent or caregiver.

Social-Emotional Development

- Delights in observing surroundings; continuously watches people and activities.
- Begins to develop an awareness of self as a separate individual from others.
- Becomes more outgoing and social in nature: smiles, coos, and reaches out.
- Distinguishes among and responds differently to strangers, teachers, parents, and siblings.
- Responds differently and appropriately to facial expressions: frowns, smiles.
- Imitates facial expressions, actions, and sounds (Figure 4-17).
- Remains friendly toward strangers at the beginning of this stage; later, is reluctant to be approached by or left with strangers; exhibits **stranger anxiety**.
- Enjoys being held and cuddled; indicates desire to be picked up by raising arms and vocalizing.
- Establishes a trust relationship with family members and teachers if physical and emotional needs are met consistently; by six months, begins to show preference for primary caregiver.
- Laughs out loud.
- Becomes upset if toy or other objects are taken away.
- Seeks attention by using body movements, verbalizations, or both.

Figure 14-17
Delights in imitating adult-made sounds.

---

stranger anxiety—a cross-cultural phenomenon in which infants begin to show distress or fear when approached by persons other than their primary caregivers.

DAILY ROUTINES

Eating

- Adjusts feeding times to the family's schedule; usually takes 3–4 feedings per day, each 6–8 ounces, depending on sleep schedule.
- *Caution:* Infants should not be allowed to drink formula or juice from a bottle or to nurse for an extended time. Extensive damage can occur when teeth are in prolonged contact with these fluids and result in a condition known as baby bottle tooth decay (BBTD) (Peterson-Sweeney & Stevens, 2010). A small amount of water offered after feedings rinses the teeth and reduces the risk of BBTD.
- Shows interest in feeding activities; reaches for cup and spoon while being fed.
- Able to wait a half hour or more after awakening for first morning feeding.
- Has less need for sucking.
- By six months, begins to accept a small amount of pureed foods, such as cereal and vegetables, when placed well back on tongue (if placed on tip, infant will push food back out).
- Closes mouth firmly or turns head away when hunger is satisfied.

Toileting, Bathing, and Dressing

- Prefers being free of clothes.
- Splashes vigorously with both hands and sometimes feet during bath time.
- Moves hands constantly; nothing within reach is safe from being spilled, placed in the mouth, or dashed to the floor.
- Pulls off own socks; plays with strings, buttons, and Velcro closures on clothing.
- Has one bowel movement per day as a general rule, often at about the same time.
- Urinates often and in large quantity; female infants tend to have longer intervals between wetting.

Sleeping

- Awakens early in the morning; usually falls asleep soon after evening meal.
- Begins to give up need for a late-night feeding.
- Sleeps 11–13 hours through the night.
- Takes two or three naps per day. (However, there is great variability among infants in terms of frequency and length of naps.)

Play and Social Activity

- Enjoys lying on back; arches back, kicks, stretches legs upward, grasps feet and brings them to mouth.
- Looks at own hands with interest and delight; may squeal or gaze at them intently.

- Plays with soft, squeaky toys and rattles; puts them in mouth and chews on them.
- "Talks" happily to self: gurgles, growls, makes high squealing sounds.
- Differentiates between people: lively with those who are familiar, might ignore or become anxious with others.
- Likes rhythmic activities: being bounced, jiggled, swayed about gently.

Learning Activities

Developmental applications for families and teachers:

4 to 8 months

- Gradually elaborate on earlier activities: imitate baby's sounds, facial expressions, and body movements; name body parts; look in the mirror together and make faces; read, talk, and sing to the baby throughout the day.
- Use the infant's name during all kinds of activities so that he or she begins to recognize it: "*Kyle* is smiling," "*Carla's* eyes are wide open." "*Tyrel* looks sleepy."
- Provide toys, rattles, and household items that make noise as baby shakes or waves them about (a set of measuring spoons or plastic keys, shaker cans, squeak toys; remember the *Rule of Fist*).
- Place objects slightly out of reach to encourage baby's movement (physical activity) and eye–hand coordination (Ward, 2010).
- Read aloud and often to baby, even the evening newspaper or your favorite magazine. Infants will not understand what you are saying, but they will begin to learn about word sounds, voice inflections, facial expressions, and that reading is an enjoyable experience.
- Play, dance, and move around with baby to music on the radio or CD; vary the tempo and movement: gentle jiggling, dancing, turning in circles; dance in front of the mirror, describing movements to the infant.
- Sing all types of songs to baby—silly songs, lullabies, popular tunes; encourage the infant to "sing" along and imitate your movements.
- Allow plenty of time for bath time. This activity provides an important opportunity for learning in all developmental areas as well as an overall enjoyment of the experience.
- Play "This little piggy," "Where's baby's (nose, eye, hand . . .)," and other simple games invented on the spot such as taking turns at shaking rattles, gently rubbing foreheads, or clapping hands.

Developmental Alerts

Check with a health care provider or early childhood specialist if, by eight months of age, the infant *does not*:

- Show an even, steady increase in weight, height, and head size (growth that is too slow or too rapid are cause for concern).
- Explore his or her own hands and objects placed in his or her hands.
- Hold and shake a rattle.
- Smile, babble, and laugh out loud.
- Search for hidden objects.
- Begin to pick up objects using a pincer grip.
- Have an interest in playing games such as pat-a-cake and peek-a-boo.
- Show interest in or respond to new or unusual sounds.
- Reach for and grasp objects.
- Sit alone.
- Begin to eat some solid (pureed) foods.

4 to 8 months

Safety Concerns

Continue to implement safety practices described for the previous stages. Always be aware of new safety issues as the baby continues to grow and develop.

Burns

- Keep electrical cords out of reach and electrical outlets covered; inspect the condition of electrical cords and replace or remove if worn or frayed.
- Take precautions to protect infants from accidentally touching hot objects (oven or fireplace doors, space heaters, candles, curling irons, burning cigarettes, hot beverage cup).

Falls

- Use approved safety gates to protect baby from tumbling down stairs; gates are also useful for keeping baby confined to an area for supervision.
- Always fasten the restraining strap when infant is placed in a highchair, stroller, or grocery cart.
- Always raise crib sides to their maximum height and lock when baby is in bed.

Poisons

- Use safety latches on cabinet doors and drawers where potentially poisonous substances (medications, cleaning supplies, cosmetics, garden chemicals) are stored.

Strangulation

- Never fasten teethers or pacifiers on a cord or around infant's neck; avoid clothing with drawstrings.
- Remove crib gyms and mobiles after baby reaches five months or begins pushing up on hands and knees.
- Use wireless baby monitor or make sure all cords are out of reach.

Eight to Twelve Months

Between eight and twelve months of age, the infant is gearing up for two major developmental events—walking and talking. These milestones usually begin about the time of the first birthday, although a child's cultural background may influence the acquisition rate and nature of these early skills (Cappiello & Gahagan, 2008). The infant is increasingly able to manipulate small objects and spends a great deal of time practicing by picking up and releasing toys or whatever else is at hand. Infants at this age are also becoming extremely sociable. They find ways to be the center of attention and to win approval and applause from family and friends (Figure 4-18). When applause is forthcoming, the infant joins in with delight. The ability to imitate improves and serves two purposes: to extend social interactions and to help the child learn many new skills and behaviors in the months of rapid development that lie ahead.

Figure 14-18
Enjoys adult attention.

8 to 12 months

DEVELOPMENTAL PROFILES AND GROWTH PATTERNS

Growth and Physical Characteristics

- Gains in height are slower than during the previous months, averaging 1/2 inch (1.3 cm) per month. Infants reach approximately 1 1/2 times their birth length by the first birthday.
- Weight increases by approximately 1 pound (0.5 kg) per month; birth weight nearly triples by one year of age: infants weigh an average of 21 pounds (9.6 kg).
- Respiration rates vary with activity: typically, 20–45 breaths per minute.

DEVELOPMENTAL PROFILES AND GROWTH PATTERNS *(continued)*

- Body temperature ranges from 96.4°F–99.6°F (35.7°C–37.5°C); environmental conditions, weather, activity, and clothing still affect variations in temperature.
- Circumferences of head and chest remain equal.
- Anterior fontanel begins to close.
- Approximately four upper and four lower incisors and two lower molars erupt.
- Arms and hands are more developed than feet and legs (cephalocaudal development); hands appear large in proportion to other body parts.
- Legs may continue to appear bowed.
- Feet appear flat because the arch has not yet fully developed.
- Visual acuity is approximately 20/100; can see distant objects (15–20 feet away) and point to them.
- Both eyes work in unison (true binocular coordination).

Motor Development

- Reaches with one hand leading to grasp an offered object or toy.
- Manipulates objects, transferring them from one hand to the other (Fagard & Lockman, 2010).
- Explores new objects by poking with one finger.
- Uses deliberate pincer grip to pick up small objects, toys, and finger foods.
- Stacks objects; also places objects inside one another.
- Releases objects or toys by dropping or throwing; cannot intentionally put an object down.
- Begins pulling self to a standing position.
- Begins to stand alone, leaning on furniture for support; moves or "cruises" around obstacles by side-stepping (Snapp-Childs & Corbetta, 2009).
- Maintains good balance when sitting; can shift positions without falling.
- Creeps on hands and knees; crawls up and down stairs (Figure 4-19)
- Walks with adult support, holding onto adult's hand; may begin to walk alone.

8 to 12 months

Figure 14-19
Safety becomes an important issue as the infant gains mobility.

> ### ▶️ TeachSource Video Connections
>
> *Fine Motor Development.* Motor development proceeds rapidly during the first year. Infants' motor abilities advance quickly from a reflexive stage to one that permits them to move about, explore, and manipulate their environment. As you watch the learning video entitled *0–2 Years: Fine Motor Development for Infants and Toddlers* on the Education CourseMate website, answer the following questions:
>
> 1. What is a pincer grasp? How does a pincer grasp differ from an ulnar or palmar grasp?
> 2. What purpose do improved fine motor skills and coordination serve?
> 3. How might cultural differences influence an infant's motor development?

Perceptual-Cognitive Development

- Watches people, objects, and activities in the immediate environment.
- Shows awareness of distant objects (15–20 feet away) by pointing at them.
- Responds to hearing tests (voice localization); however, loses interest quickly and, therefore, can be more difficult to test informally.
- Beginning to understand the meaning of some words (receptive language).
- Follows simple instructions such as "wave bye-bye," or "clap hands."
- Reaches for toys that are visible but out of reach.
- Puts everything into mouth.
- Continues to drop first item when other toys or items are offered.
- Recognizes the reversal of an object: cup upside down is still a cup.
- Imitates activities: hitting two blocks together, playing pat-a-cake.
- Drops toys intentionally and repeatedly; looks in direction of fallen object.
- Shows appropriate use of everyday items: pretends to drink from cup, puts on a necklace, hugs doll, brushes hair, makes stuffed animal "walk."
- Shows some sense of spatial relationships: puts block in cup and takes it out when requested to do so (Cuevas & Bell, 2010).
- Begins to show an understanding of causality—for example, hands the music box back to adult when the music stops to have it rewound.
- Shows some awareness of the functional relationship of objects; puts spoon in mouth, uses brush to smooth hair, turns pages of a book.
- Searches for completely hidden toy or object by the end of this period.

8 to 12 months

DEVELOPMENTAL PROFILES AND GROWTH PATTERNS *(continued)*

Speech and Language Development

- Babbles or jabbers deliberately to initiate social interaction; may shout to attract attention, listen, and then shout again if no response.
- Shakes head for "no" and might nod for "yes."
- Responds by looking for voice when name is called.
- Babbles in sentence-like sequences, *"ma ma ma ma," "ba ba ba"*; followed later by jargon (syllables and sounds common to many languages uttered with language-like inflection).
- Waves bye-bye; claps hands when asked.
- Says *"da-da"* and *"ma-ma."*
- Imitates sounds similar to those the infant has already learned to make; will also imitate motor noises, tongue clicking, lip smacking, and coughing.
- Enjoys rhymes and simple songs; vocalizes and dances to music.
- Hands toy or object to an adult when appropriate gestures accompany the request.

Social-Emotional Development

- Exhibits a definite fear of strangers; clings to or hides behind parent or caregiver (stranger anxiety); often resists separating from familiar adult (separation anxiety) (Figure 4-20).
- Wants an adult to be in constant sight; may cry and search room when no one is immediately visible.
- Enjoys being near and included in daily activities of family members and teachers; is becoming more sociable and outgoing.
- Enjoys novel experiences and opportunities to examine new objects.
- Shows need to be picked up and held by extending arms upward, crying, or clinging to adult's legs.
- Begins to exhibit assertiveness by resisting caregiver's requests; may kick, scream, toss toys, or throw self on the floor.
- Offers toys and objects to others.
- Often becomes attached to a favorite toy or blanket; cries when it is missing.
- Looks up and smiles at person who is speaking upon hearing his or her name.
- Repeats behaviors that get attention; jabbers continuously.
- Carries out simple directions and requests; understands the meaning of "no," "yes," "come here," and other common phrases.

8 to 12 months

Figure 4-20
Shows fear of adults other than primary caregivers (stranger anxiety).

DAILY ROUTINES

Eating

- Eats three meals per day plus mid-morning or mid-afternoon snacks such as juice, fruit, crackers, and cereal. Enjoys eating and usually has a good appetite.
- Begins to refuse bottle.
- Learns to drink from a cup; wants to hold it alone; will even tilt head backward to get the last drop.
- Begins to eat finger foods; might remove food from mouth, look at it, and put it back in.
- Develops certain likes and dislikes for foods.
- Continuously active; infant's hands might be so busy that a toy is needed for each hand to prevent a cup or dish from being turned over or food grabbed and tossed.

Toileting, Bathing, and Dressing

- Enjoys bath time; splashes and plays with washcloth, soap, and water toys.
- Delights in letting water drip from a sponge or washcloth; pours water from cup to cup.
- Shows great interest in pulling off hats, taking off shoes and socks.
- Fusses when diaper needs changing; might pull off soiled or wet diaper.
- Cooperates to some degree in being dressed; helps put arms in armholes, might even extend legs to have pants put on.
- Has one or two bowel movements per day.
- Remains dry after nap on occasion.

Sleeping

- Goes to bed willingly but might not fall asleep immediately; plays or walks around in crib before eventually falling asleep on top of the covers.
- Sleeps until early morning.
- Plays alone and quietly for 15–30 minutes after awakening; then begins to make demanding noises, signaling the need to be up and about.
- Plays actively in the crib when awake; crib sides must be up and securely fastened.
- Takes one afternoon nap most days; length varies from infant to infant.

Play and Social Activities

- Enjoys large motor activities: pulling to stand, cruising, standing alone, creeping.
- Places things on head: basket, bowl, cup; finds this very funny and expects others to notice and laugh.
- Puts objects in and out of each other: pans that nest, toys in and out of a box.

8 to 12 months

DAILY ROUTINES *(continued)*

- Enjoys hiding behind chairs to play "Where's baby?"
- Throws things on the floor and expects them to be returned.
- Shows interest in opening and closing doors and cupboards.
- Hands an object to an adult on request; expects to have it returned immediately.
- Responds to "no-no" by stopping; alternatively, the infant might smile, laugh, and continue inappropriate behavior, thus turning it into a game.

Learning Activities

Developmental applications for families and teachers:

- Continue to elaborate on previously suggested activities; sing, read, talk, play simple games (rolling a ball, stacking objects), and encourage the infant's efforts.
- Always pick up on the baby's lead whenever he or she initiates a new response or invents a new version of a familiar game (the roots of creativity).
- Provide safe floor space close to parent or caregiver; learning to sit, crawl, stand, and explore are an infant's major tasks during these months.
- Look at photo albums together and talk about everyday happenings in the baby's life.
- Read from sturdy, brightly colored picture books, allowing baby to help hold the book and turn pages. Point to pictures and label the object to help babies begin to make associations; "Soft brown kitten," "Happy puppy," "Big red pail."
- Talk about ongoing activities, naming and emphasizing key words: "Here is the *soap*," "You *squeeze* the sponge," "Let's *wash hands* before you eat."
- Give baby simple instructions: "Pat Mommy's head," "Point to baby's nose." Allow adequate time for response; if the infant seems interested but does not respond, demonstrate the response.
- Accept the infant's newly invented game of dropping things off of a highchair or out of the crib; act surprised, laugh, return dropped object, and do not scold. This is baby's way of learning about cause and effect, gravity, and adults' patience.
- Encourage infants to fill a container with small toys, blocks, or other items and then empty it out. (*Rule of Fist* still applies.)
- Provide push and pull toys, toys with wheels, and large balls to roll. (Helping to unpack canned foods and rolling them across the kitchen floor is an all-time favorite game!)

Developmental Alerts

Check with a health care provider or early childhood specialist if, by twelve months of age, the infant *does not*:

- Blink when fast-moving objects approach the eyes.
- Begin to develop teeth.
- Imitate simple sounds.
- Follow simple verbal requests: "come," "bye-bye."
- Pull self to a standing position.
- Transfer objects from hand to hand.
- Show anxiety toward strangers by crying or refusing to be held.
- Interact playfully with parents, caregivers, and siblings.
- Feed self; hold own bottle or cup; pick up and eat finger foods.
- Creep or crawl on hands and knees.

Safety Concerns

Continue to implement safety practices described for the previous stages. Always be aware of new safety issues as the baby continues to grow and develop.

Choking

- Cut finger foods into small bites (1/4 inch [0.63 cm] or smaller). Avoid sticky foods (e.g., raisins, caramels, peanut butter) and hard foods (e.g., raw carrots, hard candies, nuts).
- Keep small objects such as buttons, dry pet food, coins, pen tops, and small batteries out of reach; keep garbage cans closed tightly. *Any item that fits through a toilet paper tube is too small for young children.*

Drowning

- Remove unsupervised water sources, including bath water, fountains, pet dishes, and wading pools. Place safety devices on toilet lids.
- Enclose pools with fences and latched gates; install alarms on windows and doors. Never leave a young child unsupervised in a pool or bathtub, even briefly to answer the telephone.

Falls

- Always strap infants into highchairs, grocery carts, and strollers and on changing tables. Never allow them to stand up in or on these objects (unless you are holding onto the infant).
- Keep crib sides up and locked at all times.
- Pad sharp corners and edges of furniture and cabinet doors.
- Place safety gates across stairs.

Strangulation

- Purchase clothing, such as jackets, with elastic instead of pull strings in the hoods.
- Fasten cords on all blinds and curtains up high and out of children's reach.

Suffocation

- Keep plastic bags and wrappings out of baby's reach; knot and discard them immediately.
- Remove lids from airtight containers such as plastic storage tubs and toy chests.

POSITIVE BEHAVIOR GUIDANCE

There are several things adults must understand about infants' behavior: they are dependent on adults to satify all of their basic needs; crying is their primary mode of communication; they cannot be spoiled; and they should not be punished. Because caring for an infant can be stressful at times, it is important that adults take care of themselves and learn self-control and anger management skills.

Newborns:

- Respond to their cries with love, gentle handling, and calming words to build feelings of trust and security.

One to four months:

- Help infants learn to soothe and quiet themselves: hold, cuddle, or rock gently; wrap firmly in a blanket; massage their skin; offer a pacifier (some infants prefer their thumb).

Four to eight months:

- Maintain consistent eating and sleeping schedules to reduce crying and fussiness.
- Create a safe environment so mobile infants don't get into items or situations they shouldn't.
- Convey a sense of calm when responding to a fussy infant.

Eight to twelve months:

- Introduce the word "no" (gentle) to teach infants when they are doing something that could result in harm. If necessary, pick up and move the infant to a safe area until corrective measures can be taken, but do not punish him or her.
- Give attention when an infant is behaving appropriately: "You rolled the ball really far," "You came when daddy asked."

SUMMARY

The span between birth and a child's first birthday is marked by dramatic changes in all developmental areas. Gains in height and weight occur at a rate greater than at any other time during the life span. A nutritious diet is essential for assuring healthy growth; malnutrition severely limits a child's growth potential and brain development. Ongoing physical changes and motor skill development transform the infant from a nonambulatory, reflexive state to one in which

the child begins to master some purposeful control. This period also marks one of the most important stages of brain development in terms of size (number of brain cells) and establishment of neural connections—both of which are essential for the acquisition of speech and language, perceptual-cognitive, motor, and personal-social skills. Many factors influence this learning process, including genetics, culture, environment, and the expectations of individuals with whom the infant interacts.

Key Terms

in utero **p. 70**

fontanels **p. 71**

pupil **p. 73**

bonding **p. 75**

object permanence **p. 81**

depth perception **p. 88**

stranger anxiety **p. 89**

Apply What You Know

A. Apply What You Have Learned

Reread the brief developmental sketch about Juan and his parents, Anna and Miguel, at the beginning of the chapter and answer the following questions.

1. What changes can Juan's parents expect to occur in his motor development by the time he is seven months old?
2. Would you expect Juan to experience stranger anxiety if his parents don't enroll him in an early childhood program until he turns seven or eight months? Explain.
3. How would you respond to Juan's parents if they expressed concern about his disinterest in pulling himself to a standing position or taking any steps by his first birthday?

B. Review Questions

1. Explain why a ten-month-old infant might begin fussing and refusing to be left with a familiar babysitter.
2. Identify and discuss three informal methods for determining whether a newborn's hearing is functional.
3. Identify three newborn reflexes that typically disappear by one year of age. Why should you be concerned if they do not fade according to schedule?
4. What are some things that families and teachers can do with infants to promote early literacy skills?
5. Identify three perceptual-cognitive skills that appear during late infancy (8–12 months) and provide a behavioral example that illustrates each.

Helpful Websites

Center on Infant Mental Health & Development
http://www.cimhd.org

Early Head Start National Resource Center
http://www.ehsnrc.org

National Association of Child Care Resource & Referral Agencies
http://www.naccrra.org

Safe Sleep
http://www.sidsks.org/CSsafesleep.html

References

Balas, B. (2009). Using innate visual biases to guide face learning in natural scenes: A computational investigation, *Developmental Science, 13*(3), 469−478.

Cappiello, M., & Gahagan, S. (2008). Early child development and developmental delay in indigenous communities, *Pediatric Clinics of North America, 56*(6), 1501−1517.

Cuevas, K., & Bell, M. (2010). Developmental progression of looking and reaching performance on the A-not-B task, *Developmental Psychology, 46*(5), 63−71.

Fagard, J., & Lockman, J. (2010). Change in imitation for object manipulation between 10 and 12 months of age, *Developmental Psychobiology, 52*(1), 90−99.

Frank, M., Vul, E., & Johnson, S. (2009). Development of infants' attention to faces during the first year, *Cognition, 110*(2), 160−170.

Franklin, A., Bevis, L., Ling, Y., & Hurlbert, A. (2010). Biological components of colour preference in infancy, *Developmental Science, 13*(2), 346−354.

Goldstein, M., & Schwade, J. (2009). The value of vocalizing: Five-month-old infants associate their own noncry vocalizations with responses from caregivers, *Child Development, 80*(3), 636−644.

Hari, R., & Kujala, M. (2009). Brain basis of human social interaction: From concepts to brain imaging, *Physiological Reviews, 89*, 453−479.

Kawakami, F., Kawakami, K., Tomonaga, M., & Takai-Kawakami, K. (2009). Can we observe spontaneous smiles in 1-year-olds?, *Infant Behavior & Development, 32*(4), 416−421.

Ladomenou, L., Kafatos, A., Tselentis, Y., & Galanakis, E. (2010). Predisposing factors for acute otitis media in infancy, *Journal of Infection, 61*(1), 49−53.

Lagercrantz, H., & Changeux, J. (2009). Basic consciousness of the newborn, *Seminars in Perinatology, 34*(3), 201−206.

McGowan, R., Nittrouer, S., & Chenausky, K. (2008). Speech production in 12-month-old children with and without hearing loss, *Journal of Speech, Language & Hearing Research, 51*(4), 879−888.

Mundy, P., & Jarrold, W. (2010). Infant joint attention, neural networks and social cognition, *Neural Networks, 23*(8–9), 985−997.

Parsons, C., Young, K., Murray, L., Stein, A., & Kringelbach, M. (2010). The functional neuroanatomy of the evolving parent-infant relationship, *Progress in Neurobiology, 91*(3), 220−241.

Peterson-Sweeney, K., & Stevens, J. (2010). Optimizing the health of infants and children: Their oral health counts!, *Journal of Pediatric Nursing, 25*(4), 244−249.

Piaget, A. (1954). *The construction of reality in the child.* New York: Basic Books.

Robinson, C., & Sloutsky, V. (2010). Development of cross-modal processing, *Wiley Interdisciplinary Reviews: Cognitive Science, 1*(1), 135–141.

Snapp-Childs, W., & Corbetta, D. (2009). Evidence of early strategies in learning to walk, *Infancy, 14*(1), 101–116.

Vouloumanos, A., Hauser, M., Werker, J., & Martin, A. (2010). The tuning of human neonates' preference for speech, *Child Development, 81*(2), 517–527.

Ward, D. (2010). Physical activity in young children: The role of child care, *Medicine & Science in Sports & Exercise, 42*(3), 499–501.

Yasuyuki, F., & Yasuhiro, S. (2010). Neural mechanism and clinical significance of the plantar grasp reflex in infants, *Pediatric Neurology, 43*(2), 81–86.

You are just a click away from a variety of interactive study tools and helpful resources. Access the text's Education CourseMate website at **www.cengagebrain.com**, where you'll find a variety of enrichment materials, including videos, glossary flashcards, activities, tutorial quizzes, web links, and more.

CHAPTER 5
Toddlerhood: Twelve to Twenty-four Months

Learning Objectives

After reading this chapter, you should be able to:

- Describe the motor abilities of a typical one-year-old and two-year-old.
- Discuss how the speech and language skills of a one- and two-year-old differ.
- Provide two illustrations of the two-year-old's improved understanding of size and spatial relationships.
- Define the concept of egocentricity and give an example.
- Explain why toddlers are often described as picky eaters.

naeyc Standards Chapter Links:

1a, 1b and 1c: Promoting child development and learning
2a and 2c: Building family and community relationships
3c and 3d: Observing, documenting, and assessing to support young children and families
4a, 4b, 4c and 4d: Using developmentally effective approaches
5c: Using content knowledge to build meaningful curriculum

Meet Anna and Juan

Juan's parents divorced five months ago, when he was just eighteen months old. Now he and his mother, Anna, are living in a small apartment near his grandmother's house. As a single parent, Anna often feels overwhelmed by the burdens of working evenings at a local restaurant and caring for her two-year-old son. Juan spends his mornings playing alone in his bedroom or watching television while his mother sleeps. When he tires of playing with the few toys in his room, Juan often heads into the kitchen and begins pulling things from the drawers and cabinets. His activity usually awakens his mother and results

continued...

in a scolding and occasional spanking. Books, magazines, and newspapers are notably absent in their apartment. Juan's mother has little interest in reading and prefers to get her news from the television. Occasionally, Anna takes Juan to a neighborhood park to play, but most of the equipment is in poor condition and designed for older children. He usually ends up playing alone in the sandbox with Styrofoam cups, plastic spoons, and sticks he finds lying around while his mother chats with her friends.

Juan adores his father, Miguel, and spends every other weekend at his house. However, when he returns home, Anna finds Juan unmanageable and disobedient. She blames Miguel for their son's behavior problems, and they often end up arguing in front of Juan. His grandmother is concerned about the effect his parents' divorce may be having on Juan's development. He utters only two or three words that anyone can understand and shows little interest in the books his grandmother borrows from her neighbor. Increasingly, he resorts to aggression, hitting, yelling, and throwing objects whenever he becomes frustrated. He refuses to help dress himself when asked, is defiant when told to get ready for bed, and usually runs the other way when his mother calls.

Ask Yourself

1. Do you think Juan's family should be concerned about his language development? Explain.
2. What suggestions, based on the family's financial situation, could you offer to Anna for encouraging Juan's language development?
3. In what ways may Juan's environment be influencing his behavior?

Twelve to Twenty-Four Months

Toddlers are dynamos, full of unlimited energy, enthusiasm, and curiosity. Although their rate of growth slows significantly during this stage, important developmental changes are taking place. The toddler begins this period with the limited motor, social, language, and cognitive abilities of an infant and ends it with the relatively sophisticated skills of a young child.

Gradually improving motor skills allow toddlers to navigate, explore, and test their surroundings. However, this newly-emerging mobility often results in frequent bumps, falls, and other injuries due to limited control and understanding of cause and effect.

Toddlers also begin to acquire vocabulary at a fairly rapid pace which permits them to engage in more complex thinking and communication patterns. "No" becomes a favorite word and is used frequently and emphatically to express wants, needs, and frustration. Defiance (including tantrums) and negative responses become more common during this stage as toddlers begin to assert their independence. Although adults may find this behavior troublesome at times, Erikson described it as an important step in helping children achieve a sense of **autonomy** and degree of personal control over their environment (Erikson, 1959). However, because early independence is not encouraged in all cultures, teachers must be sensitive to differences in family practices and expectations for children (Raeff, 2010).

The One-Year-Old

The ability to stand upright and toddle from place to place enables one-year-olds to begin learning about the world around them. They become talkers and doers, stopping only for much-needed meals and bedtimes. Their curiosity mounts, their skills become increasingly advanced, and their energy level seems never-ending. One-year-olds believe that everything and everyone exists for their sole benefit (Piaget & Inhelder, 1967). Eventually, this **egocentricity**, or self-centeredness, gives way to a gradual respect for others. However, for now, one-year-olds are satisfied to declare everything "mine." They prefer to play alone (**solitary play**), imitating the actions of other children rather than joining in.

DEVELOPMENTAL PROFILES AND GROWTH PATTERNS

Growth and Physical Characteristics

- Grows at a considerably slower rate during this period.
- Height increases approximately 2–3 inches (5.0–7.6 cm) per year; toddlers reach an average height of 32–35 inches (81.3–88.9 cm).
- Weighs approximately 21–27 pounds (9.6–12.3 kg); gains 1/4–1/2 pound (0.13–0.25 kg) per month; weight is now approximately triple the child's birth weight.
- Breathes at a rate of 22–30 respirations per minute; rate varies with emotional state and activity.
- Heart rate (pulse) is approximately 80–110 beats per minute.

autonomy—a sense of self as separate from others.

egocentricity—believing that everything and everyone is there for your purpose.

solitary play—playing alone.

DEVELOPMENTAL PROFILES AND GROWTH PATTERNS (continued)

- Head size increases slowly and grows approximately 1/2 inch (1.3 cm) every 6 months; anterior fontanel is nearly closed at 18 months as the bones of the skull thicken.
- Chest circumference is larger than head circumference.
- Teeth begin to erupt rapidly; 6–10 new teeth will appear during this period.
- Legs may still appear bowed.
- Body shape changes; toddlers take on more adult-like appearance but still are top-heavy; abdomen protrudes, back is swayed.
- Visual acuity is approximately 20/60.

Motor Development

- Crawls skillfully and quickly to a desired location.
- Stands alone with feet spread apart, legs stiffened, and arms extended for support.
- Gets to feet unaided.
- Walks unassisted near the end of this period (most children); is still somewhat unsteady and falls often; not always able to maneuver successfully around obstacles such as furniture or toys.
- Uses furniture to lower self to floor; collapses backward into a sitting position or falls forward on hands and then sits.
- Releases an object voluntarily.
- Enjoys pushing or pulling toys while walking.
- Picks up objects and throws them repeatedly; direction becomes more deliberate.
- Attempts to run; has difficulty stopping and usually just drops to the floor.
- Crawls up stairs on all fours; goes down stairs backward in the same position.
- Sits in a small chair.
- Carries toys from place to place.
- Uses crayons and markers for scribbling; draws with whole-arm movement
- Helps feed self; wants to hold own spoon (often upside down) and cup; not always accurate at getting utensils into mouth; frequent spills should be expected (Figure 5-1).
- Helps turn pages of a book during story time.
- Stacks 2–4 objects with reasonable accuracy.

Figure 5-1
Toddlers are often adamant about feeding themselves!

►❚❚ TeachSource Video Connections

Speech and Language Development. One-year-olds are learning that language is a functional tool, useful for making requests, informing adults about their needs, and letting others know where they stand! Perhaps even more significant is their level of understanding, which far exceeds their ability to use spoken language. As you watch the learning video *0–2 years: Observation Module for Infants & Toddlers* on the Education CourseMate website, focus your attention on the one-year-old in the last one-third of the clip. Consider the following questions:

1. Were you able to understand all of what the toddler was saying? Why do you think her mother was able to do so?
2. Would you consider the toddler's speech and language skills to be developmentally typical for a one-year-old?
3. What behaviors did the toddler exhibit that would suggest she is in a stage of autonomy?

Perceptual-Cognitive Development

- Enjoys object-hiding activities:
  - Early in this period, the toddler always searches in the same location for a hidden object (if the child has watched the object being hidden). Later, the child will search in several locations (Charles & Rivera, 2009).
  - Passes toy to the other hand when offered a second object (this is referred to as *crossing the midline*—an important neurological development).
  - Manages three to four objects by setting an object aside (on lap or floor) when presented with a new toy.
- Puts toys in mouth less often.
- Enjoys looking at picture books (Figure 5-2).
- Demonstrates an understanding of functional relationships (objects that belong together):
  - Puts spoon in bowl and then uses spoon, pretending to eat.
  - Pounds wooden pegs with toy hammer.
  - Tries to make a doll stand up and pretend to walk.
- Shows or offers toy for another person to look at.
- Names many everyday objects.
- Shows increasing understanding of spatial and form discrimination (puts all large pegs in a pegboard; places three geometric shapes in large formboard or puzzle).
- Places several small items (blocks, clothespins, cereal pieces) in a container or bottle and delights in dumping them out.

Figure 5-2
Enjoys looking at picture books.

1-year-old

DEVELOPMENTAL PROFILES AND GROWTH PATTERNS *(continued)*

- Tries to make mechanical objects work after watching someone else do so.
- Uses some facial expressions, but they are not always accurate representations.

Speech and Language Development

- Produces considerable jargon (puts words and sounds together into speech-like [inflected] patterns).
- Uses one word to convey an entire thought (**holophrastic speech**); the meaning depends on the inflection ("me" might be used to request more cookies or desire to feed self). Later, the toddler produces two-word phrases to express a complete thought (**telegraphic speech**) ("more cookie," "Daddy bye-bye").
- Follows simple directions ("Give Daddy the cup").
- Points to familiar persons, animals, and toys when asked.
- Understands and identifies three body parts if someone names them (**receptive language**) ("Show me your nose [toe, ear]").
- Indicates a few desired objects and activities by name ("bye-bye," "cookie," "story", "blanket"); verbal request is often accompanied by an insistent gesture.
- Responds to simple questions with "yes" or "no" and appropriate head movement (Figure 5-3).
- Produces speech that is 25 to 50 percent **intelligible** during this period.
- Locates familiar objects upon request (if child knows location of objects).
- Acquires and uses 5–50 words (**expressive language**); typically, these are words that refer to the names of familiar objects (e.g., animals, food, toys).
- Uses gestures, such as pointing or pulling, to direct adult attention.
- Enjoys rhymes and songs; tries to join in; dances and sings along.
- Seems aware of reciprocal (back and forth) aspects of conversational exchanges; engages in some vocal turn-taking, such as making and imitating sounds.

Figure 5-3
Understands and responds to simple questions.

---

holophrastic speech—using a single word to express a complete thought.

telegraphic speech—uttering two-word phrases to convey a complete thought.

receptive language—understanding words that are heard.

intelligible—language that can be understood by others.

expressive language—words used to verbalize thoughts and feelings.

Social-Emotional Development

- Remains friendly toward others; usually less wary of strangers.
- Helps to pick up and put away toys when asked.
- Plays alone for short periods.
- Enjoys being held and read to.
- Observes and imitates adult actions in play.
- Is eager for adult attention; likes to know that an adult is near; gives hugs and kisses.
- Recognizes self in mirror.
- Enjoys the companionship of other children but seldom engages in cooperative play (Hunnius, Bekkering, & Cillessen, 2010) (Figure 5-4).
- Begins to assert independence; often refuses to cooperate with daily routines that once were enjoyable: resists getting dressed, putting on shoes, eating, taking a bath when asked; wants to try doing things without help.
- Resorts to tantrums occasionally when things go wrong or if overly tired, hungry, or frustrated (Bernier, Carlson, & Whipple, 2010).
- Shows exceeding curiosity about people and surroundings (approaches and talks to strangers, wanders away when left unattended, searches through cabinets).

Figure 5-4
Toddlers engage in solitary play but enjoy being around other children.

1-year-old

DAILY ROUTINES

Eating

- Has much smaller appetite than as an infant; lunch is often the preferred meal (Marotz, 2012).
- Goes on occasional **food jags** (willing to eat only a few preferred foods); sometimes described as a picky or fussy eater; neither requires nor wants a large amount of food.
- Holds food in mouth without swallowing it on occasion; this usually indicates that the child does not need or want more to eat.
- Uses spoon with some degree of skill (if hungry and interested in eating).
- Shows good control of cup (lifts it up, drinks from it, sets it down, holds it with one hand).
- Helps to feed self; some toddlers of this age can feed themselves independently, others still need help.

Toileting, Bathing, and Dressing

- Tries to wash self; plays with washcloth and soap.
- Helps with dressing (puts arms in sleeves, lifts feet to have socks put on). Likes to dress and undress self (takes off own shoes and socks); often puts shirt on upside down and backward or both feet in one pant leg.
- Lets adult know when diaper or pants are soiled or wet.
- Begins to gain some control of bowels and bladder (intervals between wetting/soiling becoming longer, resulting in fewer accidents). Complete control often not achieved until around age three (longer for boys).

Sleeping

- Sleeps 10–12 hours through the night. May fall asleep at dinner if nap has been missed or if the day's activities have been vigorous.
- Experiences occasional difficulty falling asleep; overflow of energy is shown in behaviors such as bouncing on the bed, calling for parent, demanding a drink or trip to the bathroom, singing, making and remaking bed—all of which seem to be ways of gradually "winding down." A short, consistent bedtime routine and quiet story promote relaxation and help the toddler prepare for sleep.
- Makes many requests at bedtime for stuffed toys, a book or two, a special blanket.

Play and Social Activity

- Develops a strong sense of property rights; "mine" is heard frequently. Sharing is difficult; often hoards toys and other items.
- Enjoys helping but often gets into trouble when left alone (smears toothpaste, tries on lipgloss, empties dresser drawers, unrolls toilet paper).

---

food jag—a phase during which a child is willing to eat only certain foods.

- Enjoys being read to; especially likes stories with repetition, such as *Is Your Mama a Llama, One Duck Stuck, Five Little Monkeys, Bang! Bang! Toot! Toot!,* and Dr. Seuss books; likes to point to and talk about pictures.
- Likes to go on walks; stops frequently to look at things (rocks, bits of paper, insects); squats to examine and pick up objects; easily distracted; much dawdling with no real interest in reaching any particular destination.
- Plays alone (solitary play) most of the time, although beginning to show some interest in other children; engages in lots of watching. Participates in some occasional **parallel play** (play alongside but not with another child). Might offer play items to another child, but there is little cooperative (purposeful) play (exception can be children who have spent considerable time in group care) (Xu, 2010).
- Seems to feel more secure and better able to settle down at bedtime if the door is left slightly ajar with a light turned on in another room.
- Continues to nap; however, naps that are too long or too late can interfere with bedtime.
- Wakes up slowly from nap; cannot be hurried or rushed into any activity.

Learning Activities

Developmental applications for families and teachers:

- Respond to the toddler's jabbering and voice inflections, both in kind (playfully) and with simple words and questions; maintain conversational turn-taking; describe what you or the child are doing (this helps children associate words with actions and objects).
- Encourage the toddler to point to familiar objects in picture books, catalogues, and magazines; name the objects and encourage (do not insist) the toddler to imitate.
- Hide a toy or other familiar object in an obvious place and encourage the toddler to find it (give clues as needed).
- Provide blocks, stacking rings, shape-sorting boxes, and nesting cups; such toys promote problem-solving and hand-eye coordination.
- Allow frequent water play; the sink is always a favorite when an adult is working in the kitchen. (*Caution:* An absorbent towel or rug catches spills and reduces the chance of slips or falls.) A plastic bowl or dishpan filled with an inch or so of water can be equally intriguing when set on the floor.
- Put favorite toys in different parts of the room so the toddler must crawl, cruise, or walk to reach them (thus practicing motor skills).

---

parallel play—playing alongside or near another person but not involved in their activity.

- Provide toys that can be pushed or pulled; a stable plastic or wooden riding toy to steer and propel with the feet; arrange safe, low places for climbing over, under, and on top of (label activities to help toddlers make connections). Make sure some toys are gender neutral (boats, trucks, and farm animals for girls; books, art materials, dress-up clothes, and people figures for boys).

- Take short walks and talk about what you see (bugs, clouds, colors); labeling reinforces language development.

- Turn off the television. Young children learn from doing, not through passive activity.

- Encourage active play to promote healthy development, reduce the risk of obesity, and help toddlers release excess energy. Have them toss or kick a soft ball back and forth, blow and chase bubbles, or pick up and drop small objects (clothespins, blocks) into a bowl or bucket across the room.

Developmental Alerts

Check with a health care provider or early-childhood specialist if, by 24 months of age, the child *does not:*

- Attempt to talk or repeat words.
- Understand some new words.
- Respond to simple questions with "yes" or "no."
- Walk alone (or with very little help).
- Exhibit a variety of emotions: anger, delight, fear, surprise.
- Show interest in pictures.
- Recognize self in a mirror (smile at, point to, or state own name).
- Make eye contact when responding to questions or making a request (unless this is a cultural taboo).
- Attempt self-feeding (hold own cup to mouth and drink).

Safety Concerns

Continue to implement safety practices described for the previous stages. Always be aware of new safety issues as the child continues to grow and develop.

Burns (Thermal and Electrical)

- Cover all electrical outlets with plastic caps.
- Protect toddlers from touching hot objects: oven doors, space heaters, water pipes, fireplace doors, outdoor grills, toasters.
- Keep electrical appliance cords (e.g., coffee pot, curling iron) up and out of reach.
- Apply sunscreen to prevent sunburns; dress toddlers in long sleeves and a hat if outdoors for long periods.

Choking

- Remove objects and toys with small pieces (less than 1 1/2 inch [3.75 cm] in diameter) such as coins, watch or calculator batteries, marbles, pen tops, beads, buttons, gum and hard candies, paper clips, latex balloons, and plastic bags.
- Cut foods into small pieces; insist that children sit down to eat; avoid foods such as popcorn, pretzels, hot dogs (unless cut crosswise and in small pieces), raw carrots, whole grapes, nuts, and hard candies.

Water Hazards

- Eliminate accessible water sources: unsupervised swimming or wading pool, mop bucket, fish tank, outdoor water feature; purchase and use locking devices on toilet seats; *children can drown in less than 2 inches (5 cm) of water.*
- Install a fence, gates, locks, and alarm system to protect toddlers from wandering into unsupervised backyard pools or hot tubs.

Falls

- Place safety gates across stairwells; secure them properly to door frame. Gates can also be used to confine toddlers to rooms where they can be closely supervised.

- Keep doors to outside, garage, bathrooms, and stairwells locked.
- Pad sharp corners of tables and chairs.
- Eliminate tripping hazards: electrical cords, rugs, wet spills, highly waxed floors; clear pathways of furniture and toys.

Poisons

- Store medications (e.g., vitamins, cough syrups, ointments, and prescription drugs), automotive and garden chemicals, and cleaning supplies in a locked cabinet. (High shelves are not always safe from children who can climb.)
- Check for and remove poisonous plants from indoor and outdoor environments. (Contact a local county extension agent for information.)

Strangulation

- Avoid clothing with drawstrings around the head or neck.
- Limit strings on pull toys to no longer than 14 inches (35 cm) in length; supervise their use closely. Remove toys, mobiles, or clothing with strings from toddler's bed before sleeping.
- Fasten cords from curtains or blinds so they are high and inaccessible to children.

2-year-old

The Two-Year-Old

This year can be terrific as well as a challenge—for the child, family, and teachers. Exasperated adults often describe a two-year-old as impossible (or demanding, unreasonable, contrary). However, the two-year-old's fierce determination, tantrums, and inability to accept limits are part of normal development and seldom under the child's control (Calkins & Williford, 2009) (Figure 5-5). The two-year-old faces demands that can be overwhelming at times: new skills and behaviors to be learned and remembered, needs and feelings that are difficult to express, learned responses to be perfected, and puzzling adult expectations with which to comply. However, toddlers are also gaining an emerging sense of self-confidence as their developmental skills and awareness improve. This can result in moment-to-moment struggles as they try to resolve conflicting desires for independence (autonomy) or dependence (Erikson, 1959). Is it any wonder that two-year-olds are frustrated, have difficulty making choices, and say no even to things they really want?

2-year-old

Figure 5-5
Toddlers often exhibit a strong sense of determination.

Most two-year-olds are able to identify themselves as either being a girl or a boy. However, they also believe gender can be changed by simply wearing different clothing or desiring it to happen. Daily occurrences (e.g., media, toys, adult expectations, peer responses) continue to shape and influence children's concept of gender.

Although this year of transition may be somewhat trying for all, many positive things also happen. Two-year-olds are noted for their frequent and spontaneous outbursts of laughter and affection. New skills are learned quickly as a result of self-discovery, play, and hands-on-activities (Verhoeven et al., 2010). Toddlers' use of videos, computer games, and television programs does not support this type of learning and, thus, does not give children any educational advantage (Linebarger & Vaala, 2010). Through repeated trial-and-error, two-year-olds begin to function more ably and amiably as newly acquired skills and earlier learning are consolidated.

DEVELOPMENTAL PROFILES AND GROWTH PATTERNS

Growth and Physical Characteristics

- Gains an average of 2–2.5 pounds (0.9–1.1 kg) per year; weighs approximately 26–32 pounds (11.8–14.5 kg) or about 4 times the weight at birth.

- Grows approximately 3–5 inches (7.6–12.7 cm) per year; average height is 34–38 inches (86.3–96.5 cm) tall.

- Assumes a more erect posture; abdomen is still large and protruding and back somewhat swayed due to weak abdominal muscles that are not fully developed.

- Respirations are slow and regular (approximately 20–35 breaths per minute).
- Body temperature continues to fluctuate with activity, emotional state, and environment.
- Brain reaches about 80 percent of its adult size.
- Eruption of teeth is nearly complete; second molars appear, for a total of 20 deciduous, or baby, teeth.

Motor Development

- Walks with a more erect, heel-to-toe pattern; able to maneuver around obstacles in pathway.
- Runs with greater confidence; has fewer falls.
- Squats for long periods while playing.
- Climbs stairs unassisted (but not with alternating feet), holding onto the railing for support.
- Balances on one foot (for a few moments), jumps up and down but might fall.
- Begins to achieve toilet training during this year (depending on the child's level of physical and neurological development), although accidents should still be expected; children will indicate readiness for toilet training (e.g., understands concepts of wet/dry, is able to pull clothing up/down, communicates needs, understands and follows directions).
- Throws large ball underhand without losing balance.
- Holds cup or glass (be sure it is unbreakable) in one hand.
- Unbuttons large buttons; unzips large zippers.
- Opens doors by turning doorknobs.
- Grasps large crayon with fist; scribbles enthusiastically on a large piece of paper (Figure 5-6).
- Climbs up on chair, turns around, and sits down.
- Enjoys pouring and filling activities—sand, water, Styrofoam peanuts.
- Stacks 4–6 objects on top of one another.
- Uses feet to propel wheeled riding toys.

Perceptual-Cognitive Development

- Follows simple requests and directions: "Find your sweater," "Come here."

Figure 5-6
Holds crayon in fist and scribbles.

- Exhibits eye–hand movements that are better coordinated; can put objects together, take them apart; fits large pegs into pegboard (Weibe, Lukowski, & Bauer, 2010).
- Begins to use objects for purposes other than intended (may push a block around as a pretend boat, use a box as a drum, turn a bucket into a hat).
- Completes simple classification tasks based on one dimension (separates toy dinosaurs from toy cars, blocks from markers); this is an important development for learning future math skills.

2-year-old

DEVELOPMENTAL PROFILES AND GROWTH PATTERNS *(continued)*

2-year-old

- Stares for long moments; seems fascinated by, or engrossed in, figuring out a situation (where the tennis ball has rolled, where the dog went, what has caused a particular noise).
- Engages in self-selected activities for longer periods (sits quietly, remains focused) (Figure 5-7).
- Shows discovery of cause and effect (squeezing the cat makes her scratch or run away, turning the door handle makes it open).
- Knows where familiar persons should be; notes their absence; finds a hidden object by looking in the last hiding place first.
- Names objects in picture books; might pretend to pick something off the page and taste or smell it.
- Recognizes and expresses pain; can point to its location.

Speech and Language Development

- Enjoys being read to if allowed to participate by pointing, making relevant noises, and turning pages.
- Realizes that language is effective for getting others to respond to needs and preferences. Makes simple requests ("More cookies?"); refuses adult wishes ("No!").
- Uses 50 to 300 words; vocabulary continuously increasing.
- Has broken the **linguistic code**; that is, much of a two-year-old's talk has meaning to him or her but not always to adults (Vygotsky's "self-talk").
- Understands significantly more language than is able to communicate verbally; most two-year-olds' receptive language is more advanced than their expressive language (Berk, 2008).
- Utters three- and four-word statements; uses conventional word order to form more complete sentences.
- Refers to self as "me" or sometimes "I" rather than by name ("Me go bye-bye"); has no trouble verbalizing "mine."

Figure 5-7
Toddlers are able to focus on an activity for longer periods.

---

linguistic code—verbal expression that has meaning to the child.

- Expresses negative statements by tacking on a negative word such as "no" or "not" ("Not more milk," "No bath").

- Asks repeatedly, "What's that?"

- Uses some plurals but not always correctly ("See the gooses"); often over-generalizes grammatical rules. Talks about objects and events not immediately present, as in "We saw ducks." (This is both a cognitive and a linguistic advance.)

- Experiences occasional stammering and other common **dysfluencies**.

- Produces speech that is as much as 65–70 percent intelligible.

2-year-old

Social-Emotional Development

- Shows signs of empathy and caring (comforts another child who is hurt or frightened); at times, can be overly affectionate in offering hugs and kisses to children (sociocultural differences and expectations may influence the nature of this behavior) (Kärtner, Keller, & Chaudhary, 2010; Nichols, Svetlova, & Brownell, 2010).

- Continues to use physical aggression if frustrated or angry; this response is more exaggerated for some children than for others; physical aggression usually diminishes as verbal skills improve (Gloeckler & Niemeyer, 2010; Trommsdorff, 2009).

- Expresses frustration through temper tantrums; frequency of tantrums typically peaks during this year; cannot be reasoned with while tantrum is in progress.

- Finds it difficult to wait or take turns; often impatient (Figure 5-8).

- Eager to "help" with household chores; imitates everyday activities (might try to toilet a stuffed animal or feed and bathe a doll).

Figure 5-8
Taking turns and waiting are difficult behaviors for toddlers.

---

dysfluency—repetition of whole words or phrases uttered without frustration and often at the beginning of a statement, such as, "Let's go, let's go get some cookies."

DEVELOPMENTAL PROFILES AND GROWTH PATTERNS *(continued)*

- Orders family members and teachers around; is bossy; makes demands and expects immediate compliance from adults.
- Watches and imitates the play of other children but seldom joins in; content to play alone.
- Offers toys to other children but is usually possessive of playthings; still tends to hoard toys.
- Finds it difficult to make choices; wants it both ways.
- Shows much defiance; shouting "no" becomes almost automatic.
- Wants everything just so; is quite ritualistic; expects routines to be carried out exactly as before and belongings to be in their usual place.

2-year-old

▶❚❚ TeachSource Video Connections

Toddler's Cognitive Development. Children younger than two learn about their world primarily through their senses. Hand one-year-olds a new toy, and they might look it over, shake it, pound it on the table, and then pop it into to their mouths (assuming that it is small enough). Two-year-olds begin to utilize a whole new set of emerging abilities for learning. As you watch the learning video *Infants & Toddlers: Cognitive Development & Imaginative* Play on the Education CourseMate website, consider the following questions:

1. What advanced cognitive skills are the two-year-olds in this video exhibiting?
2. What instructional strategies is the teacher using to foster and reinforce the children's learning?
3. Could the teacher expect to achieve the same learning outcomes if the children were one-year-olds instead of two-year-olds? Explain.

DAILY ROUTINES

Eating

- Has fair appetite; interest in food fluctuates with periods of growth; lunch is often the preferred meal.
- Sometimes described as a picky or fussy eater; usually has strong likes and dislikes (which should be respected); may go on temporary food jags (eating only certain foods such as peanut butter and jelly sandwiches, macaroni and cheese) (Mascola, Bryson, & Agras, 2010).
- Prefers simple, recognizable foods; dislikes mixtures; wants foods served in familiar ways.
- Needs between-meal snacks, which should be of good nutritive value (fresh fruits or vegetables, cheese/whole-grain crackers, yogurt), with junk foods limited.
- Feeds self with increasing skill but may be "too tired" or disinterested at times.

- Has better control of cup or glass, although frequent spills are likely to happen.
- Learns table manners through verbal instruction and by imitating those of adults and older children.

Toileting, Bathing, and Dressing

- Enjoys bath if allowed ample playtime (*must never be left alone*); tries to wash self; might object to being washed and squirm when being dried off.
- Dislikes, even resists, having hair shampooed.
- Tries to help when being dressed; needs simple, manageable clothing; can usually undress self without much effort (Figure 5-9).
- Shows signs of readiness for bowel training (some children may have already mastered bowel control); uses appropriate words; becomes upset when pants are soiled and may run to the bathroom or hide.
- Stays dry for longer periods of time (one sign of readiness for toilet training); other signs include interest in watching others use toilet, holding a doll or stuffed animal over toilet, clutching self, willingness to sit on potty for a few moments, expressing discomfort about being wet or soiled.

Sleeping

- Sleeps between 9–12 hours at nighttime.
- Still requires afternoon nap; needs time to wake up slowly.
- Resists going to bed; however, usually complies if given ample warning and can depend on a familiar bedtime routine (story, talk time, special toy) (Mindella et al., 2010).
- Takes awhile to fall asleep, especially if overly tired; might sing, talk to self, bounce on bed, call for parents, make and remake the bed (again, ways of winding down).

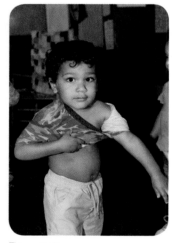

Figure 5-9
Attempts to dress self but still needs some adult help.

Play and Social Activity

- Enjoys dressing up and imitating family activities (wearing father's hat makes the child a "daddy"; putting on high-heeled shoes make the child a "mommy").
- Likes to be around other children but does not always play well with them (observes intently, imitating other children's actions [parallel play] but is unlikely to join in).
- Displays extreme negativism toward parents and caregivers at times—an early step toward establishing independence; shouts "no" or runs when asked to pick up toys, get ready for bed, or come to the dinner table.
- Pretends to have an imaginary friend as a constant companion.
- Explores everything in the environment, including other children; might shove or push other children as if to test their reaction.

2-year-old

Learning Activities

Developmental applications for families and teachers:

- Play games, such as large lotto and picture dominoes, that are based on matching colors, animals, facial expressions, and everyday objects.

- Offer manipulative materials to foster problem-solving and hand–eye coordination: large beads for stringing; brightly colored cubes; puzzles; large, plastic, interlocking bricks, nesting toys.

- Provide toy replicas of farm and zoo animals, families, dishes and cooking utensils, cars, trucks, and planes for sorting and imaginative play.

- Read to the child regularly; provide colorful picture books for naming objects and describing everyday events; use simple, illustrated storybooks (one line per page) so the child can learn to "tell" the story; ask the child to turn the pages.

- Share nursery rhymes, simple finger plays, and action songs; respond to, imitate, and make up simple games based on the child's spontaneous rhyming or chanting.

- Set out (and keep a close eye on) washable paints, markers, chalk, large crayons, and large paper for artistic expression.

- Encourage make-believe activities: save empty cereal and cracker boxes, plastic juice containers with intact labels, and recyclable bags for a pretend store; set out dress-up clothes and an unbreakable mirror or plastic gardening supplies.

- Provide wagons; large trucks and cars that can be loaded, pushed, or sat upon; doll carriage or stroller; a rocking boat; bean bags and rings for tossing.

- Create opportunities for musical enjoyment; encourage children to play musical instruments, invent and sing songs, dance, wave about scarves or crepe paper streamers to musical rhythms, pretend to be animals.

- Play games that involve sorting simple objects: laundry (towels in one pile, socks in another); colored blocks (red in one stack, blue in the other).

- Let children help with household chores: dusting furniture, "washing" the car, sweeping the sidewalk, "painting" with a brush and water.

Developmental Alerts

Check with a health care provider or early childhood specialist if, by the third birthday, the child *does not:*

- Eat a fairly well-rounded diet, even though amounts are limited.
- Walk confidently with few stumbles or falls; climb steps with help.
- Avoid bumping into objects.

- Carry out simple, two-step directions: "Come to Daddy and bring your book"; express desires; ask questions.
- Point to and name familiar objects; use two- or three-word sentences.
- Enjoy being read to; help to hold the book, name and point to objects.
- Show interest in playing with other children (watching, perhaps imitating).
- Indicate a beginning interest in toilet training (runs to bathroom, pulls pants down, uses appropriate words).
- Sort familiar objects according to a single characteristic such as type, color, shape, or size.
- Make eye contact when making a request or responding to questions (unless this is a cultural taboo).

2-year-old

Safety Concerns

Continue to implement safety practices described for the previous stages. Always be aware of new safety issues as the child continues to grow and develop.

Burns

- Set temperature of hot water heater no higher than 120°F (49°C).
- Purchase and use protective devices on bathtub and sink faucets.
- Keep hot liquids (e.g., coffee cups, kettles) out of reach.

Choking

- Continue to cut food into small pieces; insist that children sit down to eat; avoid popcorn, hot dogs (unless cut crosswise in small pieces), raw carrots, whole grapes, nuts, and hard candies.

Water

- Supervise any accessible water source (e.g., wading pool, fish tank, garden pond or fountain, bathtub). *Children can drown in less than 2 inches (5 cm) of water. Never leave children unattended.*

Play Environment

- Fasten bookcases, filing cabinets, dressers, and shelves securely to a wall or floor to prevent them from tipping over.
- Place toys on lower shelves so they are accessible.
- Keep doors to the outside and stairwells locked.
- Cover electrical outlets and remove unnecessary electrical cords.

Poisons

- Store all medicines (including vitamins and nonprescription drugs), automotive and garden chemicals, and cleaning supplies in a locked cabinet. (High shelves are not safe from children who can climb.)
- Check for and remove poisonous plants from indoor and outdoor environments.

Strangulation

- Avoid dress-up clothing that could become entangled around a child's neck (e.g., neckties, drawstrings).

2-year-old

POSITIVE BEHAVIOR GUIDANCE

Adults are responsible for protecting toddlers from harm and teaching them about social and cultural expectations. Toddlers only understand the world from their own self-centered perspective and must gradually learn how they are supposed to fit in through repeated trial and error. This process requires ongoing adult guidance, patience, and nurturing support.

One-year-olds:

- Acknowledge and encourage children's efforts even if they aren't perfect.
- Minimize the need for rules by childproofing the environment.
- Maintain predictable routines and schedules.
- Set limits that are reasonable and developmentally appropriate.
- Provide short explanations and guide the child's actions: "Gentle touches" (take the child's hand and pet the dog); "No hitting" (pick child up and move him/her to another area; distract or redirect the child's attention by offer another toy or activity).
- Enforce limits consistently so the child understands your expectations.

Two-year-olds:

- Give children your attention and let them know when they are behaving appropriately.
- Recognize that children will forget and repeat undesirable behaviors.
- Accept the toddler's intense desire for autonomy. Offer a choice instead of insisting that they do things your way: "Do you want to wear the red shirt or the blue shirt?", "Would you like to read a story or put a puzzle together after you put on your pajamas?"
- Choose your battles. Ignore a negative behavior as long as it doesn't cause harm to the child or to others. Remember, toddlers want your attention!
- Set a positive example. Toddlers imitate the way they see others behaving.

SUMMARY

Although toddlers' growth rate begins to slow, their bodies continue to undergo important physical changes. Improving motor skills typically outpace toddlers' cognitive development—their understanding of cause and effect, ability to judge size and distance, and grasp of functionality—placing them at high risk of unintentional injury. Their vocabulary (expressive language) remains quite limited, but their ability to understand language (receptive language) is considerably

more advanced. Dramatic increases in the number of words and their usage occur between the first and second birthdays. Toddlers enjoy being read to, singing, repeating simple words, and imitating adult behavior. Curiosity frequently gets them into trouble as they experiment with everyday objects, explore every nook and cranny, and attempt to take things apart. Efforts to achieve greater control or autonomy can result in bouts of defiance, frustration, and temper tantrums. Despite their sometimes challenging behaviors, toddlers are endearing bundles of unlimited joy and potential!

Key Terms

autonomy **p. 107**

egocentricity **p. 107**

solitary play **p. 107**

holophrastic speech **p. 110**

telegraphic speech **p. 110**

receptive language **p. 110**

intelligible **p. 110**

expressive language **p. 110**

food jag **p. 112**

parallel play **p. 113**

linguistic code **p. 118**

dysfluency **p. 119**

Apply What You Know

A. Apply What You Have Learned

Reread the brief developmental sketch about Juan and his family at the beginning of the chapter and answer the following questions.

1. What language skills would you expect a typically developing two-year-old to have?
2. Do you consider Juan's displays of anger and aggression to be typical or atypical of a toddler? Explain.
3. From a developmental perspective, explain why Juan continues to get into his mother's kitchen cabinets and dresser drawers despite repeated warnings to stop.
4. Because Anna sleeps in the morning while Juan is playing, what special precautions should she take in their apartment to ensure his safety?

B. Review Questions

1. Describe two developmentally appropriate activities that would promote a two-year-old's self-care skills; motor skills; language development.
2. Why are toddlers more likely to experience tantrums? In what ways would you expect to see a one-year-old to begin asserting his or her autonomy?
3. Why are toddlers at high risk for unintentional injury? What steps must adults take to reduce this risk?
4. What is holophrastic speech? Provide three examples to illustrate this form of speech. At what age are children most likely to exhibit holophrastic speech?
5. Describe three activities designed to help two-year-olds learn about the concept of size.

Helpful Websites

Centers for Disease Control & Prevention
http://www.cdc.gov/parents

First Signs
http://www.firstsigns.org

Child Development Institute
http://www.childdevelopmentinfo.com

Zero to Three
http://www.zerotothree.org

References

Berk, L. E. (2008). *Child Development.* (8th ed.). New York: Allyn & Bacon.

Bernier, A., Carlson, S., & Whipple, N. (2010). From external regulation to self-regulation: Early parenting precursors of young children's executive functioning, *Child Development, 81*(1), 326–339.

Calkins, S. D., & Williford, A. P. (2009). Taming the terrible twos: Self-regulation and school readiness. In O. A. Barbarin & B. H. Wasik (Eds.), *Handbook of Early Child Development and Early Education: Research to Practice* (pp. 172–198). New York: Guilford.

Charles, E., & Rivera, S. (2009). Object permanence and method of disappearance: Looking measures further contradict reaching measures, *Developmental Science, 12*(6), 991–1006.

Erickson, E. (1959). Identity and the life cycle, *Psychological Issues, 1,* 1–171.

Gloeckler, L., & Niemeyer, J. (2010, Spring). Social-emotional environments: Teacher practices in two toddler classrooms, *Early Childhood Research & Practice, 12*(1). Accessed online at http://ecrp.uiuc.edu/v12n1/gloeckler.html.

Hunnius, S., Bekkering, H., & Cillessen, A. (2010). The association between intention understanding and peer cooperation in toddlers, *European Journal of Developmental Science, 3*(4), 368–388.

Kärtner, J., Keller, H., & Chaudhary, N. (2010). Cognitive and social influences on early prosocial behavior in two sociocultural contexts, *Developmental Psychology, 46*(4), 905–914.

Linebarger, D., & Vaala, S. (2010). Screen media and language development in infants and toddlers: An ecological perspective, *Developmental Review, 30*(2), 176–202.

Marotz, L. (2012). *Health, safety, and nutrition for the young child.* (8th ed.). Belmont, CA: Wadsworth Cengage Learning.

Mascola, A., Bryson, S., & Agras, S. (2010). Picky eating during childhood: A longitudinal study to age 11 years, *Eating Behaviors, 11*(4), 253–257.

Mindella, J., Sadehb, A., Kohyamac, J., & Howd, T. (2010). Parental behaviors and sleep outcomes in infants and toddlers: A cross-cultural comparison, *Sleep Medicine, 11*(4), 393–399.

Nichols, S., Svetlova, M., & Brownell, C. (2010). Toddler's understanding of peers' emotions, *Journal of Genetic Psychology, 171*(1), 35–53.

Piaget, J., & Inhelder, B. (1967). *The child's conception of space.* New York: Norton.

Raeff, C. (2010). Independence and interdependence in children's developmental experiences, *Child Development Perspectives, 4*(1), 31–36.

Trommsdorff, G. (2009). Culture and development of self-regulation, *Social and Personality Psychology Compass, 3*(5), 687–701.

Verhoeven, M., Junger, M., van Aken, C., Deković, M., & van Aken, M. (2010). Parenting and children's externalizing behavior: Bidirectionality during toddlerhood, *Journal of Applied Developmental Psychology, 32*(1), 93–105.

Weibe, S., Lukowski, A., & Bauer, P. (2010). Sequence imitation and reaching measures of executive control: A longitudinal examination in the second year of life, *Developmental Neuropsychology, 35*(5), 522–538.

Xu, Y. (2010), Children's social play sequence: Parten's classic theory revisited, *Early Child Development & Care, 180*(4), 489–498.

You are just a click away from a variety of interactive study tools and resources. Access the text's Education CourseMate website at **www.cengagebrain.com**, where you'll find a variety of enrichment materials, including videos, glossary flashcards, activities, tutorial quizzes, web links, and more.

CHAPTER 6
Early Childhood: Three-, Four-, and Five-Year-Olds

Learning Objectives

After reading this chapter, you should be able to:

- Contrast the major developmental characteristics of typical three-, four-, and five-year-olds with those of toddlers.
- Describe the food preferences, eating habits, and calorie needs of typical three-, four-, and five-year-olds.
- Discuss the preschooler's need for adult attention and trace the ways these needs change with increasing independence.
- Describe at least five ways that adults can support the preschool-child's cognitive development.

naeyc Standards Chapter Links:

1a, 1b, and 1c: Promoting child development and learning
2a and 2c: Building family and community relationships
3c and 3d: Observing, documenting, and assessing to support young children and families
4a, 4b, 4c, and 4d: Using developmentally effective approaches to connect with children and families
5c: Using content knowledge to build meaningful curriculum

Meet Four-Year-Old Juan and His Mother, Anna

Anna's interest in resuming her education was sparked after she attended a recruiting program sponsored by the local community college. When Anna discovered there was space for Juan at the child care center on campus, she was even more determined. Anna knows that Juan's language and social development are delayed and believes he will benefit from having more opportunities to interact with children his own age.

Each morning, Anna drops Juan off at the child care center while she attends classes and works in the school cafeteria. However, Juan has been slow to adjust to his new school. He often

continued...

prefers to play alone, seldom stays involved in any activity for more than a few minutes, and insists on carrying his blanket wherever he goes.

Despite her busy schedule, Anna sets time aside in the evenings to play with Juan. They talk about things he has done in school that day and sometimes work together on building or art projects. Before Juan heads to bed, they always sit quietly and read several story books together. Anna is becoming increasingly confident in her ability to encourage Juan's development ever since attending a parent education class at the college. She now realizes how simple, everyday things she does with her son help him learn. Anna thinks she would enjoy working with young children and is seriously considering becoming an early education teacher.

Ask Yourself

1. Would you consider Juan's personal-social development appropriate for his age?
2. In what ways is Anna encouraging Juan's language and literacy development?
3. What signs of stress is Juan displaying as he tries to adjust to a new experience?

Three-, Four-, and Five-Year Olds

Three-, four-, and five-year-olds are typically full of energy, eagerness, and curiosity (Figure 6-1). They seem to be constantly on the move as they engross themselves totally in whatever captures their interest at the moment. During these preschool years, children are perfecting their motor skills. They exhibit creativity and imagination in everything they do, from their artwork and storytelling to dramatic play. Vocabulary and intellectual skills are expanding rapidly, enabling children to express ideas, solve problems, and plan ahead. Some children may be learning to speak a second language, which can affect other aspects of their development (Bialystok & Craik, 2010).

Preschool-age children are becoming more aware of concepts such as death and gender, but immature cognitive abilities still limit their full understanding. Children younger than five may acknowledge that someone or some thing has died but express hope that death can be reversed (Slaughter & Griffiths, 2007). By age seven, they understand death as universal—that it happens to everyone—and, shortly thereafter, children are able to accept that all body functions cease at the time of death. Similar changes occur in children's cognitive understanding of gender. Most five-year-olds are able to identify themselves as being either a boy or girl but they also believe that gender can be temporarily changed by wearing different outfits or acting out different roles (Martin & Ruble, 2010).

Preschool children strongly believe in their own opinions but, at the same time, they begin to understand that others have needs and feelings too. They are also developing

Figure 6-1
Children are exceptionally curious and inquisitive at this age.

3-year-old

limited ability to control their own behavior (Schaefer et al., 2009). They strive for independence yet need reassurance that an adult is available to give assistance, to comfort, to mediate, or to rescue if need be.

 ## The Three-Year-Old

Three-year-olds tend to be more peaceful, relaxed, and cooperative. Conflicts with adults that grew out of the two-year-old's struggle for independence are now fewer and less intense. Three-year-olds experience fewer emotional outbursts, comply with adult requests most of the time, and are able to delay their need gratification longer than before. However, there are distinct cultural differences in the importance given to developing these qualities at a young age (Trommsdorff, 2009). Three-year-olds are also becoming more aware and accepting of others and, thus, are able to participate in group play. They take obvious delight in themselves and life in general and show an irrepressible urge to find out all about everything in the world around them.

DEVELOPMENTAL PROFILES AND GROWTH PATTERNS

Growth and Physical Characteristics

- Growth is steady, although slower than during the first two years.
- Height increases 2–3 inches (5–7.6 cm) per year; average height is 38–40 inches (96.5–101.6 cm), nearly double the child's birth length.
- Adult height can be predicted from measurements at three years of age; males are approximately 53 percent of their adult height; females are 57 percent.

DEVELOPMENTAL PROFILES AND GROWTH PATTERNS *(continued)*

- Gains an average of 3–5 pounds (1.4–2.3 kg) per year; weight averages 30–38 pounds (13.6–17.2 kg).
- Heart rate (pulse) averages 90–110 beats per minute.
- Respiratory rate is 20–30, depending on activity level.
- Body temperature averages 96°F–99.4°F (35.5°C–37.4°C); affected by exertion, illness, and stress.
- Legs grow more rapidly in length than do arms, giving the three-year-old a taller, thinner, adult-like appearance.
- Head and chest circumference are nearly equal.
- Neck appears to lengthen as "baby fat" disappears.
- Posture is more erect; abdomen no longer protrudes.
- Has a full set of baby teeth (20 teeth).
- Needs to consume approximately 1,500 calories daily.
- Visual acuity is approximately 20/40, using the Snellen E chart.

Motor Development

- Walks up and down stairs unassisted, using alternating feet; might jump from bottom step, landing on both feet.
- Balances momentarily on one foot.
- Kicks a large ball.
- Feeds self; needs minimal assistance.
- Jumps in place.
- Pedals a small tricycle or riding toy.
- Catches a large bounced ball with both arms extended.
- Enjoys swinging on a swing (not too high or too fast); laughs and asks to be pushed.
- Shows improved control of crayons or markers; uses vertical, horizontal, and circular strokes.
- Holds crayon or marker between first two fingers and thumb (**tripod grasp**), not in a fist as earlier (Figure 6-2).
- Turns pages of a book one at a time.
- Enjoys building with blocks.

Figure 6-2
Holds marker in a tripod grasp.

tripod grasp—hand position whereby an object, such as a pencil, is held between the thumb and first and second fingers.

- Builds a tower of eight or more blocks.
- Plays with clay; pounds, rolls, and squeezes it with enthusiasm.
- Begins to show **hand dominance**.
- Carries a container of liquid, such as a cup of milk or bowl of water, without much spilling; pours liquid from pitcher into another container.
- Manipulates large buttons and zippers on clothing.
- Washes and dries hands; brushes own teeth but not thoroughly.
- Achieves complete bladder control, for the most part, during this time.

▶️ TeachSource Video Connections

Preschooler's Motor Development. Three-year-olds have mastered most basic gross motor skills and will now concentrate their efforts on improving strength, accuracy, and coordination. As you watch the learning video *2–5 Years: Gross Motor Development for Early Childhood* on the Education CourseMate website, consider the following questions:

1. What gross motor skills did the children display in the opening scenes of this video?
2. What gross motor skills would you expect a typically developing three-year-old to be capable of performing?
3. What indoor and outdoor activities could you plan to help three-year-olds practice and improve their gross motor skills?

Perceptual-Cognitive Development

- Listens attentively to age-appropriate stories.
- Makes relevant comments during stories, especially those that relate to home, family, and familiar events.
- Spends considerable time looking at books; may pretend to read to others by explaining the pictures.
- Requests stories with riddles, guessing, and suspense.
- Points with a fair degree of accuracy to correct pictures when given sound-alike words (*keys–cheese; fish–dish; sand–band; cat–bat*).
- Plays realistically
  - Feeds doll, puts it down for a nap, covers it up to stay warm (Figure 6-3).
  - Hooks truck and trailer together, loads truck, drives away making "motor" noises.

Figure 6-3
Engages in realistic make-believe play.

---

hand dominance—preference for using one hand over the other; most individuals are said to be either right-handed or left-handed.

DEVELOPMENTAL PROFILES AND GROWTH PATTERNS *(continued)*

- Experiments with things to see how they work; takes objects apart and reassembles them into new "inventions" (Johansson & Sandberg, 2010).

- Places eight to ten pegs in a pegboard or six round and six square blocks in a formboard.

- Attempts to draw; copies circles, squares, and some letters, but imperfectly.

- Identifies triangle, circle, square; can point to requested shape.

- Sorts objects logically on the basis of one dimension, such as color, shape, or size; usually chooses color or size as a basis for classification (all red beads in one pile, green beads in another) (Williamson, Jaswal, & Meltzoff, 2010).

- Shows understanding of basic size-shape comparisons much of the time; will indicate which is bigger when shown a tennis ball and a golf ball; also understands "smaller of the two."

- Names and matches, at minimum, primary colors (red, yellow, blue).

- Arranges cubes in a horizontal line; also positions cubes to form a bridge.

- Counts objects out loud.

- Points to picture that has "more" (cars, planes, or kittens) (Huang, Spelke, & Snedeker, 2010).

- Shows some understanding of duration of time by using phrases such as "all the time," "all day," "for two days"; some confusion remains: "I didn't take a nap tomorrow."

- Uses objects symbolically in play (block of wood might be a truck, a ramp, a bat).

Speech and Language Development

- Talks about objects, events, and people not present: "Jerry has a pool in his yard."

- Talks about the actions of others: "Daddy's mowing the grass."

- Adds information to what has just been said: "Yeah, and then he grabbed it back."

- Answers simple questions appropriately.

- Asks many questions, particularly about location and identity of objects and people (Figure 6-4).

- Uses an increasing number of speech forms that keep conversation going: "Why can't I?" "Where are we going now?" (Göksun, Hirsh-Pasek, & Golinkoff, 2010).

Figure 6-4
Asks many questions!

- Calls attention to self, objects, or events in the environment: "Watch my helicopter fly."
- Promotes the behavior of others: "Let's jump in the water. You first."
- Joins in social interaction rituals: *"Hi," "Bye," "Please," "Let's go."*
- Comments about objects and ongoing events: "There's a house"; "The tractor's pushing a boat."
- Vocabulary has increased; now uses 300 to 1,000 words.
- Recites nursery rhymes, sings songs.
- Uses understandable speech most of the time.
- Produces expanded noun phrases: "big, brown dog."
- Produces verbs with "ing" endings; uses "-s" to indicate more than one; often puts "-s" on already pluralized forms (geeses, mices, deers).
- Indicates negatives by inserting "no" or "not" before a simple noun or verb phrase ("Not baby").
- Answers "What are you doing?", "What is this?", and "Where?" questions dealing with familiar objects and events.

Social-Emotional Development

- Seems to understand taking turns but is not always willing to do so (Figure 6-5).
- Laughs frequently; is friendly and eager to please.

Figure 6-5
Learning to play well with others takes time and practice.

3-year-old

DEVELOPMENTAL PROFILES AND GROWTH PATTERNS *(continued)*

- Has occasional nightmares and fears about the dark, monsters, or fire.
- Joins in simple games and group activities, sometimes hesitantly.
- Talks to self often.
- Identifies self as a "boy" or "girl" (Chemey & Dempsey, 2010).
- Observes other children playing; might join in for a short time; often plays parallel to other children.
- Defends toys and possessions; is becoming aggressive at times, grabbing a toy, hitting another child, hiding toys.
- Engages in make-believe play alone and with other children (Nicolopoulou et al., 2010).
- Shows affection toward children who are younger or children who get hurt.
- Sits and listens to stories up to 10 minutes at a time; does not bother other children who are listening to the story; becomes upset if disturbed or interrupted.
- May continue to have a special blanket, stuffed animal, or toy for comfort.

DAILY ROUTINES

Eating

- Prefers small servings; appetite is fair. Dislikes many cooked vegetables; eats almost everything else; should not be forced to eat (Worobey et al., 2010).
- Feeds self independently if hungry. Uses spoon in semi-adult fashion; may spear food with fork (Figure 6-6).
- Eats slowly at times; plays around with food when not hungry.
- Pours milk and juice with fewer spills; serves individual portions from a serving dish with some adult prompting; "Fill it up to the line"; "Take only two spoonfuls."
- Drinks a great deal of milk. (Be sure child does not fill up on milk to the exclusion of other much-needed foods.)

Toileting, Bathing, and Dressing

- Helps wash self in bathtub but is not always thorough; often resists getting out of tub.

Figure 6-6
Handles utensils with relative skill.

- Brushes own teeth, but adults should continue to monitor child's technique.
- Manages most of own toilet needs during the daytime. (Boys, especially, may continue to have daytime accidents resulting in wet pants.)
- Some children sleep through the night without wetting the bed; others are in transition—they might stay dry at night for days or weeks, then go back to night-wetting for a period.
- Is better at undressing than dressing, although is capable of putting on some articles of clothing.
- Manipulates zippers, large buttons, and snaps with improving ability.

Sleeping

- Sleeps 10–12 hours most nights; often wakes up early in the morning.
- Begins to give up afternoon naps; however, continues to benefit from a midday quiet time.
- Prepares for bed independently most of the time; has given up many earlier bedtime rituals but still needs a bedtime story or song and tucking-in.
- Has dreams that might cause the child to awaken.
- Sometimes wanders at night; quiet firmness might be needed in returning child to his or her own bed.

Play and Social Activity

- Wants to be included in everything; the "me too" age.
- Joins in spontaneous group play for short periods; very social; beginning to play cooperatively more often.
- Argues or quarrels with other children on occasion; adults should allow children to settle their own disagreements unless physical harm is threatened.
- Dresses up and participates in dramatic play reflecting everyday activities. Some children still exhibit strong **gender** and role stereotypes: "Boys can't be nurses"; "Only girls can be dancers."
- Responds well to options rather than to commands: "Do you want to put your pajamas on before or after the story?"
- Continues to find sharing difficult, but seems to understand the concept.

Learning Activities

Developmental applications for families and teachers:

- Limit children's video and television viewing to no more than two hours a day. All content should be developmentally appropriate; young children understand media as real, not as fiction or entertainment. Active play promotes learning and decreases the risk of obesity.

---

gender—reference to being either male or female.

- Encourage children to create new uses for safe household items and discards: blanket over a table to create a cave or tent; spoons for pretend cooking; discarded mail for playing post office; hose with trickle of water for washing tricycle or wagon; plastic milk carton for a floating boat; paint brush and water for "painting" outdoor structures.

- Provide more complex manipulative materials: parquetry blocks; pegboards with multicolored pegs; various items to count, sort, and match; construction sets with medium-size, interlocking pieces.

- Offer nontoxic art and craft materials that encourage experimentation: crayons, washable markers, chalk, playdough, round-tipped scissors, papers, glue, paints, and large brushes (supervision is required).

- Keep a plentiful supply of books about animals, families, everyday events, alphabet and counting activities, poems and rhymes on hand; continue daily reading sessions. Ask children to retell stories using puppets or have them create their own story ending.

- Make regular trips to the library; allow plenty of time for children to make their own book selections. Include some nonfiction books on topics that interest children, such as animals, the ocean, and planets.

- Spend time together outdoors: encourage active games—kick, hit, or throw balls; catch bugs; jump rope; fly kites, or, play tag. Children should engage in at least 60 minutes of adult-led and 60 minutes of unstructured physical activity every day.

- Provide wheeled riding toys, wheelbarrow and garden tools, doll strollers, or shopping carts to build eye–hand–foot coordination (e.g., steering, maneuvering).

- Take children on walks, *at the child's pace*; allow ample time for children to explore, examine, and collect rocks, bugs, leaves, seed pods; name and talk about things along the way.

Developmental Alerts

Check with a health care provider or early childhood specialist if, by the fourth birthday, the child *does not*:

- Have intelligible speech most of the time; have children's hearing checked if there is any reason for concern.

- Understand and follow simple commands and directions.

- State own name and age.

- Play near or with other children.

- Use three- to four-word sentences.

- Ask questions and maintain eye contact.

- Stay with an activity for 3–4 minutes; play alone several minutes at a time.
- Jump in place without falling.
- Balance on one foot, at least briefly.
- Help with dressing self.
- Engage in pretend play, using common objects for imaginative purposes.

Safety Concerns

4-year-old

Continue to implement safety practices described for the previous stages. Always be aware of new safety issues as the child continues to grow and develop.

Burns

- Keep hot items out of children's reach.
- Place lighted candles, matches, and cigarette lighters where they are inaccessible.
- Monitor children carefully when grills, fireplaces, candles, or fireworks are lit.

Choking

- Avoid foods that can cause choking: popcorn, nuts, raw carrots, hard candies, grapes, hot dogs.
- Cut food into small pieces and insist that children sit quietly when eating.
- Supervise children closely when they are eating items with sticks, such as a lollipop or Popsicle.

Drowning

- Continue to supervise children closely when around any source of water; always empty wading pools when not in use.
- Fence in permanent pools; use pool alarm; keep gates closed and riding toys away from pool area.
- Learn CPR!

Falls

- Insist that children wear sturdy, flat-soled shoes to prevent injuries. Shoes with hard or slippery soles, sandals and slip-ons increase the risk of tripping or falling.

Poisons

- Avoid use of pesticides and chemicals on grass where children play; residues can get on hands and into sandboxes.
- Store hazardous substances, such as cleaning supplies, lawn chemicals, and medications, in locked cabinets.

Traffic

- Insist on holding the child's hand when walking in parking lots or crossing streets.
- Always buckle child securely into an appropriate car seat.

The Four-Year-Old

Tireless bundles of energy, brimming over ideas, overflowing with chatter and activity—these are the characteristics typical of most four-year-olds. Bouts of stubbornness and arguments between child and adults can be frequent as children test limits and work to achieve greater independence. Many are loud, boisterous, even belligerent; they try adults' patience with nonsense talk and silly jokes, constant chatter, and endless

questions. At the same time, they have many lovable qualities. They are enthusiastic, eager to be helpful, imaginative, and able to plan ahead to some extent: "When we get home, I'll make you a picture."

Although today's children are growing up in environments dominated by electronic media—hand-held games, computers, software, cell phones, videos—evidence supporting their contribution to learning remains limited (Plowman, McPake, & Stephen, 2010). What we do know is that children learn by experimenting, experiencing, and interacting with other children. Electronic media can limit these processes, promote sedentary behavior, and thus should be used cautiously until children are older.

DEVELOPMENTAL PROFILES AND GROWTH PATTERNS

Growth and Physical Characteristics

- Gains approximately 4–5 pounds (1.8–2.3 kg) per year; weighs an average of 32–40 pounds (14.5–18.2 kg).
- Grows 2–2.5 inches (5.0–6.4 cm) in height per year; is approximately 40–45 inches (101.6–114 cm) tall.
- Heart rate (pulse) averages 90–110 beats per minute.
- Respiratory rate ranges from 20–30, varying with activity and emotional state.
- Body temperature ranges from 98°F–99.4°F (36.6°C–37.4°C).
- Requires approximately 1,700 calories daily.
- Hearing acuity can be assessed by child's correct usage of sounds and language as well as by the child's appropriate responses to questions and instructions.
- Visual acuity is approximately 20/30 as measured on the Snellen E chart.

Motor Development

- Walks a straight line (tape or chalk line on the floor).
- Hops on one foot.
- Pedals and steers a wheeled toy with confidence; turns corners, avoids obstacles and oncoming "traffic."
- Climbs ladders, trees, playground equipment.
- Jumps over objects 5 or 6 inches (12.5 to 15 cm) high; lands with both feet together.
- Runs, starts, stops, and moves around obstacles with ease.
- Throws a ball overhand; distance and aim are improving.
- Builds a tower with 10 or more blocks.

- Forms shapes and objects out of clay: cookies, snakes, simple animals.
- Reproduces some shapes and letters (Figure 6-7).
- Holds a crayon or marker by using a tripod grasp.
- Paints and draws with purpose; might have an idea in mind but often has trouble implementing it, so calls the creation something else.
- Becomes more accurate at hitting nails and pegs with hammer.
- Threads small wooden beads on a string.

Figure 6-7
Reproduces some shapes and letters.

4-year-old

Perceptual-Cognitive Development

- Stacks at least five graduated cubes from largest to smallest; builds a pyramid of six blocks.
- Indicates whether paired words sound the same or different (*sheet–feet, ball–wall*).
- Names 18–20 uppercase letters near the end of this year; some children might be able to print several letters and write their own name; might recognize some printed words (especially those that have a special meaning for the child).
- A few children will begin to read simple words in books such as alphabet books with only a few words per page and many pictures (Goodman, Libenson, & Wade-Woolley, 2010).
- Selects and enjoys stories about how things grow and operate.
- Delights in wordplay, creating silly language.
- Understands the concepts of "tallest," "biggest," "same," and "more"; selects the picture that has the "most houses" or the "biggest dogs."
- Rote counts to 20 or more; has limited understanding of what numbers represent.
- Understands the sequence of daily events: "When we get up in the morning, we get dressed, have breakfast, brush our teeth, and go to school."
- Sorts, classifies, and patterns objects with various attributes (smallest to biggest; color and shape; things that float or sink) (Figure 6-8).
- Recognizes and identifies missing puzzle parts (of person, car, animal) when looking at the picture.

Figure 6-8
Understands and recognizes shape, color, and size differences.

4-year-old

DEVELOPMENTAL PROFILES AND GROWTH PATTERNS *(continued)*

Speech and Language Development

- Uses the prepositions *on*, *in*, and *under* correctly for the most part.
- Uses possessives consistently (*hers, theirs, baby's*).
- Answers "Whose?" "Who?" "Why?" and "How many?".
- Produces elaborate sentence structures: "The cat ran under the house before I could see what color it was" (Rice et al., 2010).
- Uses almost entirely intelligible speech.
- Begins to use the past tense of verbs correctly: "Mommy closed the door," "Daddy went to work" (Grant & Suddendorf, 2010).
- Refers to activities, events, objects, and people that are not present.
- Changes tone of voice and sentence structure to adapt to listener's level of understanding: To baby brother, "Milk gone?" To mother, "Did the baby drink all of his milk?"
- States first and last name, gender, siblings' names, and sometimes home telephone number.
- Answers appropriately when asked what to do if tired, cold, or hungry.
- Recites and sings simple songs and rhymes.

▶❚❚ TeachSource Video Connections

Preschoolers and Language Development. Four-year-olds chatter endlessly. They have much to say and, in the process, are learning how to use language for thinking, problem-solving, and communicating their ideas to others. Cultural patterns influence how children develop and use written and spoken language. As you watch the learning video *2–5 Years: Language Development for Early Childhood* on the Education CourseMate website, consider the following questions:

1. What language development does the term *over-regularization* describe?
2. What changes do most four-year-olds experience in the language development?
3. What grammatical irregularities did you note in four-year-old Caroline's description of recent bowling and putt-putt golf experiences?
4. Would you consider her grammatical usage typical for a four-year-old? Explain.

Social-Emotional Development

- Is outgoing and friendly (cultural differences may reinforce or not encourage this behavior); can be overly enthusiastic at times.
- Changes moods rapidly and unpredictably; might laugh one minute, cry the next; tantrum over minor frustrations (a block structure that will not balance); sulk over being left out or denied a request (Cipriano & Stifter, 2010).

- Holds conversations and shares strong emotions with imaginary playmates or companions; having an invisible friend is fairly common (Vygotsky's self-talk).

- Boasts, exaggerates, and bends the truth with made-up stories or claims of boldness; tests the limits with "bathroom" talk.

- Cooperates with others more often now; participates in group activities, role-playing, and make-believe activities.

- Shows pride in accomplishments; seeks frequent adult approval.

- May tattle on other children and appear selfish at times; still has trouble understanding turn-taking in some situations (Ingram & Bering, 2010).

- Insists on trying to do things independently but can become so frustrated as to verge on tantrums when problems arise (paint that drips, paper airplane that will not fold correctly).

- Relies (most of the time) on verbal rather than physical aggression; may yell angrily rather than hit to make a point; threatens: "You can't come to my birthday party if I can't play."

- Uses name-calling and taunting as ways of excluding other children: "You're such a baby."

- Establishes close relationships with playmates; beginning to have "best" friends (Figure 6-9).

Figure 6-9
Begins to have a "best" friend.

4-year-old

DAILY ROUTINES

Eating

- Appetite fluctuates; hungry and eager to eat at one meal, disinterested in eating at the next.

- May develop dislikes of certain foods and refuse them to the point of tears if pushed (such pressure can cause serious adult–child conflict).

- Able to use all eating utensils; quite skilled at spreading jelly or butter or cutting soft foods such as bread with a plastic or dinnerware knife.

DAILY ROUTINES *(continued)*

- Eating and talking get in each other's way; talking usually takes precedence over eating.
- Shows interest in helping with meal preparations (dumping premeasured ingredients, washing vegetables, setting the table).

Toileting, Bathing, and Dressing

- Takes care of own toileting needs; often demands privacy in the bathroom.
- Performs bathing and toothbrushing tasks with improved skill and attention; still needs some adult assistance and routine (subtle) inspection.
- Dresses self; can lace own shoes, button buttons, buckle belts. Becomes frustrated if problems arise while getting dressed, yet stubbornly refuses much-needed adult help.
- Can help sort and fold his or her own clean clothes, put clothes away, hang up towels, pick up and dust room; however, is easily distracted.

Sleeping

- Averages 10–12 hours of sleep at night; may still take an afternoon nap.
- Bedtime usually not a problem if cues, rather than orders, signal the time (when the story is finished, when the clock hands are in a certain position).
- Nighttime fear of the dark is common: a hallway light left on is usually helpful.
- Getting up to use the bathroom may require help in settling back down to sleep.

Play and Social Activities

- Playmates are important; plays cooperatively most of the time; can be bossy.
- Takes turns; shares (most of the time); wants to be with children every waking moment.
- Needs (and seeks out) adult approval and attention; might comment, "Look what I did," "See my boat."
- Understands and needs limits (but not too constraining); will abide by rules most of the time.
- Brags about possessions; shows off; boasts about family members.

4-year-old

Learning Activities

Developmental applications for families and teachers:

- Join in simple board and card games (picture lotto, Candyland) that depend on chance, not strategy; emphasis should be on playing, not winning. (Learning to be a good sport does not come until much later.)

- Provide puzzles with 5–20 pieces (number depends on the child), counting and alphabet games, matching games such as more detailed lotto.

- Offer a variety of basic science and math materials: ruler, compass, magnifying glass, small scales, plastic eye droppers; encourage activities such as collecting leaves, growing worms, sprouting seeds.

- Appreciate (and sometimes join in) the child's spontaneous rhyming, chanting, silly name-calling, jokes, and riddles.

- Continue daily read-aloud times; encourage children to supply words or phrases, to guess *what comes next*, to retell the story (or parts of it) by telling what happened first, what happened last; introduce the idea of looking things up in a simple picture dictionary or encyclopedia. Go to the library regularly, allowing the child ample time to choose books.

- Participate in 30–60 minutes of vigorous physical activity with your child each day: go for a walk; play in the park; ride bikes; provide balls for kicking, throwing, and hitting; enroll in swim, tumbling, or dance classes; play in the sprinkler or "swim" in an inflatable pool (*always requires an adult present*).

4-year-old

Developmental Alerts

Check with a health care provider or early childhood specialist if, by the fifth birthday, the child *does not*:

- State own name in full.
- Identify simple shapes: circle, square, triangle.
- Catch a large ball when bounced (have child's vision checked).
- Speak and be understood by strangers (have child's hearing checked).
- Have good control of posture and movement.
- Hop on one foot.
- Show interest in and respond to surroundings; ask questions, stop to look at and pick up small objects.
- Respond to statements without constantly asking to have them repeated.
- Dress self with minimal adult assistance; manage buttons, zippers.
- Take care of own toilet needs; have good bowel and bladder control with infrequent accidents.

Safety Concerns

Continue to implement safety practices described for the previous stages. Always be aware of new safety issues as the child continues to grow and develop.

Burns

- Teach children the dangers of fire.
- Make sure smoke and carbon monoxide detectors are operational. Use cooking opportunities to help children learn appropriate safety practices.

Dangerous Objects

- Keep all chemicals, cleaning supplies, personal care products, medications, guns, and dangerous tools in locked storage; curiosity peaks during this stage.

Falls

- Always insist that children wear a bike helmet and pads when biking or skating.
- Rethink the use of trampolines; many children sustain serious injuries, including head and spinal cord injuries (Esposito, 2009).

Personal Safety

- Teach children their full name, telephone number, what to do if they become lost, and how to dial 911. Increased independence may cause children to wander too far from parents and teachers.

Toys

- When purchasing toys, evaluate their safety (e.g., rounded edges, not easily broken, nontoxic, nonflammable, no protruding wires, no electrical connections).
- Avoid toys with small parts if there are younger children in the home or school setting.

Suffocation

- Remove doors from old freezer or refrigerator before disposing of it.
- Select toy boxes with removable lids or use open containers to prevent children from being trapped by a fallen top. Remove lids from large plastic storage bins.

5-year-old

The Five-Year-Old

More in control of themselves, both physically and emotionally, most five-year-olds are in a period of relative calm and are becoming increasingly self-confident and reliable. Their world is expanding beyond home, family, and schools or child care centers. Friendships and group activities begin to assume greater importance (Schaefer et al., 2009).

Five-year-olds devote much of their time and attention to the practice and mastery of skills in all developmental areas (Figure 6-10). However, their quest for mastery, coupled with a high energy level and robust self-confidence, can lead to frequent mishaps. Eagerness to do and explore often interferes with the ability to foresee danger or harmful consequences. Therefore, measures to protect children and prevent unintentional injury must be priority for families and caregivers (Marotz, 2012). At the same time, adults must not be so overly protective that good intentions interfere with the child's sense of curiosity, competence, and self-esteem.

Figure 6-10
Practice leads to mastery.

DEVELOPMENTAL PROFILES AND GROWTH PATTERNS

Growth and Physical Characteristics

- Gains 4–5 pounds (1.8–2.3 kg) per year; weighs an average of 38–45 pounds (17.3–20.5 kg).
- Grows an average of 2–2.5 inches (5.1–6.4 cm) per year; is approximately 42–46 inches (106.7–116.8 cm) tall.
- Heart rate (pulse) is approximately 90–110 beats per minute.
- Respiratory rate ranges from 20–30, depending on activity and emotional status.
- Body temperature is stabilized at 98°F–99.4°F.
- Head size is approximately that of an adult's.
- Begins to lose baby (deciduous) teeth (Figure 6-11).
- Body is adult-like in proportion.
- Requires approximately 1,800 calories daily.
- Visual acuity is approximately 20/20 on the Snellen E chart.
- Visual tracking and **binocular vision** are well developed.

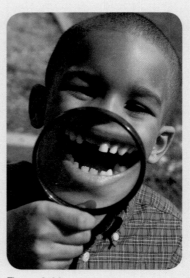

Figure 6-11
Begins losing "baby" teeth.

---

binocular vision—both eyes working together, sending a single image to the brain.

DEVELOPMENTAL PROFILES AND GROWTH PATTERNS *(continued)*

Motor Development

- Walks backward, toe to heel.
- Walks unassisted up and down stairs, alternating feet.
- Learns to turn somersaults (should be taught the right way to avoid injury).
- Touches toes without flexing knees.
- Walks a balance beam.
- Learns to skip using alternate feet.
- Catches a ball thrown from 3 feet away.
- Rides a tricycle or wheeled toy with speed and skillful steering; some children learn to ride bicycles, usually with training wheels.
- Jumps or hops forward 10 times in a row without falling.
- Balances on either foot for 10 seconds with good control.
- Builds three-dimensional structures with small cubes by copying from a picture or model.
- Reproduces many shapes and letters (square, triangle, *A, I, O, U, C, H, L, T*).
- Demonstrates fair control of a pencil or marker; begins to color within the lines.
- Cuts on the line with scissors (but not perfectly) (Figure 6-12) .
- Establishes hand dominance for the most part.

Figure 6-12
Is learning to cut on a line.

Perceptual-Cognitive Development

- Forms rectangle from two triangular pieces.
- Builds steps with set of small blocks.
- Understands and demonstrates concept of *same* shape, *same* size.
- Sorts objects on the basis of two dimensions, such as color and form.
- Sorts a variety of objects so that all things in the group have a single common feature (classification skill: all are food items or boats or animals) (Bennett & Müller, 2010).

- Understands the concepts of smallest and shortest; places objects in order from shortest to tallest, smallest to largest.
- Identifies objects with specified serial position: first, second, last.
- Rote counts to 20 and above; many children can count to 100 (Barrouillet, Thevenot, & Fayol, 2010).
- Recognizes numerals from 1 to 10.
- Understands the concepts of more/less than: "Which bowl has less water?"
- Understands the terms *dark*, *light*, and *early:* "I got up early, before anyone else. It was still dark."
- Relates clock time to daily schedule: "Time to go to bed when the little hand points to 8."
- Some children can tell time on the hour: five o'clock, two o'clock.
- Knows what a calendar is for.
- Recognizes and identifies penny, nickel, and dime; beginning to count and show interest in saving money.
- Knows alphabet; many children can name uppercase and lowercase letters and some letter sounds.
- Understands the concept of half; can say how many pieces an object has when it has been cut in half.
- Asks innumerable questions: Why? What? Where? When?
- Eager to learn new things.

5-year-old

Speech and Language Development

- Has vocabulary of 1,500 words or more.
- Tells a familiar story while looking at pictures in a book.
- Uses functional definitions (a ball is to bounce; a bed is to sleep in; a book is to read).
- Identifies and names four to eight colors.
- Recognizes the humor in simple jokes; makes up jokes and riddles.
- Produces sentences with five to seven words; much longer sentences are not unusual.
- States own birthday, name of home town, and names of family members.
- Answers telephone appropriately; calls an adult to the telephone or takes a brief message.
- Produces speech that is almost entirely intelligible.
- Uses *would*, *could*, and *should* appropriately.
- Uses past tense of irregular verbs consistently (*went, caught, swam*).
- Uses past-tense inflection (-ed) appropriately to mark regular verbs (*jumped, rained, washed*).

5-year-
old

DEVELOPMENTAL PROFILES AND GROWTH PATTERNS *(continued)*

▶❚❚ TeachSource Video Connections

Social Skill Development. Five-year-olds are imaginative, engaging, and social by nature. They usually get along well with other children, preferring to play with one or two friends at a time. However, they can also become bossy when things do not go their way. As you watch the learning video *Preschool: Social Development, Cooperative Learning and Play* on the Education CourseMate website, consider the following questions:

1. What social skills must a child have to engage successfully in cooperative or constructive play groups?
2. In what ways can teachers encourage children's development of positive social skills?
3. What skills do children acquire as a result of group participation that cannot be gained from solitary play?

Figure 6-13
Is sociable and enjoys spending time with friends.

Social-Emotional Development

- Enjoys friendships; often has one or two special playmates. (Figure 6-13).
- Shares toys, takes turns, plays cooperatively (with occasional lapses); is often quite generous (Rochat et al., 2009).
- Participates in group play and shared activities with other children; suggests imaginative and elaborate play ideas.
- Is usually affectionate and caring, especially toward younger or injured children and animals.

- Follows directions and carries out assignments most of the time; generally does what parent or teacher requests.
- Continues to need adult comfort and reassurance but might be less open in seeking and accepting comfort.
- Has better self-control; experiences fewer dramatic swings of emotions.
- Likes to tell jokes, entertain, and make people laugh.
- Takes pride in accomplishments; boasts at times and seeks adult acknowledgment and approval.

DAILY ROUTINES

5-year-old

Eating

- Has a good appetite but not at every meal.
- Likes familiar foods; prefers most vegetables raw rather than cooked.
- Often adopts food dislikes of family members, teachers, peers, or all three.
- "Makes" breakfast (pours cereal, gets out milk and juice) and lunch (spreads peanut butter and jam on bread).

Toileting, Bathing, and Dressing

- Takes full responsibility for his or her own toileting needs; might put off going to the bathroom until an accident occurs or is barely avoided.
- Bathes fairly independently but may need some help getting started.
- Dresses self completely; learning to tie shoes, sometimes aware when clothing is on wrong side out or backward.
- Careless with clothes at times; leaves them scattered about and forgets where they were left; needs many reminders to pick them up.
- Uses tissue for blowing nose but often does a careless or incomplete job; forgets to throw tissue away; needs reminder to wash hands.

Sleeping

- Manages all routines associated with getting ready for bed independently; can help with younger brother's or sister's bedtime routine.
- Averages 10 or 11 hours of sleep per night. Some five-year-olds may still nap.
- Dreams and nightmares are common.
- Delays going to sleep if the day has been especially exciting or if long-anticipated events are scheduled for the next day.

DAILY ROUTINES *(continued)*

Play and Social Activities

- Carries out family chores and routines; is usually helpful and cooperative.

- Knows the "right" way to do something and often has the "right" answers to questions; seems somewhat opinionated and rigid in beliefs at times.

- Remains attached to home and family; willing to have an adventure but wants it to begin and end at home; fearful that parents may leave or not return.

- Plays well with other children most times, but three might be a crowd: two five-year-olds will often exclude the third.

- Shows affection and is protective toward younger siblings; may feel overburdened at times if younger child demands too much attention.

5-year-old

Learning Activities

Developmental applications for families and teachers:

- Provide inexpensive materials (newsprint, old magazines, wallpaper books, paint samples, fabric scraps) for cutting, pasting, painting, coloring, folding; turn a cardboard box into a loom for weaving; offer easy sewing activities and smaller beads for stringing; gather wood scraps, glue, and tools for simple carpentry projects.

- Collect props and dress-up clothes that allow more detailed pretend play (e.g., family roles, occupations); visit and talk about community activities—house construction, post office and mail deliveries, farmers' market; encourage play with puppets; assist in creating a stage. (A large cardboard box works well.)

- Continue to read aloud regularly and frequently; expose children to books on a wide variety of topics.

- Encourage children's increasing interest in paper-and-pencil, number-, letter-, and word-recognition games that they often invent but may need adult help to play.

- Plan cooking experiences that involve children: washing and chopping vegetables; cutting out cookies; measuring, mixing, and stirring.

- Set up improvised target games that promote eye–hand coordination (bean bag toss, bowling, ring toss, horseshoes, low hoop and basketball); ensure opportunities for vigorous play (wheeled toys; jungle gyms and parallel bars; digging, raking, sweeping, and hauling).

Developmental Alerts

Check with a health care provider or early childhood specialist if, by the sixth birthday, the child *does not*:

- Alternate feet when walking up and down stairs.
- Speak in a moderate voice—not too loud, too soft, too high, or too low.
- Follow simple three-step directions in stated order: "Please go to the cupboard, get a cup, and bring it to me."
- Use four to five words in acceptable sentence structure.
- Cut on a line with scissors.
- Sit still and listen to an entire short story (5–7 minutes).
- Maintain eye contact when spoken to (unless this is a cultural taboo).
- Play well with other children; listen, take turns, offer assistance.
- Perform most self-grooming tasks independently (brush teeth, wash hands and face).

5-year-old

Safety Concerns

Continue to implement safety practices described for the previous stages. Always be aware of new safety issues as the child continues to grow and develop.

Falls

- Monitor parks and play areas for potential hazards—broken glass, sharp objects, defective structures, holes, inadequate cushioning material under play equipment.

Toys

- Refrain from purchasing toys that involve projectiles or require electricity; battery-operated toys are safer.

Traffic

- Teach street safety, especially to children who walk to and from school; review safe practices often.
- Use recommended car seats and safety restraints appropriate for the child's increasing weight and height.

Personal Safety

- *Never* leave children in a vehicle unattended for any length of time; temperatures (heat or cold) inside of a closed vehicle can quickly become deadly. Unattended children may also be targeted by potential kidnappers.
- Teach children to run away and seek adult help if approached by a stranger. Tell them to yell, "You're not my mommy (daddy)." Establish a code word to help children recognize a trusted adult.
- Teach children how to swim and about water safety rules.

Poisoning

- Use only nontoxic art supplies; check product labels carefully (see *www.cpsc.gov* for product information).
- Remind children to always check with an adult before putting nonfood items (such as pills or berries) in their mouth.

POSITIVE BEHAVIOR GUIDANCE

Adults play an essential role in helping preschoolers develop self-control. They must set behavioral expectations that are developmentally realistic for children, state them in positive terms, and enforce them consistently. It is also important that adults provide unconditional love and serve as positive role models for children.

Three-year-olds:

- Set limits and use short, simple statements to explain why they are necessary.
- Acknowledge children when they are behaving appropriately.
- Remain calm and patient; keep your own anger and frustration under control.
- Redirect the child's activity: if the child is throwing sand, ask him to help you sweep the sand back into the sandbox.

Four-year-olds:

- Offer choices: "Do you want to wear your sandals or sneakers?"
- Use natural consequences: "If you spill the paint there won't be any left for our picture." "If you bump into the other children with your bike, you will need to leave the area."
- Provide simple directions and warnings so children know what to expect next: "Lunch will be served in a few minutes so we need to begin picking up the toys."

Five-year-olds:

- Involve children in problem-solving: "Which toy do you think your brother would like?" "Where should we look for your jacket?"
- Remove children from an activity if inappropriate behavior continues and give them time to think about their actions.
- Include children in setting rules to increase compliance: "What should we do if someone pushes another child?"

SUMMARY

Preschoolers—three-, four-, and five-year-olds—are on the move every waking moment and eager to learn about everything. They want and continue to need a great deal of adult support and approval, although this becomes less significant as they move out of the preschool and into the primary school years. Families and teachers play a major role in providing safe environments, guidance, and

learning opportunities that enable preschoolers to practice, refine, and extend the skills that define healthy development. At the same time, adults must set limits to protect children from the unforeseen consequences of their exuberance and insistence on doing things by themselves. Suggestions for supporting children's development in each domain and identifying potential developmental delays are described in each of the age-related sections.

Key Terms

tripod grasp **p. 132**
hand dominance **p. 133**

gender **p. 137**
binocular vision **p. 147**

Apply What You Know

A. Apply What You Have Learned

Reread the brief developmental sketch about Anna and Juan at the beginning of the chapter and answer the following questions.

1. Assuming that Juan's motor development is progressing typically, what skills would you expect to observe?
2. What social behaviors would be characteristic of a four-year-old?
3. How would you respond to Anna's question if she asked, "How much responsibility can I expect Juan to assume for his own personal care at his age?"
4. In addition to reading bedtime stories, what other types of activities might Anna engage in with Juan to further his language development?

B. Review Questions

1. Describe three motor skills that appear between three and five years of age.
2. Describe three major speech and language skills that appear between three and five years of age (in order).
3. What self-help skills would you expect a typically developing four-year-old to be capable of performing?
4. Should a teacher be concerned about a four-year-old who exhibits frequent mood swings or often tattles? Why or why not?
5. Describe how a teacher might use a cooking activity to promote five-year-olds' perceptual-cognitive development.

Helpful Websites

Center for Child Well-being
http://www.childwellbeing.org/

Society for Research on Child Development
http://www.srcd.org/

U.S. Consumer Product Safety Commission (CPSC) (pool safety campaign)
http://www.poolsafety.gov

References

Barrouillet, P., Thevenot, C., & Fayol, M. (2010). Evidence for knowledge of the syntax of large numbers in preschoolers, *Journal of Experimental Child Psychology, 105*(3), 264–271.

Bennett, J., & Müller, U. (2010). The development of flexibility and abstraction in preschool children, *Merrill-Palmer Quarterly, 56*(4), 455–473.

Bialystok, E., & Craik, F. (2010). Cognitive and linguistic processing in the bilingual mind, *Current Directions in Psychological Science, 19*(1), 19–23.

Chemey, I., & Dempsey, J. (2010). Young children's classification, stereotyping and play behaviour for gender neutral and ambiguous toys, *Educational Psychology, 30*(6), 651–669.

Cipriano, E., & Stifter, C. (2010). Predicting preschool effortful control from toddler temperament and parenting behavior, *Journal of Applied Developmental Psychology, 31*(3), 221–230.

Esposito, P. (2009). The reemergence of the trampoline as a recreational activity, *Current Sports Medicine Reports, 8*(5), 273–277.

Göksun, T., Hirsh-Pasek, K., & Golinkoff, R. (2010). How do preschoolers express cause in gesture and speech?, *Cognitive Development, 25*(1), 56–68.

Goodman, I., Libenson, A., & Wade-Woolley, L. (2010). Sensitivity to linguistic stress, phonological awareness and early reading ability in preschoolers, *Journal of Research in Reading, 33*(2), 113–127.

Grant, J., & Suddendorf, T. (2010). Young children's ability to distinguish past and future changes in physical and mental states, *British Journal of Developmental Psychology, 28*(4), 853–870.

Huang, Y., Spelke, E., & Snedeker, J. (2010). When is four far more than three? Children's generalization of newly acquired number words, *Psychological Science, 21*(4), 600–606.

Ingram, G., & Bering, J. (2010). Children's tattling: The reporting of everyday norm violations in preschool settings, *Child Development, 81*(3), 945–957.

Johansson, I., & Sandberg, A. (2010). Learning and participation: Two interrelated key-concepts in the preschool, *European Early Childhood Education Research Journal, 18*(2), 229–242.

Marotz, L. (2012). *Health, safety, and nutrition for the young child.* (8th Ed.). Belmont, CA: Wadsworth Cengage Learning.

Martin, C., & Ruble, D. (2010). Patterns of gender development, *Annual Review of Psychology, 61,* 353–381.

Nicolopoulou, A., Barbosa, A., Ilgaz, H., & Brockmeyer, C. (2010). Using the transformative power of play to educate hearts and minds: From Vygotsky to Vivian Paley and beyond, *Mind, Culture & Activity, 17*(1), 42–58.

Plowman, L., McPake, J., & Stephen, C. (2010). The technologisation of childhood? Young children and technology in the home, *Children & Society, 24*(1), 63–74.

Rice, M., Smolik, R., Perpich, D., Thompson, T., Rytting, N., & Blossom, M. (2010). Children 3 to 9 years with and without language impairments, *Journal of Speech, Language & Hearing Research, 53*(2), 333–349.

Rochat, P., Dias, M., Broesch, T., Passos-Ferreira, C., Winning, A., & Berg, B. (2009). Fairness in distributive justice by 3- and 5-year olds across seven cultures, *Journal of Cross-Cultural Psychology, 40*(3), 416–442.

Schaefer, D., Light, J., Fabes, R., Hanish, L., & Martin, C. (2009). Fundamental principles of network formation among preschool children, *Social Networks, 32*(1), 61–71.

Slaughter, V., & Griffiths, M. (2007). Death understanding and fear of death in young children, *Clinical Child Psychology & Psychiatry, 12*(4), 525–535.

Trommsdorff, G. (2009). Culture and development of self-regulation, *Social & Personality Psychology Compass, 3*(5), 687–701.

Williamson, R., Jaswal, V., & Meltzoff, A. (2010). Learning the rules: Observation and imitation of a sorting strategy by 36-month-old children, *Developmental Psychology, 46*(1), 57–65.

Worobey, H., Ostapkovich, K., Yudin, K., & Worobey, J. (2010). Trying versus liking fruits and vegetables: Correspondence between mothers and preschoolers, *Ecology of Food & Nutrition, 49*(2), 87–97.

You are just a click away from a variety of interactive study tools and resources. Access the text's Education CourseMate website at **www.cengagebrain.com**, where you'll find a variety of enrichment materials, including videos, glossary flashcards, activities, tutorial quizzes, web links, and more.

CHAPTER 7
Early Childhood: Six-, Seven-, and Eight-Year-Olds

Learning Objectives

After reading this chapter, you should be able to:

- Describe several sensory learning experiences that would be developmentally appropriate for six-, seven-, and eight-year-olds.
- Explain why behavior problems and emotional outbursts might reappear during this developmental stage.
- Compare and contrast the speech and language skills of six- and eight-year-olds.
- Explain and demonstrate Piaget's concept of conservation.
- Discuss the role of friendships in children's development.

naeyc Standards Chapter Links:

1a, 1b, and 1c: Promoting child development and learning
2a and 2c: Building family and community relationships
3c and 3d: Observing, documenting, and assessing to support young children and familie
4a, 4b, 4c and 4d: Using developmentally effective approaches
5c: Using content knowledge to build meaningful curriculum

Meet Juan and His Friend Sergio

For weeks, Juan has repeatedly asked his mother when school will begin. Soon to turn seven, he is eagerly anticipating the start of first grade, riding on a school bus, and eating lunch in the school cafeteria. Juan met his new teacher, Mr. Rosales, last week during the open house and is excited about having a "man teacher." His mother, Anna, thinks Juan will benefit from having a male role model since his father has stopped their weekend visits.

Juan is also happy that his best friend, Sergio, will be in the same class. Unlike Juan, who is an only child, Sergio is the youngest of five brothers and three sisters. His parents work long hours and show

continued…

6- to 8-
year-olds

little interest in his school activities or homework. They view their primary role as caretakers and believe the teachers are responsible for helping their son to learn. Sergio struggles to write his name, has difficulty sorting objects by category, and is unable to recognize and order numbers consistently. His kindergarten teacher was reluctant to advance him to the first grade, but Mr. Rosales assured her that he would devote extra time and attention to mentoring Sergio. Mr. Rosales is aware that Sergio's family speaks little English at home and has limited resources.

Juan thinks it is "pretty neat" that he will go to school all day like his mother, who plans to finish her associate's degree in early childhood education this spring. She is proud of her son's progress in school and works with him at home so that he continues to do well. Juan's advanced reading and writing skills are apparent in the imaginative stories he composes on the computer when he and his mother visit their local library. When he is finished, Juan often seeks out the librarian so he can read his story to her. Juan is also excited about learning to tell time and repeatedly wants his mother to ask him what time it is.

Ask Yourself

1. What environmental factors may help to explain why Juan and Sergio are performing differently in school?
2. What steps is Juan's mother taking to support his literacy development?

Six-, Seven-, and Eight-Year-Olds

The period following the preschool years is especially remarkable. Children are in a stage of developmental integration—organizing and combining various developmental skills to accomplish increasingly complex tasks. At this age, boys and girls alike are becoming more competent at managing their own personal needs—washing, dressing, toileting, eating, getting up, and getting ready for school. They observe family rules regarding mealtimes, television, chores, and needs for privacy. They can be trusted to run errands and carry out simple responsibilities at home and school without frequent reminders. In other words, children are in control of themselves and their immediate world. Above all, six-, seven-, and eight-year-olds are ready and eager to attend school, even though they may be somewhat apprehensive when the time actually arrives. Going to school creates anxieties about things such as arriving on time, remembering to bring back assigned homework, having a new teacher, taking tests, or walking home alone (Rood et al., 2010).

Learning to read is the most complex perceptual task the child encounters following the preschool years (Charlesworth, 2011; Piaget, 1926). Recognizing visual letter symbols and associating them with their spoken sound is an important component

of **emerging literacy**. It also means that children must learn to combine letters to form words and to put these words together to form intelligible thoughts that can be read or spoken. Complex as the task is, most children become more adept at reading between six and eight years of age; for some, the skill is soon taken for granted.

Sensory activities continue to be essential for children's learning (Figure 7-1). Developmental kindergartens and primary classes recognize this as fundamental practice (Ray & Smith, 2010). They provide sensory experiences that encourage children to manipulate a variety of materials—blocks; puzzles; paints, glue, paper, and found materials; sand, water, and dirt; musical instruments; and, measurement devices. They also include project-based opportunities such as cooking, gardening, carpentry, science, and dramatic play that reinforce learning across all developmental areas. The National Association for the Education of Young Children (NAEYC) strongly endorses a **hands-on learning** approach with six-, seven-, and eight-year-olds as well as with younger children. This philosophy is clearly stated in NAEYC's *Developmentally Appropriate Practice in Early Childhood Programs Serving Children Birth through Age 8* (NAEYC, 2009). Particularly noteworthy are the subsections entitled "Principles of child development and learning that inform practice" and "Guidelines for developmentally appropriate practice" that outline the rationale for individualizing children's educational opportunities. Above all, this position statement acknowledges that each child is a unique individual whose developmental abilities, family and cultural heritage, needs,

Figure 7-1
Children continue to learn best through sensory experiences.

emerging literacy—early experiences, such as being read and talked to, naming objects, and identifying letters, that prepare a child for later reading, writing, and language development.

sensory—refers to the five senses: hearing, seeing, touching, smelling, and tasting.

hands-on learning—a curriculum approach that involves children as active participants, encouraging them to manipulate, investigate, experiment, and solve problems.

and learning style differ from those of other children. Similar recommendations have been adopted by other early childhood professional organizations, including family child care and school-age programs.

Play continues to be one of the most important activities for fostering cognitive and social skill development in the early grades (Rushton, Juola-Rushton, & Larkine, 2010). For the most part, six-, seven-, and eight-year-olds play well with other children, especially if the group is not too large. There is keen interest in making friends, being a friend, and having friends. At the same time, there also can be quarreling, bossing, and excluding: "If you play with Lynette, then you're not *my* friend." Some children show considerable aggression, but it often tends to be verbal, aimed at hurting feelings rather than at causing physical harm.

Friends are usually playmates the child has ready access to in the neighborhood and at school. Friends often are defined as someone who is "fun," "pretty," "strong," "nice," or "awesome." Friendships at this age are easily established and readily abandoned; few are stable or long-lasting (Diamond & Hong, 2010).

Throughout the primary school years, many children seem almost driven by the need to do everything right, yet they enjoy being challenged and completing tasks. They like to build models, do craft projects, play computer and board games, and participate in organized activities. Most children enjoy these early school years. They become comfortable with themselves, their families, and their teachers.

▶❚❚ TeachSource Video Connections

Cognitive Development. Advances in cognitive abilities, including improving memory capacity, information processing, and abstract thinking, begin to open new opportunities for complex learning. As you watch the learning video *5–11 Years: Lev Vygotsky, the Zone of Proximal Development, and Scaffolding* on the Education CourseMate website, consider the following questions:

1. Describe Vygotsky's Zone of Proximal Development.
2. What is the teacher's role in this form of learning?
3. Do you consider this instructional approach to be developmentally appropriate or inappropriate for six-year-olds? Explain.
4. What is scaffolding?
5. How did the teacher respond to children's incorrect answers?

The Six-Year-Old

Exciting adventures begin to open up to six-year-olds as their coordination improves and their size and strength increase. New challenges are often met with a mixture of enthusiasm and frustration. Six-year-olds typically have difficulty making choices and, at times, are overwhelmed by unfamiliar situations. At the same time, changes in their

cognitive abilities enable them to see rules as useful for understanding everyday events and the behavior of others. Children should have opportunities for vigorous play each day to promote physical development, decrease the risk for obesity, and channel excess energy.

For many children, this period also marks the beginning of formal, subject-oriented schooling. It should be noted that formal academic activities at this age are considered developmentally inappropriate by many early childhood educators (Ray & Smith, 2010; Russell, 2010). Behavior problems and signs of stress or tension such as tics, nail-biting, hair-twisting, bed-wetting, or sleeping difficulties may flare up as new experiences are encountered. Generally, these pass as children become familiar with

6-year-old

new expectations and the responsibilities associated with going to school. Despite the turmoil and trying times (for adults as well), most six-year-olds experience an abundance of happy times marked by a lively curiosity, an eagerness to learn, an endearing sense of humor, and exuberant outbursts of affection and good will (Figure 7-2).

Figure 7-2
Six-year-olds are curious and eager to learn.

DEVELOPMENTAL PROFILES AND GROWTH PATTERNS

Growth and Physical Characteristics

- Growth occurs slowly but steadily.
- Height increases 2–3 inches (5–7.5 cm) each year: girls are an average of 42–46 inches (105–115 cm) tall; boys are an average of 44–47 inches (110–117.5 cm).
- Weight increases 5–7 pounds (2.3–3.2 kg) per year: girls weigh approximately 38–47 pounds (19.1–22.3 kg); boys weigh approximately 42–49 pounds (17.3–21.4 kg).
- Weight gains reflect significant increases in muscle mass.
- Heart rate (80 beats per minute) and respiratory rates (18–28 breaths per minute) are similar to those of adults; both rates vary with activity.
- Body takes on a lanky appearance as long bones of the arms and legs begin a phase of rapid growth.

DEVELOPMENTAL PROFILES AND GROWTH PATTERNS *(continued)*

6-year-old

- Loses baby (**deciduous**) **teeth**; permanent (secondary) teeth erupt, beginning with the two upper front teeth; girls tend to lose teeth at an earlier age than do boys.
- Visual acuity should be approximately 20/20; children testing 20/40 or less should have a thorough professional evaluation (Ethan et al., 2010).
- Farsightedness is not uncommon and may be outgrown as children mature.
- Develops more adult-like facial features and overall physical appearance.
- Requires approximately 1,600 to 1,700 calories per day.

Motor Development

- Has increased muscle strength; typically, boys are stronger than girls of similar size.
- Gains greater control over large and fine motor skills; movements are becoming more precise and deliberate, although some clumsiness persists.
- Enjoys vigorous physical activity (running, jumping, climbing, and throwing) (Figure 7-3).
- Moves constantly, even when trying to sit still.

Figure 7-3
Engaging in physical activity each day is an essential step in obesity prevention.

- Has increased dexterity and eye–hand coordination along with improved motor functioning, which facilitates learning to ride a bicycle (without training wheels), swim, swing a bat, or kick a ball.
- Enjoys art projects (likes to paint, model with clay, "make things," draw and color, put things together, and work with wood).
- Writes numbers and letters with varying degrees of precision and interest; may reverse or confuse certain letters (*b/d, p/g, g/q, t/f*).
- Traces around hand and other objects.
- Folds and cuts paper into simple shapes.
- Ties own shoes (still a struggle for some children).

Perceptual-Cognitive Development

- Shows increased attention span; works at tasks for longer periods of time, although concentrated effort is not always consistent.

---

deciduous teeth—initial set of teeth that eventually fall out; often referred to as *baby teeth*.

- Understands concepts such as simple time markers (today, tomorrow, yesterday) or uncomplicated concepts of motion (cars go faster than bicycles).
- Identifies seasons and major holidays and the activities associated with each.
- Enjoys the challenge of puzzles, counting and sorting activities, paper-and-pencil mazes, and games that involve counting or matching letters and words with pictures.
- Recognizes some words by sight; attempts to sound out words (some children may be reading well by this time).
- Identifies familiar coins (pennies, nickels, dimes, and quarters).
- Names and correctly holds up right and left hands fairly consistently.
- Clings to certain beliefs involving magic or fantasy (the Tooth Fairy swapping a coin for a tooth; the Easter Bunny bringing eggs).
- Has limited understanding about death and dying (believes it can be reversed or that he or she caused it to happen; often expresses fear that parents might die, especially mother) (Favazza, 2010).

6-year-old

Speech and Language Development

- Talks nonstop (this behavior may not be encouraged in all cultures); sometimes described as a chatterbox.
- Acquires language pattern reflective of his or her cultural background.
- Carries on adult-like conversations; asks many questions.
- Learns as many as five to ten new words each day; vocabulary consists of approximately 10,000 to 14,000 words.
- Uses appropriate verb tenses, word order, and sentence structure.
- Uses language rather than tantrums or physical aggression to express displeasure: "That's mine! Give it back, or I'm telling."
- Talks self through steps required in simple problem-solving situations (although the logic may be irregular and unclear to adults).
- Imitates slang and profanity; finds "bathroom" talk extremely funny.
- Delights in telling jokes and riddles; often, the humor is far from subtle (Figure 7-4).

Figure 7-4
Finds humor in almost everything.

DEVELOPMENTAL PROFILES AND GROWTH PATTERNS *(continued)*

- Enjoys being read to and making up stories.
- Is capable of learning more than one language; does so spontaneously in a bilingual or multilingual family (Marchman, Fernald, & Hurtado, 2010).

Social-Emotional Development

6-year-old

- Experiences sudden mood swings: can be "best friends" one minute, "worst of enemies" the next; loving one day, uncooperative and irritable the next; especially unpredictable toward mother or primary caregiver.
- Becomes less dependent on family as friendship circle expands; still needs closeness and nurturing, yet has urges to break away and "grow up" (Piaget, 1929).
- Needs and seeks adult approval, reassurance, and praise; anxious to please; may complain excessively about minor hurts or illnesses to gain attention.
- Continues to be self-centered (egocentric); still sees events almost entirely from own perspective (views everything and everyone as there for child's own benefit).
- Easily disappointed and frustrated by self-perceived failure.
- Has difficulty composing and soothing self; dislikes being corrected or losing at games; might sulk, cry, refuse to play, or reinvent rules to suit own purposes.
- Is enthusiastic and inquisitive about surroundings and everyday events.
- Shows little or no understanding of ethical behavior or moral standards; often fibs, cheats, or takes items belonging to others.
- Knows when he or she has been "bad"; values of "good" and "bad" are based on school and family expectations and rules.
- May become increasingly fearful of thunderstorms, the dark, unidentified noises, dogs, and other animals (Berger, 2010).

DAILY ROUTINES

Eating

- Has a healthy appetite most of the time; often takes larger helpings than is able to finish. May skip an occasional meal; usually makes up for it later.
- Has strong food preferences and definite dislikes; willingness to try new foods is unpredictable.
- Uses table manners that often do not meet adult standards; may revert to eating with fingers; puts too much food into mouth at one time; continues to spill milk or drop food in lap.

- Has difficulty using table knife for cutting and fork for anything but spearing food.
- Finds it difficult to sit quietly through an entire meal; wiggles and squirms, gets off (or "falls" off) chair, drops utensils.

Personal Care and Dressing

- Balks at having to take a bath; finds many excuses for delaying or avoiding a bath entirely.
- Manages toileting routines without much adult help; sometimes is in a hurry or waits too long so that "accidents" happen.
- Reverts to occasional accidental soiling or wetting of pants especially during new experiences, such as in the first weeks of school or when under stress.
- Sleeps through most nights without having to get up to use the bathroom. *Note:* Some children, especially boys, may not maintain a dry bed for another year or so.
- Performs self-care routines such as handwashing, bathing, and toothbrushing in a hurry; not always careful or thorough; still needs frequent supervision and demonstrations to make sure routines are carried out properly.
- Expresses interest in selecting own clothes; still needs some guidance in determining occasion and seasonal appropriateness.
- Drops clothing on floor or bed, loses shoes around the house, and flings jacket down; often forgets where items were left (Figure 7-5).

Figure 7-5
Often forgetful when it comes to caring for clothes.

Sleeping

- Requires 9–11 hours of uninterrupted sleep.
- Sleeps through the night; some children continue to have nightmares and sleep disturbances (Hoban, 2010).
- Sometimes requests a night-light, special blanket, or favorite stuffed toy (may want all three).
- Finds numerous ways to avoid bedtime; when finally in bed, falls asleep quickly.
- Finds ways to amuse self with books, toys, television, or coloring if awake before the rest of the family.

Play and Social Activities

- Has strong sense of self, evident in terms of preferences and dislikes; uncompromising about wants and needs. (Often these do not coincide with adult plans or desires.)

6-year-old

DAILY ROUTINES *(continued)*

- Is possessive about toy, books, parents, and friends but is able to share on some occasions.
- Forms close, friendly relationship with one or two other children (often slightly older); play involves working together toward specific goals.
- Becomes intolerant of being told what to do; may revert to tantrums on occasion.
- Seeks teacher's attention, praise, and reassurance; now views teacher (rather than parent) as the ultimate source of "truth."

6-year-old

Learning Activities

Developmental applications for families and teachers:

- Provide materials for coloring, cutting, pasting, and painting.
- Offer paper-and-pencil games (dot-to-dot, number-to-number, word search, hidden objects; copying and tracing activities).
- Provide (and frequently join in) simple card games (Hearts, Uno, Flinch) and boardgames (Scrabble Junior, Candyland, checkers), especially those in which competitiveness is minimal.
- Keep a plentiful supply of books and magazines on hand for children to look at as well as for adults to read with children; encourage children to make up and tell their own stories. Make weekly trips to the library.
- Share children's interest in collecting objects (seashells, colored stones, bugs); help them to group, label, and display objects.
- Teach children what to do if they become lost or are approached by a stranger.
- Provide an assortment of dress-up clothes for boys and girls; use children's interests and familiar community workers as a guide for role-playing.
- Encourage simple cooking, carpentry, and construction activities with blocks, cars, trucks, planes, and zoo and farm animals. (Avoid battery-driven and mechanical toys that offer little involvement, hence limited learning, once the novelty has worn off.)
- Encourage at least 60 minutes of vigorous physical activity daily (bicycling; inline skating; swimming; gardening; throwing, catching, batting, and kicking balls; walking). Limit time spent on computer and electronic games which encourage sedentary behavior and reduce children's active play (a major cause of obesity).
- Involve children in cooking activities; use these opportunities to build language, math, science, and problem-solving skills.

Developmental Alerts

Check with a health care provider or early childhood specialist if, by the seventh birthday, the child *does not*:

- Show signs of ongoing growth (increasing height and weight); continuing motor development such as running, jumping, and balancing.

- Show some interest in reading and trying to reproduce letters, especially his or her own name.

- Follow simple, multiple-step directions: "Finish your book, put it on the shelf, and then get your coat on."

- Follow through with instructions and complete simple tasks (putting dishes in the sink, picking up clothes, or finishing a puzzle). *Note:* All children forget. Task incompletion is not a problem unless a child *repeatedly* leaves tasks unfinished.

- Begin to develop alternatives to excessive use of inappropriate behavior to get his or her way.

- Develop a steady decrease in tension-type behavior that may be associated with the start of school or participation in an organized activity (repeated grimacing or facial tics, eye twitching, grinding of teeth, nail biting, regressive soiling or wetting, frequent stomachaches, or refusing to go to school).

6-year-old

Safety Concerns

Continue to implement safety practices described for the previous stages. Always be aware of new safety issues as the child continues to grow and develop.

Burns

- Keep matches and lighters in locked storage.

Falls

- Make sure clothing fits properly; skirts and pants that are too long can cause a child to trip or become entangled in play equipment. Remind children to keep shoes tied or Velcro straps fastened.
- Require children to wear helmets and other appropriate protective gear whenever they ride bikes, skateboards, or scooters.

Equipment

- Store machinery and sharp instruments in a safe place, out of children's reach.
- Teach children proper use of scissors, knives, hammers, and kitchen equipment.
- Set parental controls on televisions (V-chip) and computers to protect children from unwanted content.

Traffic

- Review safety rules to follow in and around motor vehicles, when crossing streets, or riding a bicycle.

Teach children to dismount and walk their bike across streets.

- Discuss appropriate behavior on buses if your child rides one to school.
- Insist that children always wear a seatbelt when riding in motor vehicles.

Water

- Enroll children in swimming lessons and teach them correct safety rules to follow around pools. Have proper rescue equipment accessible.
- *Never leave children unattended near water.*

The Seven-Year-Old

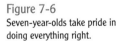

7-year-old

Seven-year-olds are becoming more aware of themselves as individuals. They work hard at being responsible, being "good," and doing it "right" (Figure 7-6). They tend to take themselves seriously—too seriously at times. When they fail to live up to their own self-imposed expectations, they might sulk or become frustrated or withdrawn. It is as if children at seven are trying to think things through and integrate what they already know with the flood of new experiences coming their way (Cowan et al., 2010). Worrying about what might or might not come to pass is also typical; for example, anticipating yet dreading second grade can create anxiety. Maybe the work will be too hard; maybe the teacher won't be nice; or maybe the other kids won't be friendly.

At the same time, children of this age have many positive traits. They are more reasonable and willing to share and cooperate. They are becoming better listeners and better at understanding and following through on what they are told. They are able to stay on task longer and strive mightily to do everything perfectly (which only increases their worry load). Because of these complicated feelings, parents and teachers need to exercise patience and tolerance. Unpredictable mood swings reflect the child's overwhelming efforts to cope with the conflicts inherent in being a seven-year-old.

Figure 7-6
Seven-year-olds take pride in doing everything right.

DEVELOPMENTAL PROFILES AND GROWTH PATTERNS

Growth and Physical Characteristics

- Weight increase tends to be relatively small; a gain of 6 pounds (2.7 kg) per year is typical. Seven-year-olds weigh approximately 50–55 pounds (22.7–25 kg).

- Height increases an average of 2.5 inches (6.25 cm) per year. Girls are approximately 44–44.5 inches (110–116.3 cm) tall; boys are approximately 46–49.5 inches (115–124 cm) tall.

- Muscle mass is fairly equal for boys and girls.

- Physical growth continues slowly and steadily; some girls may overtake some boys in height.

- Posture is more erect; arms and legs continue to lengthen, giving children a longer, leaner appearance.

- Energy level comes and goes, fluctuating between spurts of high energy and intervals of temporary fatigue.

- Still experiences a number of colds and other minor illnesses; however, these occur less frequently than at age six.

- Eyeballs continue to change shape and size; children's eyes should be checked periodically to ensure good vision.

- Hair often grows darker in color.

- Permanent teeth continue to replace baby teeth.

Motor Development

- Exhibits large and fine motor control that is more precisely tuned: balances on either foot; runs up and down stairs with alternating feet; throws and catches smaller balls; practices batting balls; manipulates a computer mouse, knitting needles, or paintbrush with greater accuracy (Figure 7-7).

- Approaches more challenging physical activities, such as climbing up or jumping down from high places, with caution.

- Practices a new motor skill over and over until mastered and then drops it to work on something else.

- Finds floor more comfortable than furniture when reading, playing games, or watching television; legs are often in constant motion.

Figure 7-7
Manipulates objects with improved skill and accuracy.

7-year-old

DEVELOPMENTAL PROFILES AND GROWTH PATTERNS *(continued)*

- Uses knife and fork appropriately but inconsistently.
- Holds pencil in a tight grasp near the tip; rests head on forearm, lowers head almost to the tabletop when doing pencil-and-paper tasks.
- Produces letters and numbers in a deliberate and confident fashion (characters are increasingly uniform in size and shape; might run out of room on line or page when writing).

Perceptual-Cognitive Development

- Understands concepts of space and time in ways that are both logical and more practical (a year is "a long time"; a hundred miles is "far away") (Jordan, Glutting, & Ramineni, 2010).

- Begins to grasp Piaget's concepts of **conservation**; for example, the shape of a container does not necessarily reflect the quantity it can hold (Figure 7-8). (Children are now entering Piaget's stage of *concrete operations*.)

Figure 7-8
Children are beginning to understand that two differently shaped containers can hold the same amount of liquid.

- Gains a better understanding of cause and effect: "If I'm late for school again, I'll be in big trouble"; "Ice cubes will melt if they get too warm."
- Tells time by the clock and understands calendar time—days, months, years, and seasons.
- Plans ahead: "I'm saving this cookie for later tonight."
- Shows marked fascination with magic tricks; enjoys putting on shows for family and friends.
- Finds reading easier; many seven-year-olds read for their own enjoyment and delight in retelling story details.
- Has better reading than spelling skills.
- Enjoys counting and saving money.
- Continues to reverse some letters and substitute sounds on occasion; this is typical development and does not indicate a reading or learning disability.

Speech and Language Development

- Engages in storytelling; likes to write short stories and tell imaginative tales.
- Uses adult-like sentence structure and language in conversation; patterns reflect cultural and geographical differences.

7-year-old

---

conservation—the stage in children's cognitive development at which they understand that an object's physical qualities (e.g., weight, mass) remain the same despite changes in its appearance; for example, flattening a ball of Play-Doh does not affect its weight.

- Becomes more precise and elaborate in use of language; greater use of descriptive adjectives and adverbs.

- Uses gestures to illustrate conversations.

- Criticizes own performance: "I didn't draw that right," "Her picture is better than mine."

- Verbal exaggeration commonplace: "I ate ten hot dogs at the picnic."

- Offers explanations of events in terms of own preferences or needs: "It didn't rain yesterday because I was going on a picnic."

- Describes personal experiences in great detail: "First we parked the car, then we hiked up this long trail, then we sat down on a broken tree near a lake and ate...."

- Understands and carries out multiple-step instructions (up to five steps); may need to have directions repeated because of not listening to entire request the first time.

- Enjoys writing email messages and simple notes to friends.

Social-Emotional Development

- Is cooperative and affectionate toward adults and less frequently annoyed with them; sees humor in everyday happenings and is more outgoing.

- Likes to be the "teacher's helper"; is eager for teacher's attention and approval but less obvious about seeking it.

- Seeks out friendships; friends are important but can find plenty to do if no one is available.

- Quarrels less often, although squabbles and tattling continue to occur in both one-on-one and group play.

- Complains that family decisions are unjust; that a particular sibling may get to do more or is given more.

- Blames others for own mistakes; makes up alibis for personal shortcomings: "I could have made a better one, but my teacher didn't give me enough time."

- Prefers same-gender playmates; more likely to play in groups (Figure 7-9).

- Worries about not being liked; feelings easily hurt; might cry, be embarrassed, or state adamantly, "I will never play with you again," when criticized.

- Takes responsibilities seriously; can be trusted to carry out directions and commitments; worries about being late for school or not getting work done.

Figure 7-9
Spends most time with same-gender friends.

7-year-old

TeachSource Video Connections

Cognitive Development and Concrete Operations. Children are developing an increasingly sophisticated understanding of how things work, their causes and effects, and how various manipulations can alter the outcome. These cognitive advances pique children's curiosity and interest in undertaking new activities. As you watch the learning video *5–11 Years: Piaget's Concrete Operational Stage* on the Education CourseMate website, consider the following questions:

1. Which cognitive abilities make it possible for seven-year-olds to understand Piaget's theory of conservation?
2. Which changes in children's cognitive skills are evident during Piaget's concrete operational stage?
3. In what ways do these newly emerging cognitive abilities influence children's development in other domains such as motor, speech and language, and social-emotional?
4. Do all children experience this stage of cognitive development? How might cultural or developmental differences influence this process?

7-year-old

DAILY ROUTINES

Eating

- Eats most foods; is better about sampling unfamiliar foods or taking small tastes of disliked foods, but may still refuse a few strong "hates."
- Shows interest in food; likes to help with grocery shopping and meal preparation.
- Uses table manners that adults might consider far from perfect but improving; less spilled milk and other accidents due to silliness, impulse, or haste to finish.
- Uses eating utensils with relative ease; seldom eats with fingers; some children still have trouble cutting meat.
- Is sometimes distracted during mealtimes by conversations and things going on elsewhere in the house or outdoors; at other times, is focused on eating and getting done.

Personal Care and Dressing

- Reluctant to begin bath; however, once in the tub, seems to relax and enjoy the experience; is able to manage own bath or shower with minimal assistance.
- Dresses self, although slow and distracted at times; can speed up the process when time becomes critical or there is something else they want to do.
- Buttons and zips own clothes; ties own shoes; not always careful or precise (buttons askew, zipper undone, shoelaces soon dragging).
- Shows little interest in clothes; wears whatever is laid out or available.
- Shows more interest in combing or brushing own hair.

- Has achieved complete bowel and bladder control; individual rhythm is well established; may resist having bowel movements at school.
- Less likely to get up during the night to use the toilet.

Sleeping

- Averages 10–11 hours of sleep at night; children who are in bed fewer hours often have trouble getting up in the morning (Giannotti & Cortesi, 2010).
- Sleeps soundly with few if any bad dreams; instead, often dreams about their own exploits and adventures (Burnham & Conte, 2009).
- Gets ready for bed independently most nights but still enjoys being tucked in or read to.
- Wakes up early most mornings; occupies self in bed with toys, counting out savings in piggy bank, looking at baseball card collection, reading, and so forth.

Play and Social Activities

- Participates in organized group activities (Boys' and Girls' Clubs, Cub Scouts and Brownies, 4-H, swim and soccer teams).
- Dislikes missing school or social events; wants to keep up with friends and classmates.
- Has interest in coloring and cutting things out, with a friend or alone.
- Engages in favorite play activities such as bicycle riding, climbing activities, basketball, skating, and computer games.
- Likes to play competitive board and card games but may bend the rules when losing.
- Turns activities into challenges. "Let's see who can throw rocks the farthest." "I can run to the corner faster than you can."

7-year-old

Learning Activities

Developmental applications for families and teachers:

- Take trips to the library for children's story time and dramatic play activities as well as for checking out books.
- Sign up for free or low-cost community offerings of interest to the child (art, science, swimming, T-ball, tumbling, yoga, or zoo and museum programs).
- Utilize the outdoors for learning; take family "collecting walks" in a park, on the beach, or around the neighborhood; support children's interests in collecting and organizing found treasures (Figure 7-10).
- Accumulate small working tools and equipment (simple carpentry and gardening tools; science materials for growing a potato vine or maintaining an ant farm; a small aquarium).

7-year-old

Figure 7-10
The outdoors provides a wealth of learning opportunities.

- Gather materials for creating art projects, models, or science experiments (pieces of wood, Styrofoam, various weights and textures of cardboard and paper, beads, fabric, ribbon, yarn, and so forth).
- Offer dress-up clothes and props for planning and staging shows; attend the children's "performances."
- Assemble a box of discarded small appliances (clock, hair drier, electric can opener, mixer–with *cords removed*) and tools for taking them apart.
- Provide a doll house, farm or zoo set, space station, or airport, complete with small-scale people, animals, and equipment.

Developmental Alerts

Check with a health care provider or early childhood specialist if, by the eighth birthday, the child *does not*:

- Attend to the task at hand; show longer periods of sitting quietly, listening, and responding appropriately.
- Follow through on simple instructions.
- Go to school willingly most days (of concern are excessive complaints about stomachaches or headaches when getting ready for school).
- Make friends (observe closely to see whether the child plays alone most of the time or withdraws consistently from contact with other children).
- Sleep soundly most nights. (Frequent or recurring nightmares are usually few at this age.)
- See or hear well at times (squints, rubs eyes excessively; asks frequently to have things repeated).

- Handle stressful situations without undue emotional upset (excessive crying, sleeping or eating disturbances, withdrawal, frequent anxiety).
- Assume responsibility for personal care (dressing, bathing, feeding self) most of the time.
- Show improved motor skills.

Safety Concerns

Continue to implement safety practices described for the previous stages. Be aware of new safety issues as the child continues to grow and develop.

Firearms

- Store unloaded guns in a locked cabinet with ammunition kept in another location. Teach children never to pick up or touch a gun and to report immediately if one is found. Check with families of your children's friends to determine whether guns are present and properly stored in their house.

Play Environments

- Review rules for safe play and the use of playground equipment when away from home. Be aware of your child's friends and types of play in which they tend to engage. Remind children to wash their hands after playing, especially after touching any animals.

Tools/Equipment

- Do not let children use power mowers or other motorized yard equipment (e.g., weed eaters, hedge trimmers); keep children away when equipment is in use.

Water

- Continue to supervise children at all times when they are in a pool, lake, or around any body of water.
- Teach children to swim and to follow water safety rules. Insist that children wear approved floatation vests when in or around large bodies of water (fishing, boating, skiing).

8-year-old

The Eight-Year-Old

Eight-year-olds display a great enthusiasm for life. Energy is concentrated on improving skills they already possess and enhancing what they already know. Eight-year-olds, once again, experience strong feelings of independence and are eager to make decisions about their own plans and friends. Interests and attention are increasingly devoted to peers and team or group activities rather than to family, teachers, or siblings. Sometime near midyear, boys and girls begin to go their separate ways and form new interests in same-gender groups (Halim & Ruble, 2010).

A small percentage of children may begin to engage in aggressive, intimidating, or **bullying** behaviors. Their targets are often peers who are perceived as loners, likely to react or retaliate, lacking in self-confidence, having special needs, or unable to stand up for themselves (Nipedal, Nesdale, & Killen, 2010). Occasional incidences of name-calling,

---

bullying—verbal and physical behavior that is hurtful, intentional, and repeatedly directed toward a person or child who is viewed as weaker.

threatening, or hitting are not uncommon at this age. However, a pattern of intentional and hurtful behavior that escalates as children approach adolescence distinguishes bullying from typical developmental expectations.

Researchers continue to study why some children have more difficulty controlling aggressive behavior than do others. Their findings suggest that bullies typically fall into two categories (Reavis, Keane, & Calkins, 2010). The first includes children who are self-assured, impulsive, angry, and lacking in empathy and who use their physical strength to intimidate. The second group consists of children who tend to be passive, less likely to initiate bullying, but willing to join in after it has begun. These children often possess poor social skills, low self-esteem, and might themselves be victims of abuse or neglect. They also have difficulty knowing how to initiate appropriate social interaction and how to control their own impulsive behaviors.

Anti-bullying programs are being implemented in many schools and communities in response to state legislation and findings that demonstrate short-term and long-term consequences of bullying on children's development (Swearer et al., 2010). These initiatives are aimed at promoting positive social, communication, and anger management skills; boosting children's self-esteem; and reducing harassing behaviors. Prevention efforts are also focusing on the victims, helping them learn empowering behaviors such as walking away, avoiding bullies, problem-solving, informing an adult, and peaceful conflict resolution skills (Sherer & Nickerson, 2010).

8-year-old

DEVELOPMENTAL PROFILES AND GROWTH PATTERNS

Growth and Physical Characteristics

- Continues to gain 5–7 pounds (2.3–3.2 kg) per year; an eight-year-old weighs approximately 55–61 pounds (25–27.7 kg). Girls typically weigh less than boys.
- Height increases are slow but steady, averaging 2.5 inches (6.25 cm) per year; girls are generally taller (46–49 inches [115–122.5 cm]) than boys (48–52 inches [120–130 cm]).
- Body shape takes on a more mature appearance; arms and legs grow longer, creating an image that is tall and lanky.
- Normal vision acuity is 20/20; periodic vision check assure that children are able to see.
- Some girls may begin to develop breasts and pubic hair and experience menses (Copeland et al., 2010).
- Mood swings may become more apparent as changes in hormonal activity occur.
- Overall state of health improves; experiences fewer illnesses.

Motor Development

- Enjoys vigorous activity; likes to dance, inline skate, swim, wrestle, ride bikes, play basketball, jump rope, and fly kites (Figure 7-11).

- Seeks out opportunities to participate in team activities and games such as soccer, baseball, and kickball.
- Exhibits significant improvement in agility, balance, speed, and strength.
- Copies words and numbers from a blackboard with increasing speed and accuracy; has good eye–hand coordination.
- Possesses seemingly endless energy.

Perceptual-Cognitive Development

- Collects objects; organizes and displays items according to more complex systems; bargains and trades with friends to obtain additional pieces.
- Saves money for small purchases; eagerly develops plans to earn cash from odd jobs; studies catalogues and magazines for ideas of items to purchase.
- Begins taking an interest in what others think and do; understands there are distant countries and differences of opinion and cultures.

Figure 7-11
Enjoys good health and vigorous activity.

8-year-old

- Accepts challenge and responsibility with enthusiasm; delights in being asked to perform tasks, both at home and in school; is interested in being rewarded for efforts.
- Likes to read and work independently; spends considerable time planning and making lists.
- Understands perspective (shadow, distance, shape); drawings reflect more realistic portrayal of objects.
- Grasps the basic principles of conservation. (A tall, narrow jar might look different from one that is short and wide but they both can hold the same amount of liquid.)
- Uses more sophisticated logic to understand everyday events; for example, is systematic in looking for a misplaced jacket, backpack, or toy.
- Adds and subtracts multiple-digit numbers; learning multiplication and division.
- Looks forward to school and is disappointed when ill or unable to attend.

Speech and Language Development

- Delights in telling jokes and riddles.
- Understands and carries out multiple-step instructions (up to five steps); may need to have directions repeated because they did not listen to the entire request.
- Reads with ease and understanding.

DEVELOPMENTAL PROFILES AND GROWTH PATTERNS *(continued)*

- Composes and sends imaginative and detailed messages to friends and family via email, texting, or webcam (Figure 7-12).
- Uses language to criticize and compliment others; repeats slang and curse words.
- Understands and follows rules of grammar in conversation and written form.
- Is intrigued with learning secret word codes and using code language.
- Converses fluently with adults; able to think and talk about past and future: "What time is my swim meet next week?" "Where did we go on vacation last summer?"

Social-Emotional Development

- Begins to form opinions about moral values and attitudes; declares things either right or wrong (Xu et al., 2010).
- Plays with two or three "best" friends, most often of the same age and gender; also enjoys spending some time alone (Poulin & Chan, 2010).

Figure 7-12
Composes messages and stories with imaginative detail.

- Seems less critical of own performance but is easily frustrated and upset when unable to complete a task or when the product does not meet expectations.
- Participates in team games and activities; group membership and peer acceptance are important.
- Continues to blame others or makes up alibis to explain his or her own shortcomings or mistakes.
- Enjoys talking on the telephone with friends and family.
- Understands and respects the fact that some children are more talented in certain areas such as drawing, sports, reading, art, or music.
- Desires adult attention and recognition; enjoys performing for adults and challenging them in games.

8-year-old

TeachSource Video Connections

Moral Development. As children mature, they begin to develop a greater understanding of social expectations, the consequences of their choices, and the ability to "know better." As you watch the learning video *5–11 Years: Moral Development in Middle Childhood* on the Education CourseMate website, consider the following questions:

1. Why are six- and seven-year-olds only able to view a person's behavior as being either "right" or "wrong?"
2. What is guilt?
3. How would a child in the preconventional stage of moral development respond to another child who takes an extra cookie at lunch time and hides it in his pocket? How might the response differ if the child were in the conventional stage?

DAILY ROUTINES

Eating

- Looks forward to meals; boys are often hungry and will eat more than girls. Serving nutrient-dense foods (fruits, vegetables, whole grains, low-fat dairy, lean meat) and limiting calorie-dense items (candy, cookies, chips, soft drinks, French fries) meets critical growth requirements and reduces the risk of **obesity** (Marotz, 2012). Calories taken in need to be balanced with physical activity to prevent excessive weight gain.
- Is willing to try new foods and some of the foods previously refused.
- Takes pride in using good table manners, especially when eating out or when company is present; at home, manners are of less concern.
- Finishes meals quickly to resume previous activities; may stuff mouth with too much food or not chew food thoroughly in order to hurry.

Personal Care and Dressing

- Develops a pattern for bowel and bladder functions; usually has good control but may need to urinate more frequently when under stress.
- Hurries through hand washing; dirt often ends up on the towel rather than washed down the drain.
- Enjoys bath and playing in water; easily sidetracked when supposed to be getting ready to bathe; some children are able to prepare their own bath or shower.
- Takes greater interest in appearance, selecting and coordinating own outfits, brushing hair, and looking good.

8-year-old

---

obesity—although no uniform definition exists, experts usually consider a child whose height-weight ratio (BMI) exceeds the 85th percentile for age to be overweight and obese if it is greater than the 95th percentile.

DAILY ROUTINES *(continued)*

- Helps care for own clothes; hangs clothes up most times, helps with laundry by folding and returning items to dresser.
- Ties own shoes skillfully but often too busy to be bothered.

Sleeping

- Sleeps soundly through the night (averages 10 hours); efforts to delay bedtime might suggest less sleep is needed.
- Begins to question established bedtime; wants to stay up later; becomes easily distracted and involved in other activities while getting ready for bed.
- Sometimes wakes early and gets dressed while family members are still sleeping.

Play and Social Activities

- Enjoys competitive activities and sports (soccer, baseball, swimming, gymnastics); eager to join a team; just as eager to quit if there is too much forced competition.
- Begins to adopt a know-it-all attitude toward the end of the eighth year; becomes argumentative with peers (and adults).
- Likes to play board, electronic, and computer and card games; often interprets rules to improve her or his own chances of winning.
- Seeks acceptance from peers; begins to imitate clothing fads, hairstyles, behavior, and language of admired peers.

8-year-old

Learning Activities

Developmental applications for families and teachers:

- Provide (and join in) games that require a moderate degree of strategy (chess, checkers, dominoes, card games, magic sets, and educational computer games).
- Encourage creativity; provide materials for painting, crafts, cooking, gardening, or building projects.
- Make frequent trips to the library; provide books to read as well as stories on CDs and DVDs.
- Invest in an inexpensive camera and encourage children to experiment; have them write stories and create journals about their pictures.
- Arrange for opportunities to develop skills in noncompetitive activities—swimming, dancing, tumbling, skating, basketball, karate, bowling, or playing a musical instrument; this is a time for exploring many interests; seldom is there a long-term commitment.

- Assign routine tasks, such as feeding the dog, folding laundry, dusting furniture, bringing in the mail, watering plants, or setting the dinner table, to foster a sense of responsibility and self-esteem.

Developmental Alerts

Check with a health care provider or early childhood specialist if, by the ninth birthday, the child *does not*:

- Exhibit a good appetite and continued weight gain. (Some children, especially girls, might already begin to show early signs of an eating disorder.) Medical evaluation should be sought for excessive weight gains or losses.

- Experience fewer illnesses.

- Show improved motor skills in terms of agility, speed, and balance.

- Understand abstract concepts and use complex thought processes to problem-solve.

- Look forward to school and the challenge of learning on most days.

- Follow through on multiple-step instructions.

- Express ideas clearly and fluently.

- Form friendships with other children and participate in group activities.

8-year-old

Safety Concerns

Continue to implement safety practices described for the previous stages. Be aware of new safety issues as the child continues to grow and develop.

Animals

- Remind children to respect animals (not to approach unfamiliar animals and to refrain from yelling or making sudden movements).
- Teach children to recognize poisonous snakes and to leave them alone.
- Insist on thorough hand washing after touching any animal to avoid illness.

Backpacks

- Provide backpacks with dual shoulder straps to prevent injury; load the heaviest items against the child's back; packs should weigh less than 20 percent of the child's body weight. Wheeled backpacks are preferable.

Media

- Monitor children's computer use; set parental controls (security) to limit access to unwanted Internet sites.
- Talk to children about not giving out personal information to protect their online safety.
- Know what television programs children are watching (at home, at friends' houses) and what music they are listening to.

Toys

- Supervise use of more advanced toys such as chemistry or woodworking sets and those that involve motors, electricity, or propellants.

- Require children to wear a helmet and appropriate protective gear when biking, skating, roller-blading, or skateboarding.

Water

- Require children to wear a life jacket whenever boating, skiing, or participating in other water sports.

POSITIVE BEHAVIOR GUIDANCE

Although six-, seven-, and eight-year-olds begin to question and test limits, they also need and want rules that are easy to understand, provide structure, and are enforced consistently. They must be allowed to develop increasing independence, but only with continued adult supervision.

Six-, seven-, and eight-year-olds:

- Adults serve as role models for children by displaying positive behavioral responses and self-control. Set a good example: take a deep breath, maintain eye contact, and respond in a calm, nonthreatening manner.

- Establish rules in positive terms so they teach children the behaviors considered to be appropriate; "We always go down the slide on our bottoms, feet first," "Hands must be washed before we can eat."

- Acknowledge the child's feelings and frustrations. Listen to his or her explanations even though you may not agree with what is said.

- Help children learn effective problem-solving, communication, and conflict resolution skills.

- Use logical consequences or withhold privileges when rules have been broken: "I can't let you go to Laura's house because you didn't clean up your room as asked."

- Acknowledge children's appropriate behavior, "You really helped me out by putting away the groceries."

- Use time outs to help children regain their composure. Briefly explain why this action is being taken and send children to their room or a quiet area; this allows time to think about the misbehavior and to regain emotional control.

- Ignore behaviors not likely to cause harm to the child or to others. When the child ends the undesirable behavior be sure to give some form of attention or acknowledgement.

SUMMARY

The transition to formal schooling marks a distinctive change for many children. New experiences and opportunities are generally met with a combination of enthusiasm and improving abilities as well as periodic reluctance and frustration. Children often set high expectations for themselves, then falter when these standards cannot be met. However, they are eager to learn and able to accomplish many complex skills, including reading, writing, telling time, counting money, and following detailed instructions during this stage. They become imaginative storytellers, jokesters, and even "magicians." Friends and friendships are increasingly important as children's interests and independence expand. They also begin to understand the meaning and complexity of everyday events, form moral values and opinions, and recognize cultural and individual differences. By the end of this period, children are fully capable of managing their own personal care and grooming needs but may still need occasional adult reminders.

Key Terms

emerging literacy **p. 161**

sensory **p. 161**

hands-on learning **p. 161**

deciduous teeth **p. 164**

conservation **p. 172**

bullying **p. 177**

obesity **p. 181**

Apply What You Know

A. Apply What You Have Learned

Reread the brief developmental sketch about Juan and Sergio at the beginning of the chapter and answer the following questions.

1. Which initial forms of screening would you arrange for Sergio to ensure that his learning delays were not being caused by a health-related condition?
2. Which motor skills would you expect Juan to exhibit if his development was typical for a seven-year-old?
3. Is it appropriate for Juan's mother to encourage his participation in a local youth soccer league? Explain your answer from a developmental perspective.

B. Review Questions

1. Compare and contrast the cognitive skills of a typical six-year-old and an eight-year-old.
2. Should you be concerned about a seven-year-old who weighs 75 pounds? Explain.
3. What classroom activities can a teacher plan to reinforce eight-year-olds' interest in reading and writing?
4. Describe three perceptual skills that indicate a readiness to begin reading.
5. Identify three reasonable expectations for a six-year-old in terms of home routine.

Helpful Websites

Academic benchmarks
http://www.academicbenchmarks.com/search/
(interactive map of states)

Healthy Child Care America
http://www.healthychildcare.org/

Healthy Youth
http://www.cdc.gov/HealthyYouth/physicalactivity
(for info on healthy eating & activity)

References

Berger, M. (2010). "It's the sight not the bite": A model and reinterpretation of visually-based developmental fears, *Clinical Psychology Review, 30*(6), 779–793.

Burnham, M., & Conte, C. (2009). Developmental perspective: Dreaming across the lifespan and what this tells us, *International Review of Neurobiology, 92,* 47–68.

Charlesworth, R. (2011). *Understanding child development.* Belmont, CA: Wadsworth Cengage Learning.

Copeland, W., Shanahan, L., Miller, S., Costello, J., Angold, A., & Maughan, B. (2010). Outcomes of early pubertal timing in young women: A prospective population-based study, *American Journal of Psychiatry, 167,* 1218–1225.

Cowan, N., Morey, C., AuBuchon, A., Zwilling, C., & Gilchrist, A. (2010). Seven-year-olds allocate attention like adults unless working memory is overloaded, *Developmental Science, 13*(1), 120–133.

Diamond, K., & Hong, S. (2010). Young children's decisions to include peers with physical disabilities in play, *Journal of Early Intervention, 32*(3), 163–177.

Ethan, D., Basch, C., Platt, R., Bogen, E., & Zybert, P. (2010). Implementing and evaluating a school-based program to improve childhood vision, *Journal of School Health, 80*(7), 340–345.

Favazza, P. (2010). Loss and grief in young children, *Young Exceptional Children, 13*(2), 86–99.

Giannotti, F., & Cortesi, F. (2010). Family and cultural influences on sleep development, *Child & Adolescent Psychiatric Clinics of North America, 18*(4), 849–861.

Halim, M., & Ruble, D. (2010). Gender identity and stereotyping in early and middle childhood, *Handbook of Gender Research in Psychology, 7,* 495–525.

Hoban, T. (2010). Sleep disorders in children, *Annals of the New York Academy of Sciences, 1184*(2), 1–14.

Jordan, N., Glutting, J., & Ramineni, C. (2010). The importance of number sense to mathematics achievement in first and third grades, *Learning & Individual Differences, 20*(2), 82–88.

Marchman, V., Fernald, A., & Hurtado, N. (2010). How vocabulary size in two languages relates to efficiency in spoken word recognition by young Spanish-English bilinguals, *Journal of Child Language, 37,* 817–840.

Marotz, L. (2012). *Health, safety & nutrition for the young child.* Belmont, CA: Wadsworth Cengage Learning.

National Association for the Education of Young Children (NAEYC). (2009). Developmentally appropriate practice in early childhood programs serving children

from birth through age 8. Accessed on November 7, 2010 from http://www.naeyc. org/files/naeyc/file/positions/position%20statement%20Web.pdf

Nipedal, C., Nesdale, D., & Killen, M. (2010). Social group norms, school norms, and children's aggressive intentions, *Aggressive Behavior, 36*(3), 195−204.

Piaget, J. (1926). *The language and thought of the child.* New York: Harcourt, Brace & World.

Piaget, J. (1929). *The child's conception of the world.* New York: Harcourt Brace.

Poulin, F., & Chan, A. (2010). Friendship stability and change in childhood and adolescence, *Developmental Review, 30*(3), 257−272.

Ray, K., & Smith, M. (2010). The kindergarten child: What teachers and administrators need to know to promote academic success in all children, *Early Childhood Education Journal, 38*(1), 5−18.

Reavis, R., Keane, S., & Calkins, S. (2010). Trajectories of peer victimization: The role of multiple relationships, *Journal of Developmental Psychology, 56*(3), 303−332.

Rood, L., Roelofs, J., Bögels, S., & Alloy, L. (2010). Dimensions of negative thinking and the relations with symptoms of depression and anxiety in children and adolescents, *Cognitive Therapy & Research, 34*(4), 333−342.

Rushton, S., Juola-Rushton, A., & Larkin, E. (2010). Neuroscience, play, and early childhood education: Connections, implications, and assessment. *Early Childhood Education Journal, 37*(5), 351−361.

Russell, J. (2010). From child's garden to academic press: The role of shifting institutional logics in redefining kindergarten education, *American Educational Research Journal, 47*(3), 1−32.

Sherer, Y., & Nickerson, A. (2010). Anti-bullying practices in American schools: Perspectives of school psychologists, *Psychology in the School, 47*(3), 217−229.

Swearer, S., Espelage, D., Vaillancourt, T., & Hymel, S. (2010). What can be done about school bullying?, *Educational Researcher, 39*(1), 38−47.

Xu, F., Bao, X., Fu, G., Talwar, V., & Lee, K. (2010). Lying and truth-telling in children: From concept to action, *Child Development, 81*(2), 581−596.

You are just a click away from a variety of interactive study tools and helpful resources. Access the text's Education CourseMate website at **www.cengagebrain.com**, where you'll find a variety of enrichment materials, including videos, glossary flashcards, activities, tutorial quizzes, web links, and more.

CHAPTER 8

Middle Childhood: Nine-, Ten-, Eleven-, and Twelve-Year-Olds

Learning Objectives

After reading this chapter, you should be able to:

- Describe several developmental changes that occur during early puberty.
- Describe the concept of friendship from the perspective of a nine-year-old and a ten-year-old.
- Plan developmentally appropriate activities for nine- and ten-year-olds and eleven- and twelve-year-olds.
- Compare and contrast the language development of nine- and ten-year-olds with that of eleven- and twelve-year-olds.

naeyc Standards Chapter Links:

1a, 1b, and 1c: Promoting child development and learning
2a and 2c: Building family and community relationships
3c and 3d: Observing, documenting, and assessing to support young children and families
4a, 4b, 4c, and 4d: Using developmentally effective approaches
5c: Using content knowledge to build meaningful curriculum

Meet Juan and His Stepsister, Carlin

Juan, age eleven, and his new stepfather have enjoyed each other's companionship from the very beginning. They spend considerable time together, attending sporting events, taking camping trips in the mountains, and building model planes. Juan likes school, especially math and computer classes, and has many "best friends." His teacher considers Juan a good student and appreciates his offers to help around the classroom. Juan's parents are continually amazed by his seemingly endless appetite and energy.

Juan has slowly been adjusting to the idea of having a stepsister.

continued...

Carlin, a caring and talkative nine-year-old, is somewhat less enthusiastic than Juan about school. During the last parent–teacher conference, Carlin's teachers expressed concern about her inability to remain seated and focused on assignments for longer than five or ten minutes at a time. Carlin's mother has made similar observations at home, often becoming exasperated because Carlin has difficulty following multistep directions and tends to be disorganized. Carlin "forgets" that the dog needs to be fed, that she was supposed to set the dinner table, or when her homework is due. She has few friends and prefers to play with Juan and his friends. However, Juan finds it annoying when she tags along and frequently begs his stepfather to make her stop.

Ask Yourself

1. How would you describe a typical eleven-year-old's development based on this scenario?

2. Which of Carlin's behaviors would cause you to recommend her referral to an early childhood specialist for additional evaluation?

Nine-, Ten-, Eleven-, and Twelve-Year Olds

The stretch of years from age eight to early adolescence is usually an enjoyable and relatively peaceful time for all concerned. Spontaneous behavior is gradually channeled into more goal-directed efforts as children begin making the transition from a state of dependence to one of greater independence. Although they are no longer young children, they are also not yet capable adults. This tension contributes to struggles with self-concept, self-esteem, and desire for complete autonomy.

The middle years are marked by a hunger for knowledge and understanding. Most children have adjusted to being at school for six or more hours each day. The stresses, strains, and frustrations of learning to read, write, do basic arithmetic, and follow directions are long forgotten. Language usage becomes more sophisticated and adult-like. During this period, children also develop an increasingly complex ability to think in the abstract, understand cause and effect, and use **logic** for solving problems and figuring out how things work. They comprehend that things really are the same in spite of being used for alternative purposes or seen from a different perspective—a shovel can be used not only for digging but also for prying the lid off of a paint can; a mixing bowl can be traced to draw a perfect circle.

---

logic—process of reasoning based on a series of facts or events.

Figure 8-1
Children grow and develop at
very different rates.

Changes in physical growth and development vary greatly from child to child during this period and reflect, in part, ethnic and cultural differences (Figure 8-1). Girls typically experience a growth spurt (height and weight) that is significantly greater than that of boys. Research finds that some girls as young as eight or nine begin to experience hormonal changes associated with puberty (Walvoord, 2010).

Middle childhood is also a time when some children may begin to experiment with new behaviors such as wearing alternative clothing and hair styles, quitting a long-time sport or favorite musical instrument, forming associations with a "different crowd," or dieting. Families may find these changes distressing, but they are part of an important developmental process that shapes self-identity and helps children determine what is ultimately right for them. A small percentage of children may also begin to experiment with substances such as legal or illegal drugs, tobacco, alcohol, or inhalants which can pose a serious threat to their well-being and may require professional intervention and treatment (Costello & Angold, 2010).

Although children's ideas about gender identity and behavior are relatively set by middle childhood, some male–female contrasts become evident. Boys' ideas about what is masculine tend to follow a more stereotypical path (e.g., football, baseball, competitive video games), while girls may be completely at ease with their femininity and begin to branch out and explore a range of activities, such as hunting, fishing, carpentry, cross-country running, and team sports. However, there is also little tolerance for crossing gender lines, especially when it comes to males who hang around with girls, exhibit "unmanly" behavior, or dress in feminine clothing (Ewing & Troop-Gordon, 2011). It must also be remembered that a child's ethnic and cultural heritage continues to be a strong determinant in shaping gender behavior and role expectations.

Despite frequent protests and rejections, children still want and need their family's continued trust and support. It is important that families and teachers maintain

9- to 10-year-olds

an ongoing dialogue with children about subjects such as personal health, substance abuse (drugs, alcohol, smoking), and sex education (typical development, pregnancy, protection from sexually transmitted diseases) because many of these decisions have serious, long-term consequences (Graber & Nichols, 2010; Lemstra et al., 2010). When adults treat these issues in an open and nonthreatening manner, it conveys understanding and compassion to children. It also fosters their sense of self-esteem and enhances the likelihood that children will continue to seek adult input in the future.

Nine- and Ten-Year-Olds

Most nine- and ten-year-olds have entered a phase of relative contentment—sometimes described as the calm before the storm of adolescence. Although nine-year-olds may still display some emotional highs and lows, these outbursts gradually mellow by age ten. Home and family continue to provide a source of security and comfort for most children. Hugs and kisses are still offered as signs of affection for family members.

Most nine- and ten-year-olds also find school enjoyable. They eagerly anticipate classes and meeting with friends and are disappointed if they must miss out on school activities. Teachers are respected and their attention is highly coveted. Small homemade gifts and offers of assistance are made in the hope of pleasing one's teacher. Although children's attention span is longer, they still need frequent opportunities to move about in the classroom and to participate in vigorous outdoor activity (Trudeau & Shephard, 2010) (Figure 8-2).

Figure 8-2
Children continue to need ample opportunities to release excess energy.

DEVELOPMENTAL PROFILES AND GROWTH PATTERNS

Growth and Physical Characteristics

- Rate of growth is slow and irregular; girls begin to experience growth spurts that are far more dramatic than those of boys; boys are more alike in size and smaller than most girls.

- Assumes a slimmer shape as fat accumulations begin to shift.

- Growth of various body parts occurs at different rates; lower half of body grows faster; arms and legs appear long and out of proportion.

- Brain increases significantly in size; almost reaches adult size by age ten.

- Height increases by approximately 2 inches (5 cm) each year; increases are usually greater during growth spurts.

- Gains approximately 6 1/2 pounds (14.3 kg) per year.

- Loses remaining baby teeth; overcrowding might occur when larger, permanent teeth erupt into a yet small jaw.

- Girls might begin to experience prepubertal changes (e.g., budding breasts, appearance of pubic hair, rounding of hips, accentuated waistline; darkening of hair color); boys are less likely to undergo any sexual changes for another year or two.

Motor Development

- Throws a ball with accuracy; writes, sketches, and performs other fine motor skills with improved coordination. This period is marked by continued refinement of fine motor skills, especially notable among girls (Barnett et al., 2010).

- Uses arms, legs, hands, and feet with ease and improved precision; boys tend to excel in large motor activities requiring strength and speed.

- Runs, climbs, skips rope, swims, rides bikes, and skates with skill and confidence.

- Enjoys team sports but may still need to develop some of the necessary complex skills.

- Likes to use hands for arts and crafts, cooking, woodworking, needlework, painting, building models, or taking apart objects such as a clock or telephone.

- Draws pictures in detail; takes great joy in perfecting handwriting skills.

Perceptual-Cognitive Development

- Develops ability to reason based more on experience and logic than on **intuition** (Piaget's stage of **concrete operational thought**): "If I hurry and walk the dog, I can play with my friends." Still sees some situations as either/or, with "yes" or "no" answers but is beginning to think in less concrete,

---

intuition—thoughts and ideas based on a feeling or hunch.

concrete operational thought—Piaget's third stage of cognitive development; period when concepts of conservation and classification are understood.

DEVELOPMENTAL PROFILES AND GROWTH PATTERNS *(continued)*

more creative ways (Piaget, 1928). Understands abstract concepts if real (concrete) objects can be seen and manipulated: "If I eat one cookie now, only two will be left."

Figure 8-3
Hands-on involvement optimizes learning.

- Likes challenges in arithmetic but does not always understand mathematical relationships involved in complex operations such as multiplication or division.

- Learns best through hands-on learning; prefers to research information in books or online, conduct science experiments, build models, or put on a play rather than listen to teachers' lectures that produce the same information (Figure 8-3).

- Enjoys time at school; finds it difficult to sit still for periods longer than 30 minutes; forgets all about school as soon as it is over.

- Uses reading and writing skills for nonacademic activities (compiling grocery lists, composing scripts for puppet shows, drawing and labeling neighborhood maps, texting or sending email).

- Shows improved understanding of cause and effect.

- Continues to master concepts of time, weight, volume, and distance (Kamii & Russell, 2010).

- Traces events based on recall; able to think in reverse, following a series of occurrences back to their beginnings.

- Prefers reading books that are longer and descriptive, with complex plots.

Speech and Language Development

- Talks, often nonstop and for no specific reason; sometimes used as an attention-getting device; may be reserved in the classroom, boisterous and talkative at other times.

- Expresses feelings and emotions effectively through words.

- Understands and uses language as a system for communicating with others.

- Uses slang expressions commonly expressed by peers in conversation ("sweet," "cool," "awesome," "hey dude").

- Recognizes that some words have double meanings ("far out," "cool haircut," "wicked").

- Finds humor in using illogical metaphors (play on words) in jokes and riddles (Figure 8-4).

9- to 10-
year-olds

- Shows advanced understanding of grammatical sequences; recognizes when a sentence is not grammatically correct.

Social-Emotional Development

- Enjoys being with friends; seeks out friendships based on common interests and proximity (neighborhood children or classmates); is verbally critical of the opposite gender ("Boys are too rough," "Girls are babies") (Jones & Estell, 2010).

Figure 8-4
Delights in telling jokes and riddles.

- Has several "good" friends and an "enemy" or two; friends and friendships often change from day to day.

- Begins to show more interest in rules and basing games on realistic play; rules should be kept simple so everyone enjoys playing (Figure 8-5).

- Responds with name-calling and teasing when provoked; less likely to use physical aggression than previously; also understands that such behavior can affect others' feelings. Still depends occasionally on adults to settle some disputes.

Figure 8-5
Beginning to understand and play by the rules.

- Begins to develop moral reasoning; adopts social customs and moral values (understands honesty, right from wrong, fairness, good and bad, respect) (Malti & Latzko, 2010).

- Develops attachments to teachers, coaches, club leaders; may see them as heroes; often goes out of way to please and gain their attention.

- Acts with considerable confidence; knows everything and can do no wrong.

- Takes criticism as a personal attack; feelings are easily hurt; has difficulty at times dealing with failure and frustration.

9- to 10-
year-olds

 TeachSource Video Connections

Emotional Development and Bullying. Although most grade-school children achieve reasonable control of their emotions, a small percentage may engage in aggressive, antisocial behavior that is intentional. As you watch the learning video *School Age: Emotional Development* on the Education CourseMate website, consider the following questions:

1. Why is it important that teachers and families discuss the issue of bullying with children?
2. What are the consequences of being bullied?
3. Why might some children who are being bullied be reluctant to tell an adult?

DAILY ROUTINES

Eating

- Appetite fluctuates, depending on the amount and vigor of activity; consumes more with increased activity; prefers to eat when hungry rather than at prescribed times.
- Eats at any time of day, yet often is still hungry at mealtime; more receptive to trying new foods. Many children also enjoy cooking and helping with meal preparations. Prefers certain favorite foods, usually pizza, French fries, tacos, ice cream, and cookies; has few dislikes but is less fond of cooked vegetables.
- Battles over posture and table manners (elbows on the table; slouched in chair; fisted grasp of forks and spoons) but usually displays good manners at friends' houses.

Personal Care and Dressing

- Shows limited interest in personal hygiene; often needs reminders to bathe, wash hair, brush teeth, put on clean clothes.
- Requires coaxing to bathe but, after bath is started, may not want to get out.
- Takes some interest in appearance; wants to dress and look like friends; school clothes take on an important role in self-identification.
- Manages own toileting needs without reminders; seldom gets up at night unless too much liquid is consumed before bedtime.

Sleeping

- Seems unaware of fatigue and the need for sleep.
- Requires 9–10 hours of sleep to function throughout the day. Wakes up in time for school without much coaxing if getting enough sleep. Insufficient sleep interferes with learning and has been linked to increased weight gain (Buckhalt, 2011; Gutierrez & Willoughby, 2010).
- Girls may have more bedtime rituals and take longer to fall asleep than do boys.

- Nightmares and fears of the dark might redevelop; some children experience sleepwalking, waking up in the middle of the night, or bed-wetting. Parents should not criticize children who develop these problems and should seek professional help if they persist.

Play and Social Activities

- Maintains activity level that fluctuates between extremes of high intensity and almost nonexistent activity; may virtually collapse following periods of intense play.
- Spends free time reading magazines, playing computer games, watching videos, listening to music, texting, and talking with friends.
- Forms and joins clubs with secret codes, languages, and signs.
- Offers to help with simple household chores such as dusting and sweeping, vacuuming, putting away groceries, and washing the car.
- Develops new hobbies or collections based on special interests.

Learning Activities

Developmental applications for families and teachers:

- Take advantage of educational opportunities in the community. Plan outings to the beach, farmers' market, library, museum, zoo, park, aquarium, garden center, cabinet-maker, pet shop, or grocery store.
- Encourage children to appreciate diversity by learning about the customs and celebrations of other cultures. Obtain library books, visit websites, invite guests, locate musical instruments, and prepare ethnic foods for children to taste. Teach children to be accepting and avoid prejudice through your own actions and words.
- Gather sports equipment such as balls, bats, nets, and rackets; encourage children to organize and participate in group activities.
- Provide space, seeds, and tools for planting and maintaining a garden.
- Assemble materials and provide basic instructions for conducting science experiments; science activity suggestions can be found in many good books at the public library or on child-oriented websites.
- Nurture children's interest in reading, writing, and friendships by locating pen pals in another state or country; encourage children to correspond (via letter, email, webcam), read books about where their pen pal lives, and locate the state or country on a map.
- Encourage children to participate in at least 60 minutes of vigorous physical activity daily for healthy development; plan some activities that all family members can do together.
- Maintain open communication with children. Spend time together, talking about their interests and friends, and being supportive.

Developmental Alerts

Check with a health care provider or early childhood specialist if, by the eleventh birthday, the child *does not:*

- Continue to grow at a rate appropriate for the child's gender.
- Show continued improvement of fine motor skills.
- Make or keep friends.
- Enjoy going to school and show interest in learning most days. (Have children's hearing and vision tested; vision and hearing problems affect children's ability to learn and maintain their interest in learning.)
- Approach new situations with reasonable confidence; show a willingness to try.
- Handle failure and frustration in a constructive manner; learn from mistakes.
- Sleep through the night or experiences prolonged problems with bed-wetting, nightmares, or sleepwalking.

Safety Concerns

Continue to implement safety practices described for the previous stages. Always be aware of new safety issues as the child continues to grow and develop.

Media Exposure

- Be aware of online websites (and content) that children visit. Teach children Internet safety rules and the importance of not giving out personal information (name, address, telephone number) online. Block websites that you don't want children to access.
- Know what music children listen to, what video games they play, and what movies they watch, to determine whether they are being exposed to violence, sex, or drug culture.

Firearms

- Educate children about the dangers of guns and other weapons. Stress the importance of not picking up firearms and always alerting an adult if one is found.
- Store firearms and ammunition separately and keep in locked storage; never leave loaded firearms unattended.

Traffic

- Insist that children wear seat belts on every motor trip.
- Review safe practices for crossing streets, getting in and out of parked cars, riding a bicycle, skateboarding, and otherwise acting responsibly around traffic.
- Make sure children always wear helmets and appropriate protective gear when engaged in sports activities.

Water

- Provide and require children to wear approved flotation devices whenever fishing, skiing, or boating.
- Teach basic water safety and continue to supervise water-related activities.

Eleven- and Twelve-Year-Olds

For the most part, eleven- and twelve-year-olds are endearing individuals. They are curious, energetic, helpful, and usually happy (Figure 8-6). They assist with chores around the house, sometimes even volunteering before being asked. Their language, motor, and cognitive skills are reaching adult levels of sophistication. By age twelve, children have developed a sense of confidence in their capabilities and approach tasks with renewed interest. Their emotional stability is generally smoother, and they encounter fewer conflicts with family and peers (Poulin & Chan, 2010). Eleven- and twelve-year-olds enjoy participating in organized sports and physical activity. In general, their health is good, and they begin to understand that a healthy lifestyle is not only important but also requires dedicated awareness and effort. However, eleven- and twelve-year-olds also see themselves as invincible. Few children believe they will ever experience serious health conditions such as sexually transmitted diseases (STDs), lung cancer, diabetes, or heart disease despite engaging in risky behaviors (e.g., smoking, following a sedentary lifestyle, eating a high-fat diet) (Woodgate & Leach, 2010).

11- to 12-year-olds

Figure 8-6
Eleven- and twelve-year-olds are curious, energetic, and confident.

DEVELOPMENTAL PROFILES AND GROWTH PATTERNS

Growth and Physical Characteristics

- Height and weight vary significantly from child to child; body shape and proportion are influenced by heredity and environment; birth length is tripled by the end of this period.

- Girls are first to experience a prepuberty growth spurt, growing taller and weighing more than boys at this age; may gain as much as 3.5 inches (8.75 cm) and 20 pounds (44 kg) in one year; this period of rapid growth ends around age twelve for girls; boys' growth rate is much slower (Biro et al., 2010).

DEVELOPMENTAL PROFILES AND GROWTH PATTERNS *(continued)*

- Bodily changes mark approaching puberty (widening hips and budding breasts [girls], enlarging testes and penis [boys], appearance of pubic hair).

- Menstruation may begin if it has not already started; some girls have vaginal discharge sooner; some may be upset if not progressing at the same rate as other girls.

- Spontaneous erections are common among eleven- and twelve-year-old boys; pictures, physical activity, talk, and daydreams can trigger these events; some will begin to have nocturnal emissions (involuntary discharge of seminal fluid).

- Muscle mass and strength increase, especially in boys; girls often reach their maximum muscle strength by age twelve.

- Posture is more erect; increases in bone size and length cause shoulders, collarbone, rib cage, and shoulder blades to appear more prominent.

- Complaints of headaches and blurred vision are not uncommon if children are experiencing vision problems; added strain of schoolwork (smaller print, computer use, longer periods of reading and writing) may cause some children to request an eye examination.

Motor Development

- Displays movements that are smoother and more coordinated; however, rapid growth spurts can cause temporary clumsiness.

- Enjoys participation in activities such as dancing, karate, soccer, gymnastics, swimming, and organized games in which improved skills can be used and tested.

- Concentrates efforts on continued refinement of fine motor abilities through a variety of activities (model-building, rocket construction, drawing, woodworking, cooking, sewing, arts and crafts, writing letters, or playing a musical instrument); has now perfected all fundamental gross motor skills (Figure 8-7).

- Requires outlets for release of excess energy that builds during the school day; enjoys team sports, riding bikes, playing in the park, taking dance lessons, going for a walk with friends, shooting hoops, playing soccer.

- Has an abundance of energy but also fatigues quickly.

- Uses improved strength to run faster, throw balls farther, jump higher, kick or bat balls more accurately, and wrestle with friends.

Figure 8-7
Improved fine motor skills enable children to attempt and be successful at new activities.

Perceptual-Cognitive Development

- Begins thinking in more **abstract** terms; expanded memory ability enables improved long-term recall; now remembers stored information, so no longer needs to rely solely on experiencing an event to understand it (Casasanto, Fotakopoulou, & Boroditsky, 2010).

- Succeeds in sequencing, ordering, and classifying because of improved long-term memory capacity (skills necessary for solving complex mathematics problems).

- Accepts the idea that problems can have multiple solutions; often works through problems by talking aloud to oneself. Develops solutions or responses based on logic.

- Enjoys challenges, problem-solving, researching, and testing possible solutions; researches encyclopedias, the Internet, and dictionaries for information (Figure 8-8).

- Exhibits longer attention span; stays focused on completing school assignments and other tasks.

- Develops detailed plans and lists to reach a desired goal.

- Performs many routine tasks without having to think; increased memory sophistication makes automatic responses possible.

- Shows more complex understanding of cause and effect; learns from mistakes; identifies factors that may have contributed to or caused an event (combining baking soda with vinegar releases a gas; attaching a longer tail helps a kite fly higher in strong wind).

Figure 8-8
Enjoys researching and solving problems.

Speech and Language Development

- Completes the majority of language development by the end of this stage; only subtle refinements are still necessary during the next few years.

- Talks and argues, often nonstop, with anyone who will listen.

- Uses longer and more complex sentence structures.

- Masters increasingly complex vocabulary; adds 4,000–5,000 new words each year; uses vocabulary skillfully to weave elaborate stories and precise descriptions.

- Becomes a thoughtful listener.

---

abstract—the ability to think and use concepts; an idea or theory.

DEVELOPMENTAL PROFILES AND GROWTH PATTERNS *(continued)*

- Understands that word statements can have implied (intended) meanings. (When your mother asks, "Is your homework done?" she really means you had better stop playing, gather up your books, and get started.)

- Grasps concepts of irony and sarcasm; has a good sense of humor and enjoys telling jokes, riddles, and rhymes to entertain others (Glenwright & Pexman, 2010).

- Masters several language styles, shifting back and forth based on the occasion (a more formal style when talking with teachers, a more casual style with parents, and a style that often includes slang and code words when conversing with friends).

Social-Emotional Development

- Organizes group games and activities but may modify rules while the game is in progress.

- Views self-image as very important; typically defines self in terms of appearance, possessions, or activities; may also make comparisons to much admired adults.

- Becomes increasingly self-conscious and self-focused; understands the need to assume responsibility for his or her own behavior and that consequences are associated with one's actions (Howie et al., 2010).

- Begins to think and talk about occupational interests and career plans; daydreams and fantasizes about the future.

- Develops a critical and idealistic view of the world; realizes the world is larger than one's own neighborhood; expresses interest in other cultures, foods, languages, and customs (Figure 8-9).

- Adopts dress, hairstyles, and mannerisms of popular sports figures and celebrities.

- Recognizes that loyalty, honesty, trustworthiness, and being a considerate listener are prerequisites to becoming a good friend; may spend more time now with peers than with family members (Dwyer et al., 2010).

- Handles frustration with fewer emotional outbursts; is able to discuss what is emotionally troubling; accompanies words with facial expressions and gestures for emphasis.

Figure 8-9
Expresses interest in learning about other cultures and traditions.

TeachSource Video Connections

Middle Childhood and Cognitive Development. Most of the developmental skills children will need as they approach adolescence are now in place. Eleven- and twelve-year-olds are able to think abstractly, make judgments based on logic, and face challenge with a reasonable degree of competence and self-confidence. As you watch the learning video *5–11 Years: Observation Module for Middle Childhood,* on the Education CourseMate website, consider the following questions:

1. What cognitive skills are the children using to arrive at their responses to the conservation demonstration and to the question, "What did you do last night"?

2. What qualities did the first two children in the video clip use to describe themselves? Were they consistent with gender expectations?

3. Were you surprised by the responses of the first two children in the video clip to the questions about gender differences? What do you think accounted for the contrast in their answers?

4. What signs of stress or tension did you note while the first two children were being interviewed? If you were a teacher, how might you use this feedback?

11- to 12-year-olds

DAILY ROUTINES

Eating

- Eats nonstop and is always hungry; boys in particular may consume astonishing amounts and combinations of food (Figure 8-10). Boys require approximately 2,500 calories daily; girls need 2,200 calories daily.

- Has few dislikes; willing to eat less preferred foods now and then; shows interest in trying foods from other cultures.

- Needs large snack upon arriving home from school; searches cabinets and refrigerator for anything to eat. Having access to nutritious foods encourages healthy eating habits.

Figure 8-10
Seems hungry and able to eat at almost any time.

DAILY ROUTINES *(continued)*

- Makes some connection between eating (calories) and gaining or losing weight, especially girls; for example, some girls may talk about dieting (monitor closely for signs of a developing eating disorder) (Van den Berg et al., 2010; Woelders et al., 2010).

Personal Care and Dressing

- Cares for most personal needs without adult assistance.
- Bathes often and willingly; keeps self clean; often prefers showers.
- Still needs occasional reminder to wash hands.
- Brushes and flosses teeth regularly; a bright smile is important for appearance. Dental checkups are recommended every six months to monitor rapidly erupting permanent teeth and to treat existing cavities; many children already have several decayed teeth or dental fillings.
- Takes pride in appearance; likes to wear what is fashionable or what friends are wearing.

Sleeping

- Needs plenty of sleep; growth spurts and active play often leave children feeling tired.
- Heads to bed without much resistance but now wants to stay up longer on week nights and even later on weekends and nonschool days.
- Sleeps less soundly than previously; may wake up early and read or finish homework before getting up.
- Bad dreams still trouble some eleven- and twelve-year-olds.

Play and Social Activities

- Shows less interest in frivolous play; prefers goal-directed activities (money-making schemes, competing on a swim team, writing newsletters, attending summer camp).
- Gets involved in organized youth groups such as sports teams, 4-H, or Scouts or just spends time alone with a friend or two; never without something to do.
- Likes animals; offers to care for and train pets.
- Reads enthusiastically; enjoys listening to music, attending movies, watching the news, surfing on the computer, and playing video games.
- Enjoys and participates in outdoor activities such as skateboarding, inline skating, basketball, tennis, riding bikes, or walking with friends.
- Prefers to attend movies, theater, or sport performances alone with friends (not parents) on occasion.

Learning Activities

Developmental applications for families and teachers:

- Continue to maintain open communication with children. Spend time together, know what is going on in their lives, and be supportive (not judgmental). Provide children with information about their personal health (sexuality, drugs and alcohol, pregnancy, sexually transmitted diseases) and the importance of making sound decisions. Encourage them to come to you whenever they have questions or are experiencing problems.

- Encourage children's interest in reading; take them to the library or bookstore.

- Read and discuss newspaper and magazine articles together; suggest that children create their own newsletter.

- Help children develop a sense of responsibility by assigning tasks they can perform on a regular basis (caring for a pet, reading stories to a younger sibling, folding laundry, loading the dishwasher, washing dishes, sweeping the garage).

- Gather a variety of large cardboard boxes, paints, and other materials; challenge children to design a structure (a store, library, train, castle, farm, space station).

- Help children stage a play; invite them to write the script, design scenery, construct simple props, and rehearse.

- Offer to help children plan and organize a pet show, bike parade, scavenger hunt, or neighborhood fundraiser.

- Locate free or low-cost opportunities to join organized group or sporting activities; these are often available through local parks and recreation departments, YMCA / YWCAs, church youth groups, and after-school programs.

- Provide children with a variety of art materials (paints, crayons, markers, paper, old magazines and catalogues, cloth scraps); encourage children to collect natural materials such as leaves, pebbles, interesting twigs, seed pods, feathers, and grasses to use for collages.

11- to 12-year-olds

Developmental Alerts

Check with a health care provider or early childhood specialist if, by the thirteenth birthday, the child *does not*:

- Have movements that are smooth and coordinated.

- Have energy sufficient for playing, riding bikes, or engaging in other desired activities.

- Stay focused on tasks at hand.

- Understand basic cause-and-effect relationships.
- Handle criticism and frustration with a reasonable response (physical aggression and excessive crying could be an indication of underlying problems).
- Exhibit a healthy appetite. (Frequent skipping of meals is not typical for this age group; excessive eating should also be monitored.).
- Make and keep friends.

11- to 12-year-olds

Safety Concerns

Continue to implement safety practices described for the previous stages. Always be aware of new safety issues as the child continues to grow and develop.

Machinery

- Teach children how to operate small appliances and equipment safely.
- Provide basic first aid instruction for responding to injuries.

Media Exposure

- Monitor children's online activities (websites, social networking, chat rooms) for inappropriate content and correspondence.
- Reinforce the importance of online safety: not giving out personal information, not responding to marketers, setting browsers to delete cookies.
- Talk with children about **cyber-bullying** and **sexting**; let them know it is inappropriate (and illegal in some states) to engage in this activity and to inform you if they are ever recipients.
- Limit the amount of time spent online (unless related to schoolwork) or playing video games. Children need to be active; too much sedentary activity increases the risk of obesity and interferes with other learning opportunities.

Sports

- Make sure proper protective equipment is available and worn; check its condition periodically.
- Provide instruction or make sure an adult is supervising any competition; check safety of area, equipment, and practices.

Substance Abuse

- Be aware of warning signs associated with "huffing" (inhaling) hazardous vapors from common household products such as hair spray, polish remover, aerosol paints, ammonia, and gasoline. Note any unusual odor on the child's breath or clothing, slurred speech, jitteriness, poor appetite, bloodshot eyes, or reddened areas around nose or mouth.
- Discuss the hazards of prescription and non-prescription drug abuse and underage drinking.

cyber bullying—sending hurtful, threatening, or harassing messages via the Internet or cell phone.

sexting—sending sexually explicit pictures or messages via cell phone.

POSITIVE BEHAVIOR GUIDANCE

The years between nine and twelve mark the end of childhood and the approach of adolescence. It is during these years that adults need to change their disciplinary style so that children begin to assume gradual responsibility for their own behavior.

Nine-, ten-, eleven- and twelve-year-olds:

- Focus on children's positive behaviors and let them know often that you appreciate their efforts to behave in a responsible manner.

- Involve children in setting appropriate limits and expectations. They are more likely to abide by the rules if they have helped to develop them.

- Take time to hear children's side of the story before passing judgment. Let children know you understand how they feel; however, doing so doesn't necessarily suggest that you accept their behavior.

- Provide unconditional love. Everyone makes mistakes from time to time and children are still in the process of learning to make sound decisions.

- Maintain an open dialogue with children and encourage them to talk about their concerns and feelings.

- Help children develop and use problem-solving and conflict resolution skills to make responsible choices.

- Use consequences to reinforce compliance with behavioral expectations: performing poorly on a math test because the child forgot to bring his book home the night before (**natural consequence**); not being allowed to go to the movies with friends because she was late coming home the previous time (**logical consequence**).

SUMMARY

Growth patterns during this stage are irregular and inconsistent. Girls tend to grow more than do boys, with fairly significant variations occurring from child to child. Most children are rather carefree, happy, energetic, industrious, and eager to learn. They spend the years between ages nine and twelve finetuning basic skills, many of which were already in place. Advanced cognitive abilities

11- to 12-
year-olds

---

natural consequence—an outcome that occurs as a result of the behavior.

logical consequence—a planned response that is implemented if the child misbehaves.

continue to emerge, enabling children to think in the abstract, understand concepts of weight, distance, and time, follow detailed instructions, and comprehend cause-and-effect relationships. Feelings related to self-concept gradually shift from overly harsh self-criticism to increased confidence in his or her own abilities. Although friends and friendships are very important, family ties are still valued and needed. Participation in group activities and team sports provides an additional support system and serves as an outlet for excess energy, competition, development of advanced motor and social skills, and companionship.

Key Terms

logic **p. 190**

intuition **p. 193**

concrete operational thought **p. 193**

abstract **p. 201**

cyber-bullying **p. 206**

sexting **p. 206**

natural consequence **p. 207**

logical consequence **p. 207**

Apply What You Know

A. Apply What You Have Learned

Reread the brief developmental sketch about Juan and Carlin at the beginning of the chapter and answer the following questions.

1. What physical characteristics would you expect to observe in the typical eleven-year-old?
2. Would it be developmentally appropriate to expect most eleven-year-olds to like school? Why do you agree or disagree with this statement?
3. From a developmental perspective, do you think Juan's reactions to having his sister tag along are typical or atypical? Explain.
4. Would you consider Carlin's development to be typical for a nine-year-old? Explain.

B. Review Questions

1. What gender differences are nine-year-olds likely to exhibit in their social-emotional development?
2. How do nine- and eleven-year-olds differ in their ability to think abstractly?
3. What physical changes are ten-year-olds likely to experience?
4. Describe the cognitive abilities typical of most eleven- and twelve-year-olds.
5. Identify three qualities that are needed to make and keep friends.

Helpful Websites

Visit the book companion website for links to additional resources.

ConnectSafely
(social networking safety)
http://www.connectsafely.org/

National Institute of Mental Health
(teen brain development)
http://www.nimh.nih.gov/index.shtml

University of Michigan
(disability and sexuality)
http://www.med.umich.edu/yourchild/topics/disabsex.htm

References

Barnett, L., van Beurden, E., Morgan, P., Brooks, L., & Beard, J. (2010). Gender differences in motor skill proficiency from childhood to adolescence: A longitudinal study, *Research Quarterly for Exercise & Sport*, 81(2), 162–170.

Biro, F., Huang, B., Morrison, J., Horn, P., & Daniels, S. (2010). Body mass index and waist-to-height changes during teen years in girls are influenced by childhood body mass index, *Journal of Adolescent Health*, 46(3), 245–250.

Buckhalt, J. (2011). Insufficient sleep and the socioeconomic status achievement gap, *Child Development Perspectives*, 5(1), 59–65.

Casasanto, D., Fotakopoulou, O., & Boroditsky, L. (2010). Space and time in the child's mind: Evidence for a cross-dimensional asymmetry, *Cognitive Science*, 34(3), 387–405.

Costello, E., & Angold, A. (2010). Developmental transitions to psychopathology: Are there prodromes of substance use disorders?, *Journal of Child Psychology and Psychiatry*, 51(4), 526–532.

Dwyer, K., Fredstrom, B., Rubin, K., Booth-LaForce, C., Rose-Krasnor, L., & Burgess, K. (2010). Attachment, social information processing, and friendship quality of early adolescent girls and boys, *Journal of Social & Personal Relationships*, 27(1), 91–116.

Ewing, E. & Troop-Gordon, W. (2011). Peer processes and gender role development: Changes in gender atypicality related to negative peer treatment and children's friendships, *Sex Roles*, 64(1-2), 90–102.

Glenwright, M., & Pexman, P. (2010). Development of children's ability to distinguish sarcasm and verbal irony, *Journal of Child Language*, 37(2), 429–451.

Graber, J., & Nichols, T. (2010). Putting pubertal timing in developmental context: Implications for prevention, *Developmental Psychobiology*, 52(3), 254–262.

Gutierrez, J., & Willoughby, D. (2010). Slimming slumber? How sleep deprivation manipulates appetite and weight, *Nutrition Today*, 45(2), 77–81.

Howie, L., Lukacs, S., Pastor, P., Reuben, C., & Mendola, P. (2010). Participation in activities outside of school hours in relation to problem behavior and social skills in middle childhood, *Journal of School Health*, 80(3), 119–125.

Jones, M., & Estell, D. (2010). When elementary students change peer groups: Intragroup centrality, intergroup centrality, and self-perceptions of popularity, *Merrill-Palmer Quarterly, 56*(2), 164–188.

Kamii, C., & Russell, K. (2010). The older of two trees: Young children's development of operational time, *Journal for Research in Mathematics Education, 41*(1), 6–13.

Lemstra, M., Bennett, N., Nannapaneni, U., Neudorf, C., Warren, L., Kershaw, T., & Scott, C. (2010). A systematic review of school-based marijuana and alcohol prevention programs targeting adolescents aged 10–15, *Addiction Research & Theory, 18*(1), 84–96.

Malti, T., & Latzko, B. (2010). Children's moral emotions and moral cognition: Towards an integrative perspective, *New Directions for Child & Adolescent Development, 129*, 1–10.

Piaget, J. (1928). *Judgment and reasoning in the child.* New York: Harcourt, Brace & World.

Poulin, F., & Chan, A. (2010). Friendship stability and change in childhood and adolescence, *Developmental Review, 30*(3), 257–272.

Trudeau, F., & Shephard, R. (2010). Relationship of physical activity to brain health and the academic performance of schoolchildren, *American Journal of Lifestyle Medicine, 4*(2), 138–150.

Van den Berg, P., Keery, H., Eisenberg, M., & Neumark-Sztainer, D. (2010). Maternal and adolescent report of mothers' weight-related concerns and behaviors: Longitudinal associations with adolescent body dissatisfaction and weight control practices, *Journal of Pediatric Psychology, 35*(10), 1093–1102.

Walvoord, E. (2010). The timing of puberty: Is it changing? Does it matter?, *Journal of Adolescent Health, 47*(5), 433–439.

Woelders, L., Larsen, J., Scholte, R., Cillessen, A., & Engels, R. (2010). Friendship group influences on body dissatisfaction and dieting among adolescent girls: A prospective study, *Journal of Adolescent Health, 47*(5), 456–462.

Woodgate, R., & Leach, J. (2010). Youth's perspectives on the determinants of health, *Qualitative Health Research, 20*(9), 1173–1182.

You are just a click away from a variety of interactive study tools and resources. Access the text's Education CourseMate website at **www.cengagebrain.com**, where you'll find a variety of enrichment materials, including videos, glossary flashcards, activities, tutorial quizzes, web links, and more.

CHAPTER 9
Adolescence: Thirteen- to Nineteen-Year-Olds

Learning Objectives

After reading this chapter, you should be able to:

- Discuss changes in adolescent brain development and how they affect behavior.
- Explain why thirteen- and fourteen-year-olds often experience a loss of self-confidence.
- Describe the role that friends and friendships play during middle adolescence.
- Discuss the nature of social-emotional development in late adolescence.

naeyc Standards Chapter Links:

1a,1b, and 1c: Promoting child development and learning
2a and 2c: Building family and community relationships
3c and 3d: Observing, documenting, and assessing to support young children and families
4a, 4b, 4c and 4d: Using developmentally effective approaches
5c: Using content knowledge to build meaningful curriculum

Meet the Escobar Sisters

Morena and Emilia Escobar moved to the United States with their family several months before the beginning of the current school year. Both girls had attended private schools in Argentina and spoke relatively good English, which made their transition into the middle and high schools here somewhat easier. Morena, soon to be sixteen, is sociable, outgoing, and an exceptional soccer player who makes friends quickly. She enjoys learning about her new culture and participating in things that teenagers in this country typically do at her age, like watching movies with friends, texting,

continued…

shopping at the mall, talking about boys, and dating. Emilia, Morena's thirteen-year-old sister, who is an accomplished pianist and honor student, is small for her age, soft-spoken, and not as outgoing. Emilia has met several friends through her involvement on the school newspaper and governance council but spends little time with them outside of these activities.

Although the girl's parents are quite pleased with their adjustment to a new culture and schools, they have also had several concerns. Their family has always been very close and deeply religious. They believe that Morena is spending far too much time with her friends and not enough time at home with her family or devoted to her studies. They know little about her new friends and worry that Morena could easily be pressured into doing things of which they disapprove, such as drinking or experimenting with drugs, because she is eager to be accepted. Her parents have also been surprised by some of the recent changes they have observed in Morena's clothing and music choices, as well as her impulsive decisions. Although they have fewer concerns about Emilia's progress, they worry that she has become more self-conscious and moody as of late, often retreats to her bedroom in the evening, and seems to have only one close friend with whom she spends her time.

Ask Yourself

1. Do you think the developmental changes exhibited by the girls are typical, or should they be cause for concern?
2. How could the girls' parents determine if their concerns are justified or nothing to worry about?
3. In what ways may differences in cultural expectations be contributing to the parents' worries?

Thirteen- to Nineteen-Year-Olds

Adolescence marks a period of dramatic transitions, confusion, and uncertainty for children, their families, and teachers alike. Bodily changes and emerging feelings of sexuality can lead to increased self-consciousness, self-doubt, and a readjustment of self-identity. Children who were once spontaneous, cooperative, and fun-loving may become moody, questioning, and, at times, rebellious teenagers. They resent being treated as children, yet are not ready to assume full responsibility for decisions governing their own behavior until they near the end of this stage. Although they may challenge adult authority and demand independence, adolescents truly want and need their families to care and to set reasonable limits that help guard against harmful

consequences (e.g., substance abuse, sexually transmitted diseases, pregnancy, crime). Is it any wonder that few adults want to relive their adolescence, or that parents have mixed emotions as their children enter their teenage years?

Although it is easy to dwell on the negative aspects of adolescence, it is more important to remember that most children are "good kids," even those who may be difficult to manage at times (Figure 9-1). They possess many positive intellectual and personal qualities: They are eager to learn, curious, capable, industrious, inventive, and interested in making a difference. They are able to think in abstract terms, use logic to solve problems, and communicate complex thoughts with adult-like sophistication (Best & Miller, 2010). They begin to dream about career options during the early adolescent years and later pursue the training that will ultimately help achieve their goals. They embrace technology, are active participants in social networking, and rely on instant messaging to stay connected with friends and family (Jackson et al., 2010).

Why does the adolescent show such a contrast in personalities? Recent medical research has provided some clues. It has long been thought that brain development was complete by the time children reached their teen years. However, new findings based upon analyses of brain images reveal that structural changes (increased white matter, thinning of grey matter, sensitivity to brain chemicals) and reorganization (formation of new **neural connections**) continue well into the early twenties (Blakemore, 2010). The brain centers most affected by these changes include those that regulate emotion, decision-making, memory, social and sexual behavior, and impulsivity, which may help to explain the adolescent's often unpredictable and questionable behavior (Figure 9-2). These responses should not be viewed as negative qualities but rather as behaviors that

Figure 9-1
Most adolescents are 'good kids' who have many positive qualities.

neural connections—organized linkages formed between brain cells as a result of learning.

Figure 9-2
Areas of change in adolescent brain development.

13- to 14-year-olds

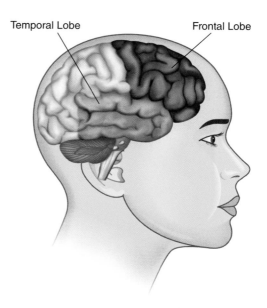

Temporal Lobe   Frontal Lobe

eventually enable adolescents to better understand themselves, determine how they fit into a society, make sound decisions, and, ultimately, to achieve adult maturity. What adolescents need most during these turbulent years are adults who provide patience, understanding, consistency, and nurturing support.

Thirteen- and Fourteen-Year-Olds (Early Adolescence)

Thirteen- and fourteen-year-olds are confronted with countless new feelings, experiences, and expectations which, at times, may prove to be overwhelming. How these events are perceived and handled is influenced by the adolescent's and families' unique cultural, social, and environmental beliefs and conditions. As thirteen-year-olds transition to junior high or middle school they often face a host of fears and uncertainties; "Will I have any friends?", "What if the classes are too hard?", "What if the teachers don't like me?" They also begin to discover a multitude of new interests and activities—organized sports, arts, academic subjects—and want to try them all but must make tough choices due to time constraints. Early adolescents are extremely curious, able to think hypothetically, and readily accepting of intellectual challenge. However, concerns about physical appearance begin to raise feelings of insecurity as hormones trigger troublesome weight gain, acne, facial hair, menstruation, voice changes, and extremities that grow at uneven rates. In some cultural groups, these changes signal an important transition from childhood to adulthood and are celebrated as a "coming-of-age." Despite the fact that thirteen-year-olds may consider themselves to be grown up and perceive rules and limits as overly confining and restrictive, they need consistent nurturing and guidance now more than ever.

Although thirteen-year-olds experience some loss of self-confidence as they adjust to the many physical and psychological changes occurring in their lives, their sense of self-identity quickly returns the following year. Fourteen-year-olds conduct themselves with greater self-assurance and emotional control, become more outgoing, have an improved (positive) outlook on life, and regard friendships with greater importance. Time outside of classes is often spent with same-gender peers—participating in extracurricular activities of mutual interest (e.g., school council, chess or glee club, theater, organized athletics, church groups, 4-H, computer gaming), gathering at a local hangout, talking on cellphones, texting, blogging, or engaging in other social networking platforms. Advancements in social and moral development are evident in the fourteen-year-olds' emerging interests in civic responsibility (giving back) and participation in community service or service learning projects. In other words, fourteen-year-olds are beginning to show significant signs of maturing.

13- to 14-year-olds

DEVELOPMENTAL PROFILES AND GROWTH PATTERNS

Growth and Physical Characteristics

- Weight gain varies by individual based on food intake, physical activity, and genetic influence.
- Continues to grow taller; boys, especially, begin to experience rapid growth spurts. Girls may experience small increases, but most have already reached their adult height.
- Head size and facial features are adult-like; arms, legs, and feet often appear large and out of proportion to the rest of the body.
- Has full set of permanent teeth except for the second and third molars (wisdom teeth).
- Still tires easily, especially with vigorous activity.
- Blood pressure reaches adult values (approximately 110/80); varies with child's weight, activity, emotional state, and ethnicity (some racial groups are prone to higher blood pressure).
- Develops facial blemishes due to hormonal changes.
- Continues to experience bodily changes associated with puberty; girls begin having regular monthly periods; boys develop facial hair, voice changes, and nocturnal emissions.
- Complains of blurred vision or fatigue while reading; should have eyes examined to rule out any acuity problem if complaints persist.

Motor Development

- Movements are often awkward and uncoordinated due to irregular and rapid growth.
- Engages in purposeful activity; less time spent "just fooling around."
- Able to sit still for longer periods but still needs frequent outlets for excess energy.

DEVELOPMENTAL PROFILES AND GROWTH PATTERNS *(continued)*

- Girls exhibit greater speed and agility; boys have better strength and endurance.

- Develops new interests in individual sports (e.g., swimming, golf, gymnastics) and team athletics (e.g., softball, soccer, basketball, football, hockey) (Figure 9-3).

Perceptual-Cognitive Development

- Uses more advanced processes (theoretical, rational, and logical) to formulate an opinion.

- Begins to analyze problems from multiple perspectives before arriving at a solution; first makes a prediction (hypothesis) and then considers multiple variables or options one at a time before arriving at a conclusion. (Piaget referred to this process as **formal operational thinking**.)

- Is able to understand and learn advanced material; thinks abstractly about complex issues but still lacks the experience necessary to always make sound decisions.

- Likes school and academic challenge: arrives early; tries new academic subjects and extracurricular activities; feels overwhelmed at times by schoolwork and tests.

Figure 9-3
New interests in sports reflect improved motor abilities.

- Fascinated with technology; uses the Internet for homework, entertainment, and communication purposes; has difficulty determining if media content is truthful and, therefore, reliable.

- Spends considerable time in self-reflection; often retreats to bedroom to think (Heatherton, 2011).

- Plans and organizes activities without adult assistance.

- Focuses most attention on the present but is beginning to make some plans for the future.

Speech and Language Development

- Is articulate in expressing ideas and thoughts; word comprehension and fluency have nearly reached adult levels.

- Pauses and thinks before responding.

---

formal operational thinking—Piaget's fourth stage of cognitive development; period when children are capable of using abstract thought to predict, test, and reason to arrive at a logical conclusion.

- Answers questions in a direct and concise manner; is less likely to engage in spontaneous conversation with family members than during earlier years.
- Spends endless time texting, emailing, and/or talking on their cellphone with friends.
- Understands irony, sarcasm, and metaphors when used in conversation.

Social-Emotional Development

- Has unpredictable periods of moodiness (usually related to hormonal changes); may act out when frustrated or faced with new or stressful challenges.
- Develops firm moral viewpoints about what is right and wrong.
- Is often opinionated and questions parental decisions; although this may result in hurt feelings, it is an important step in becoming independent.
- Embarrassed by displays of adult affection in public (e.g., father putting his arm around son's shoulder, mother hugging daughter good-bye).
- Begins to display signs of adolescent **egocentrism**; becomes increasingly self-conscious and sensitive to criticism; compares self to an **imaginary audience** (friends, movie stars, rock musicians, fashion models in magazines) and attempts to mimic their image; often expresses dissatisfaction with body appearance (especially girls) and personal achievements.
- Spends increasing time with friends rather than family (Figure 9-4).
- Has strong desire for peer acceptance; makes an effort to fit in through choice of clothes, behavior, music, and/or mutual-interest activities (Ojanen et al., 2010).
- Has mixed feelings about sexual relationships, although may begin to engage in exploratory behaviors and discussions with peers (Root & Denham, 2010).
- Is developing a stronger sense of self-identity but still wavers between feeling confident and independent one moment and insecure and needing reassurance the next.

Figure 9-4
Friends and friendships become more important than spending time with family.

egocentrism—an adolescent's belief in their own importance.

imaginary audience—a component of egocentrism whereby an adolescent believes that others care about and notice their behavior and appearance.

13- to 14-
year-olds

 TeachSource Video Connections

Understanding Adolescent Emotions. New experiences, conflicts, and challenges can be intimidating and sometimes lead to emotions that adolescents find difficult to understand and control. As you watch the learning video *Social-Emotional Development: Understanding Adolescents* on the Education CourseMate website, consider the following questions:

1. Why would meeting with the adolescent boys as a group be an effective way to help them address their anger?
2. What positive strategies were the boys able to identify for dealing with their anger and stress?
3. Why is it important that adults take time to establish rapport with adolescents and listen to their side of the story?

DAILY ROUTINES

Eating

- Continues to have a hearty appetite (especially boys); increased consumption often precedes an impending growth spurt.
- Usually eager for a snack after school, while studying, and before bedtime; food choices not always the most nutritious.
- Weight concerns may lead to self-imposed food restriction and unhealthy diets especially among girls; nutritious meals should be provided and children's intake observed carefully (avoid drawing too much attention to food intake or making negative comments about weight).
- Some children have an increased interest in cooking and preparing meals for others.

Personal Care and Dressing

- Manages own bathing and care routines but may need gentle reminders at times.
- Begins to shave or trim facial hair (boys); girls may shave legs and underarms.
- Takes pride in appearance; has definite clothing preferences.
- Selects and may help purchase some of own clothing items; choices often reflect what is considered to be "in style" with peers.

Sleeping

- Stays up later at night: studies, finishes homework, watches television, or plays computer games; often has difficulty waking up in the morning (Cain & Gradisar, 2010).
- Insufficient sleep in adolescents has been linked to depression, poor academic performance, and substance abuse (Owens, Belon, & Moss, 2010; Pieters et al., 2010).

Social Activities

- Relies on friends for companionship. Girls form a close social bond with one or two same-gender friends and confide in them about personal matters. Boys prefer doing things together with several friends or as a group.
- Shows some interest in casual dating; attends school dances, parties, and other social events; goes to the movies as a couple or with other couples in a group.
- Meets and communicates often with friends through social networking sites (Patchin & Hinduja, 2010).

Learning Activities

Developmental applications for families and teachers:

- Encourage children to explore a variety of academic subjects and extracurricular activities; refrain from criticizing or making children feel guilty if they decide to opt out after giving it their best effort.
- Support children's interest in civic responsibility; help them identify opportunities for volunteering (animal shelter, local library, neighborhood garden), fundraising for a local cause, or participating in community service projects.
- Designate one evening each week as a "family night." Plan and cook a meal, make popcorn and watch a movie, play box or electronic games, take a walk, ride bikes, swim, or engage in some other activity together. Time spent with one another strengthens communication and family ties.
- Promote children's interests in the environment and social responsibility: challenge them to design alternative energy devices, such as a solar stove, wind generator, water heater.
- Foster adolescents' creative literacy: help them compose a short novel, write and produce a play, make and edit a movie, or initiate a neighborhood newsletter .
- Interest children in researching and organizing a collection: coins, shells, baseball cards, bumper stickers, pencils, maps, insects, travel souvenirs.
- Challenge children to try a new sport: track, Frisbee golf, swimming, basketball, table tennis, soccer, handball, bowling, volleyball. Reinforce the importance of being physically active every day to maintain fitness and health.
- Assign tasks that children are responsible for completing on a regular basis: feeding and walking the dog, folding and putting away laundry, setting out the recycling containers, vacuuming, or mowing the lawn.

Developmental Alerts

Check with a health care provider or child development specialist if, by the fifteenth birthday, the child *does not*:

- Make and socialize with friends; show little interest in activities that were once enjoyable; maintain reasonable eating and sleeping habits. Sudden and/or prolonged behavioral changes may indicate an emotional problem that needs to be addressed.

- Continue to grow or experience physical changes associated with puberty.

- Demonstrate ability to think in the abstract; consider more than one solution when solving a problem.

- Read with understanding; express ideas so they are meaningful to others.

- Look forward to school or attend on a regular basis (makes frequent excuses to stay home, or skips school without parent's knowledge).

- Abide by family rules and expectations on most occasions despite protesting.

- Demonstrate moral reasoning or ability to distinguish right from wrong (engages in risky behaviors such as drinking, drugs, sexting, or petty crime).

Safety Concerns

Continue to implement safety practices described for the previous stages. Always be aware of new safety issues as the child continues to grow and develop.

Sports

- Make sure children are healthy and have medical clearance to play organized sports.
- Insist that appropriate safety equipment be worn at all times, even during practice. Check condition of equipment periodically to make sure it is intact, the correct size, and adjusted properly.
- Be familiar with the quality of supervision or coaching children receive. Are children positively reinforced to perform? Are injuries handled properly? Are rest breaks offered? Are adults trained to administer CPR and first aid?

Suicide/depression

- Note sudden changes in children's moods (irritability, aggression, withdrawal, sadness), eating routines, and/or sleep patterns. Depression and suicide thoughts often peak during early

adolescence; professional help should be sought (Smiga & Elliott, 2011; Brendgen et al., 2010).
- Monitor the adolescent's social networking and Internet use; let them know to alert an adult if ever the target of cyber-bullying.
- Maintain an open, nonjudgmental dialogue with teens; encourage them to discuss concerns with a trusted adult (Figure 9-5).

Media Exposure

- Talk with children about online safety: chat room guidelines; adult content sites; data-mining by marketers; not accepting messages from unknown persons; telling an adult if inappropriate content or communication is received.
- Locate computers out of bedrooms and into a public area where they can be observed.
- Limit the amount of time children spend online, on a cellphone, or other handheld device.

15- to 16-year-olds

Figure 9-5
Adolescents should feel comfortable talking to a trusted adult.

Risky Behaviors

- Provide adolescents with information to help them make sound decisions regarding sexual activity, alcohol consumption, illicit drugs, prescription medication abuse, tattoos, and body piercings.
- Note early behavioral and emotional signs of a potential eating disorder: consuming less food, skipping meals, weight loss, prolonged dissatisfaction with body image, vomiting, depression.
- Establish a plan to know where adolescents are at all times: when to call, where they are going, and when they can be expected to return.

Fifteen- and Sixteen-Year-Olds (Middle Adolescence)

Behavioral contrasts continue to be evident during the middle adolescence years. However, the ways in which they are experienced and expressed often vary due to differences in family, social, religious, and cultural values. Typical fifteen-year-olds exhibit many developmental traits that are similar to those of thirteen-year-olds. They once again become introspective, indifferent, rebellious, and intent on gaining their autonomy. Friends (one-on-one and in groups) gradually replace family as a source of comfort, security, and personal information. Fifteen-year-olds either like school and work hard to achieve good grades, or they become disengaged and disinterested. They find convenient reasons (e.g., school activities, errands, social events) not to stay home and, when they are at home, often retreat to their room and immerse themselves in computer games, online chatting, listening to music, daydreaming, or watching TV. Although most fifteen-year-olds enjoy excellent health, they often experience considerable stress and tension from daily occurrences (e.g., test taking, team tryouts, feelings of sexuality, friendships) (Seiffge-Krenke et al., 2010).

Figure 9-6
Adolescents continue to refine their self-identity by exploring and experimenting with everything from technology to interpersonal relationships.

15- to 16-year-olds

Many positive qualities begin to return as adolescents approach their sixteenth birthday. They develop a renewed sense of self-confidence, respect, emotional control, tolerance, and self-determination. Friends are important and continue to play a vital role. Relationships are formed on the basis of common interests, are relatively stable, and are intimate in some cases. Sexual identity is well-established, although some adolescents are reluctant to acknowledge or to discuss concerns about homosexual tendencies or gender confusion (Ryan et al., 2010). This can interfere with the adolescent's sense of acceptance or belonging and lead to significant depression (McCallum & McLaren, 2011). Sixteen-year-olds develop more advanced cognitive and analytical skills that enable **deductive reasoning**, improved decision-making, and planning ahead for the future (Best & Miller, 2010). They continue to explore and experiment with everything from clothing styles and interpersonal relationships to technology, philosophical ideas, and vocational interests (Figure 9-6). In other words, sixteen-year-olds are well on their way to becoming independent thinkers and doers.

DEVELOPMENTAL PROFILES AND GROWTH PATTERNS

Growth and Physical Characteristics

- Weight gain varies by individual and depends on food intake, physical activity, and genetics.
- Continues to grow taller; boys, especially, experience rapid growth spurts. Girls reach their approximate adult height early in this period; males do so by the end of this stage.
- Wisdom teeth (third molars) may erupt.

deductive reasoning—a process of considering hypothetical alternatives before reaching a conclusion.

- Still tires easily, especially following vigorous activity.
- Heart doubles in size and beats slower. Blood pressure reaches adult values (approximately 110/80); varies with child's weight, activity, emotional state, and ethnicity (some groups are prone to higher blood pressure).
- Experiences fewer skin eruptions (acne) as hormone levels stabilize.
- Continues to undergo gradual body changes associated with puberty.
- Arms, legs, hands, and feet may still appear large and out of proportion to the rest of the body.
- Continues to add muscle mass, especially males but also girls who are athletically active.

15- to 16-year-olds

Motor Development

- Motor coordination, speed, and endurance level off for girls; boys begin to surpass girls in these abilities and continue to improve until age twenty.
- Hand–eye coordination becomes more precise and controlled.
- Appears awkward and uncoordinated (clumsy) during periods of rapid growth; prone to more injuries during these times.

▶II Teachsource Video Connections

Technology and Learning. Technology has revolutionized our daily lives and changed the way students learn. Innovative instructional programs offer enriched opportunities for exploring and understanding complex information. As you watch the learning video *Integrating Technology to Improve Student Learning: A High School Science Simulation* on the Education CourseMate website, consider the following questions:

1. What perceptual-cognitive skills are fifteen- and sixteen-year-olds developing that enable them to grasp complex ideas, such as genetics?
2. In what ways are the students using scientific reasoning to explain genetic differences?
3. Why would the use of instructional technology appeal to adolescents?
4. What examples of the adolescent's ability to focus attention on multiple activities can be observed in the video?

Perceptual-Cognitive Development

- Solves abstract problems using deductive reasoning; is able to visualize or recall a concept, place, or thing without actually seeing or experiencing it at the time.
- Plans ahead; considers the pros and cons of several weekend activities before deciding on a final choice; makes hypothetical plans for the summer break; thinks about future career options.
- Uses **scientific reasoning** to solve increasingly complex problems; combines knowledge, experience, and logic to arrive at a solution or outcome.

scientific reasoning—critical thinking skills (identify, analyze, conclude) used to achieve a solution.

DEVELOPMENTAL PROFILES AND GROWTH PATTERNS *(continued)*

- Becomes aware of a much larger world; is curious, eager for academic challenge, and interested in trying new things.
- Is able to focus attention on several activities at the same time: listens to music on headphones or watches television while doing homework.
- Recognizes that not all information is trustworthy; evaluates an information source before accepting it as reliable.

Speech and Language Development

- Experiences modest gains in vocabulary; girls continue to score higher than boys on verbal abilities.
- Is capable of learning additional languages but requires more time and effort than when younger (an important consideration for schools given the numbers of non-English speaking children) (Livingstone & Brake, 2010; Oh & Fuligni, 2010).
- Adjusts language and communication style according to the situation: conversing on the cellphone with friends, discussing a project with teachers, or texting in cyber slang.

Figure 9-7
Begins to have interest in forming romantic relationships.

- Uses increasingly complex grammar and sentence construction to express ideas.
- Spends considerable time engaged in social networking and communicating with friends; uses technology (texting, cellphone conversations, Internet, Facebook, "tweeting").
- Understands and engages in adult humor.

Social-Emotional Development

- Establishes friendships with peers of both genders; having friends and being "popular" are important (LaFontana & Cillessen, 2010; Ojanen et al., 2010) (Figure 9-7).
- Continues to struggle with self-identity issues, especially if there are real or perceived differences from one's peers (religious beliefs, biracial, sexual orientation, adopted, ethnicity, special needs); is sensitive to peer comments.
- Develops interest in forming serious romantic relationships. This is an important step in refining one's self-identity and self-image, determining sexual orientation, establishing personal values related to intimacy and sexual behavior, and learning about the qualities desired in a partner.
- Has strong drive to achieve autonomy from family; dislikes parental authority and limits placed on activities.

15- to 16-year-olds

- Is caring, cooperative, and responsible much of the time; temperamental, moody, and rebellious on occasion, especially when wishes are not granted.
- Adopts clothing styles and behavior of peer group; may also experiment with risky behaviors (illicit drugs, tattoos, body piercings, sexual activity, tobacco, alcohol) to make a statement or gain acceptance.
- Recognizes right from wrong but makes some irresponsible decisions that contradict this understanding (Leijenhorst et al., 2010).

15- to 16-year-olds

DAILY ROUTINES

Eating

- Continues to have a healthy appetite, but is less likely to participate in family meals; often eats when hungry or convenient due to time conflicts with school or extracurricular activities.
- May severely restrict food intake to control weight gain; eating disorders (anorexia, bulimia) and severe dieting are more common among both genders during this period and can lead to serious health problems (Rodgers, Paxton, & Chabrol, 2010).
- Shows greater interest in nutrition, trying new foods, and experimenting with dietary practices (vegetarian diet, lowering fat intake), but has less interest in cooking (Salvy et al., 2011).

Personal Care and Dressing

- Takes pride in personal grooming and appearance; girls often apply makeup; boys shave.
- Bathes or showers daily; washes hair frequently.
- Usually quite particular about clothing choices; prefers items that reflect current styles and fashion trends.

Sleeping

- Requires approximately nine hours of uninterrupted nighttime sleep to maintain health and attention. Sleep deprivation can interfere with learning, diminish alertness, and contribute to moodiness, irritability, and behavior problems (Beebe, Rose, & Amin, 2010; Cain & Gradisar, 2010).
- Stays up late at night; biological changes during adolescence cause a shift in wake/sleep rhythms (toward a later bedtime); may fail to get adequate sleep due to school activities, employment, homework, or socializing with friends.

Social Activities

- Prefers spending time alone when home; often goes to own bedroom and closes the door.
- Develops new friendships; may spend more time with friends than with family; friends provide an important source of companionship, feedback, and emotional support, especially among girls.
- Enjoys challenge and competition; explores and participates in a variety of social and extracurricular activities; some adolescents may also hold down part-time jobs.

Learning Activities

Developmental applications for families and teachers:

- Provide opportunities for privacy; respect the adolescent's need for time alone; knock before entering their room.
- Encourage children's interest in developing leadership skills and assuming leadership roles at school or in local organizations.
- Offer to help arrange small social gatherings where teens can mingle in a safe setting: pool party, sleep over, watching a movie at home with friends, youth group meetings, roller skating.
- Support interests in new activities: singing, theater, art, playing a musical instrument, hunting, robotics, golf, yoga, astronomy, cooking, hiking.
- Assist teens in locating volunteer opportunities or occasional part-time work (babysitting, mowing lawns, shoveling snow, pet sitting, raking leaves).
- Plan trips centered around a learning theme: space museum, aquarium, national park, working ranch, adventure camp, history, snorkeling, another culture.
- Organize a book club; have teens take turns selecting a book for the group to read and discuss.
- Interest teens in learning about genealogy, researching their family background, and developing a family tree.
- Continue to discuss high-risk behaviors and preventive measures; provide educational reading materials and encourage teens to ask questions.
- Teach time management and organizational skills; encourage teens to set up a digital calendar where due dates for homework, tests, and activities can be noted; create a quiet area for studying and storing school materials.
- Prepare teens to handle difficult situations (offered drugs or alcohol, pressured to have sex); role play strategies for avoiding involvement.

Developmental Alerts

Check with a health care provider or child development specialist if, by the seventeenth birthday, the child *does not*:

- Have or keep friends; is not included in group activities.
- Remember or plan ahead on most occasions.
- Maintain reasonable interest in personal hygiene and daily activities, including school; sudden apathy or failing grades may be signs of depression or other mental health disorders.
- Use language correctly to express thoughts and requests; interpret or respond appropriately to nonverbal behavior.

- Grasp humor, jokes, or puns.
- Confront new situations with a relative degree of self-confidence.
- Avoid involvement in harmful behaviors (drugs, alcohol abuse, bullying, promiscuous sex, crime, truancy).

Safety Concerns

Sporting Activities

- Insist that proper protective gear be worn when participating in sporting activities: paintball (goggles); biking (helmet); skateboarding (helmet, protective knee and elbow pads); hunting (ear plugs, goggles, reflective vest); baseball and softball (helmet, mouth and shin guards), boating (life jacket).
- Seek medical evaluation for any head injury; prevent teens from returning to activity until given medical clearance.

Media Exposure

- Monitor adolescents' Internet use (e.g., social networking sites, movies, computer games, music) at home; make it a point to know what teens are accessing when visiting friends.
- Educate teens about potential risks involved in an online presence: urge caution about giving out or posting personal information; report cyber bullying and sexting to an adult; never agree to meet an online "friend" unless in a public area, with trusted friends, and after informing an adult.

Dating

- Educate teens about dating, setting limits, and maintaining healthy relationships.
- Discuss dating violence; talk about the warning signs and what to do if teens find themselves in an abusive relationship.
- Provide teens with information about pregnancy and sexually transmitted disease (STDs) prevention to help them make informed decisions.

Travel

- Insist that seatbelts be worn when riding in a vehicle with family or friends.
- Educate teens about refusing to ride with a drunk driver and to report the individual.
- Have teens call when they leave and/or arrive at their destination; let them know it isn't about trust, rather it has to do with your concerns about their safety.
- Make sure teens have emergency contact information with them, such as parents' cellphone numbers.

17- to 18-year-olds

Seventeen- and Eighteen-Year-Olds (Late Adolescence)

The remaining years of adolescence are characterized by few developmental changes that are either dramatic or significant in number. Girls have completed their physical and reproductive growth while boys continue to experience small gains in height and muscle mass into their early twenties. Cognition, social-emotional capacity, speech and language, and motor abilities are well-established by now and will undergo only minor refinement during late adolescence. Seventeen- and eighteen-year-olds have established a clear sexual identity and are comfortable with themselves, self-reliant, more emotionally stable, and philosophical about life. They are now able to shift their interests and energies from skill acquisition and peer acceptance to contemplating the

Figure 9-8
Much thought is devoted during
late adolescence to future plans
and career goals.

17- to 18-
year-olds

future (Figure 9-8). "What plans do I have following high school?" "What are my long-range career goals, and what must I do to achieve them?" "Am I interested in an intimate relationship or long-term commitment?" "How do I plan on supporting myself financially?" How adolescents ultimately resolve these decisions is strongly influenced by their cultural, economic, social, and family values (Giguère, Lalonde, & Lou, 2010). In some cultural and social groups, for example, adolescents are expected to continue living with their family and contribute financially until they marry. In contrast, it is presumed that adolescents in many Western societies will leave home and establish their independence once they have completed school.

And so, the journey through childhood nears an end as adolescents approach their nineteenth birthday. Most are ready to begin the next chapter of life and to face a host of new challenges, decisions, and opportunities as they become young adults.

DEVELOPMENTAL PROFILES AND GROWTH PATTERNS

Growth and Physical Characteristics

- Undergoes few changes in basic physical development; has almost reached adult maturity.
- Experiences small increases in height, weight, and bone mass; males continue to grow taller until their early twenties; girls have achieved their full adult height.
- Enjoys good health and few illnesses.
- Experiences a high rate of injury, death, and disability due to irrational decisions and impulsive behavior.

Motor Development

- Reaches peak muscle mass.
- Continues to develop muscular strength into the early twenties, especially males.
- Achieves precise finger dexterity and hand–eye coordination; manipulates computer and video games with great skill.
- Movements are now coordinated and controlled.

Perceptual-Cognitive Development

- Uses recall, logic, and abstract thinking to solve complex problems.
- Begins to rely on **analytical thinking** more often when planning and problem-solving than in the past; identifies and evaluates potential solutions although does not always reach a rational decision (Figure 9-9).
- Shows some gender differences in cognitive abilities: girls tend to achieve higher verbal skills; boys may excel in science and mathematics. However, these differences are becoming less significant as more opportunities and support are equalizing skill acquisition across genders (Haworth, Dale, & Plomin, 2010).
- Continues to make impulsive decisions and illogical choices that sometimes make adults wonder. Remember: adolescent brains are still undergoing development and maturation in the areas responsible for emotional control and decision-making (Blakemore, 2010).

17- to 18-year-olds

Figure 9-9
Is capable of solving complex problems based on analytical thinking.

---

analytical thinking—a cognitive process used when attempting to solve problems or make plans; identifying and evaluating the pros/cons of alternative solutions.

DEVELOPMENTAL PROFILES AND GROWTH PATTERNS *(continued)*

Speech and Language Development

- Uses correct grammar and more elaborate sentence structure; is able to critique own written work.

- Articulates complex ideas, varying the style according to the situation.

- Continues to expand vocabulary; adds words that are more advanced, sophisticated, and abstract.

- Participates heavily in social networking; uses Internet slang and shortcuts masterfully to converse (text) with friends ("b/c," because; "g2g," got to go; "sbrd," so bored; "meh," whatever; "PAW," parents are watching) (Figure 9-10).

- Understands and uses **figurative language**: "He jumped as high as the sky," "She was as quiet as a mouse," "The walls have ears."

Figure 9-10
Social networking is used to share information and stay in touch with friends.

Social-Emotional Development

- Is becoming more open and receptive to adult advice; may actually request it on occasion.

- Continues to refine a self-identity based more on realistic goals and cultural ideals and less on idealistic notions ("I want to be a famous musician, but it's going to take a lot of hard work and dedication.")

- Has more self-confidence; is less likely to be influenced by peers or to rely on them for approval.

- Sees himself or herself as part of a much larger world; continues to redefine personal values and beliefs about social roles and civic responsibilities; seeks out opportunities to become involved in community programs.

- Has better emotional control but still exhibits a range of moods and occasional impulsive behavior (Sturman & Moghaddam, 2011).

- Seeks intimate relationships based more on shared interests than pure romantic desire.

- Understands and is more likely to accept responsibility for own behaviors.

17- to 18-year-olds

---

figurative language—words or statements that have meaning other than their literal definition.

TeachSource Video Connections

Peer Influence. Friendships and peers play an essential role in adolescent development. However, the nature of these relationships changes over time. As you watch the learning video *12–18 Years: Peers and Domain Influences in Development* on the Education CourseMate website, consider the following questions:

1. What is meant by "domain-specific peer influence"?
2. What developmental areas are parents most likely to influence?
3. Why do seventeen- and eighteen-year-olds value the input of peers and parents differently?
4. Why do they appear to be more receptive to adult advice at this point in their development?

17- to 18-year-olds

DAILY ROUTINES

Eating

- Continues to have important nutrient needs (e.g., protein, calcium, vitamins, iron, zinc) that must be satisfied to assure optimum growth, health, and performance.
- Eating patterns may become more erratic as activities and schedules compete with mealtimes; skips occasional meals, overeats following vigorous workouts or during stressful periods.
- Makes more independent decisions about food choices; eats with friends and away from home more often.
- Weight concerns and emotional problems may lead to unhealthy diets and/or eating disorders.

Personal Care and Dressing

- Is self-sufficient in managing personal care responsibilities.
- Chooses clothes that are "popular" with peers or that express individuality.

Sleeping

- Requires approximately nine hours of uninterrupted nighttime sleep.
- May nap following vigorous activity or if up late the night before; napping too long can delay falling asleep at night.
- Stress, medications, and mental health disorders such as depression may interfere with sleep patterns (sleeping too much or too little).

Social Activities

- Has learned to drive and may transport self to school activities and events.
- Juggles school, homework, and employment so there is still time to take in a movie with friends, attend a sporting event or party, go out on a date, or simply join friends for something to eat.

DAILY ROUTINES *(continued)*

- Has more friends of the opposite gender, some of whom the adolescent may be dating; friendships are formed on the basis of personalities and common interests with fewer concerns about popularity.
- Spends considerable time staying in touch with friends through social networks, instant messaging, or phone calls.
- Continues to develop and experiment with new interests and activities, such as surfing, skiing, or bowling; learning another language; playing a musical instrument; discovering religion; taking up yoga; repairing cars; martial arts.

17- to 18- year-olds

Learning Activities

Developmental applications for families and teachers:

- Continue to discuss risky behaviors and safety considerations; role play strategies for resisting negative peer pressure.
- Offer guidance with experiences that may be new to the adolescent, such as opening a checking account, applying for admission to college, purchasing a first car, or obtaining employment.
- Help adolescents learn healthy stress and anger management techniques.
- Encourage and support the adolescent's interest in volunteering or becoming involved in community service activities.
- Motivate adolescents to follow a healthy diet and engage in physical activity.
- Create opportunities that give adolescents responsibility and acknowledge their efforts.
- Talk about and practice time management skills (these will be helpful as they continue their education and/or seek employment).
- Locate first aid and CPR classes and urge adolescents to complete the training.

Developmental Alerts

Check with a health care provider or child development specialist if, by the nineteenth birthday, the child *does not*:

- Maintain usual eating and sleeping routines; sudden or prolonged changes may signal substance abuse or mental health problems.
- Show interest and/or initiative in achieving independence from family.

- Link moral reasoning to behavioral choices; take responsibility for own behavior and learn from experience.
- Exhibit self-confidence and positive self-esteem in most daily activities.
- Attend school on a regular basis.
- Use reasonable judgment in regulating emotions.
- Grasp and process information when making decisions.
- Achieve functional literacy (reading and writing skills).
- Make and keep friends that have a positive influence on behavior.

Safety Concerns

Continue to implement safety practices described for the previous stages. Always be aware of new safety issues as the child continues to grow and develop.

17- to 18-year-olds

Health and Well-being

- Reinforce the importance of consuming a healthy diet and active lifestyle.
- Continue to talk with adolescents about the risks of pregnancy and sexually transmitted infections.
- Recognize the signs of undue stress; encourage teens to talk about things that are making them feel anxious; be a patient listener and provide nonjudgmental support; reinforce healthy coping skills (tackling challenges in small steps, seeing the positive side of an problem, making time for fun and relaxation (listening to music, taking a walk, talking with friends, reading a book).

Unintentional Injury

- Continue to emphasize safe driving; motor vehicle accident and fatality rates are highest among older teens, especially males (Sleet, Ballersteros, & Borse, 2010) (Figure 9-11). Prohibit the use of cellphones and texting while driving or driving under the influence of drugs or alcohol. Teens tend to believe they are invincible!
- Urge caution when participating in recreational activities such as weightlifting, hunting, riding all-terrain vehicles (ATVs), jogging, and swimming. Make sure proper equipment, training, and supervision are provided.

Number of 15–19 Year Old Males and Females Killed in Crashes, 2000–2006

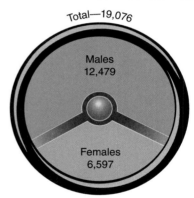

Total—19,076

Males 12,479

Females 6,597

Figure 9-11
Adolescent motor vehicle fatalities.
Source: http://www.cdc.gov/Features/dsTeenDriving/

- Educate adolescents about the risk and warning signs of concussions (traumatic brain injury, or TBI) that may be sustained during athletic activities. Stress the importance of seeking medical attention and clearance before activity is resumed.
- Ensure that adolescents complete appropriate safety training if they use firearms for hunting or target practice.

Violence (suicide, homicide)

- Recognize the early warning signs of depression, mood disorders, sexual abuse, and potential suicide; adolescents' sexual orientation increases the likelihood of malicious harassment and bullying (Hirsch, Carlson, & Crowl, 2010).
- Educate adolescents about their increased vulnerability to the effects of drugs and alcohol; maturational changes in brain structure and function can interfere with rational thought,

intensify sensitivity to substances, and increase the probability of addiction (Bava & Tapert, 2010).

- Know who the adolescent's friends are, where they hang out, and what they do when they are together.
- Foster resilience and empower teens to resist peer pressure; continue to strengthen the adolescent's communication skills, self-esteem, and healthy mentoring relationships with caring adults.

POSITIVE BEHAVIOR GUIDANCE

Behavioral guidance and limit-setting remain important adult responsibilities. However, the expectations and way in which these roles are performed are highly influenced by a person's social and cultural background. Adolescents who are raised in societies where parent–child relationships demand respect and obedience are less likely to experience conflict than their counterparts in Western countries where autonomy is strongly encouraged. Teens need and want continued adult support, respect, and direction in making sound decisions despite their frequent objections. At the same time, adults can promote adolescents' quest for autonomy by gradually relinquishing parental control and involving them in responsible decision-making.

Thirteen- and fourteen-year-olds:

- Let teens know you are available to talk (in a nonjudgmental manner); encourage them to discuss concerns with family or a trusted adult; make a point to spend time together as a family.
- Choose your battles; decide which conflicts are most important to address.
- Adolescents face a host of new experiences and must learn how to make responsible choices. Understand that they won't always make the right decisions but they will, hopefully, learn from their mistakes.
- Listen to the adolescent's side of the story; learn why he or she chose to violate a rule. It isn't necessary to agree, but it is important to respect their opinions, build a healthy relationship, and help them to understand why the rule was necessary.
- Involve adolescents in establishing rules, responsibilities, and consequences for unacceptable behavior. Enforce rules consistently to build respect and accountability.

Fifteen- and sixteen-year-olds:

- Make an effort to know the adolescent's friends and the values they share; meet them at school functions; invite them over to hang out. Friends can be a source of positive social-emotional support or the basis for negative peer pressure.

- Never hit, humiliate, or call the adolescent sarcastic names. Overreacting, disciplining when you are angry, or using physical force sets a poor example and teaches negative ways of handling a situation.

- Negotiate to reduce frequent disagreements and help adolescents understand the rational for the rule; involve your teen in defining the behavior in question, identifying reasonable solutions, arriving at a mutual decision, implementing, enforcing, and monitoring how well the solution is working.

- Use logical consequences: take the cellphone away if too much time is spent talking with friends and homework is ignored; set a curfew thirty minutes earlier if the teen was thirty minutes late.

- Acknowledge and reinforce responsible behavior; teens want adults to notice and be proud of their accomplishments.

- Address harmful or risky behaviors in a direct, firm, and consistent manner. Let adolescents know that their poor choices indicate a lack of readiness to make mature decisions.

Seventeen- and eighteen-year-olds:

- Continue to provide a safe, structured environment; maintain and enforce reasonable limits.

- Convey a sense of trust and respect, even though teens may make occasional mistakes in judgment. Encourage them to talk about and learn from mistakes.

- Give adolescents increased responsibility for handling their own affairs (checking account, laundry, scheduling, bill payments, clothing purchases) and acknowledge their efforts.

- Let adolescents know you are available to talk; they continue to need support and reassurance as they encounter new and challenging experiences.

SUMMARY

Perhaps the analogy of an extended remodeling project can best be used to understand and summarize the child's journey through adolescence. Twelve-year-olds enter this stage with a relatively strong foundation that consists of basic developmental skills across all domains. Changes associated with puberty and brain development require periods of major reorganization and readjustment. Thirteen-year-olds are confronted with many new opportunities and experiences which can be exhilarating and overwhelming at times. By age fourteen, adolescents have become more comfortable with these physical and situational changes and regain some of the self-confidence lost during the previous year. They have fewer worries about appearance, friendships, school, and decisions as their cognitive skills become more complex and enable abstract thinking. Fifteen-year-olds once again face a period of self-doubt and self-questioning as they grapple with desires to gain autonomy. They are introspective, reliant on friends for emotional support, impulsive, capable of deductive thinking, and captivated with technology. Sixteen-year-olds have greater emotional stability and a renewed sense of self-confidence, self-identity, self-determination, and interest in forming serious relationships. During late adolescence, teens become more self-reliant, comfortable with their sexual identity, open to adult advice, capable of complex learning, and philosophical about the future.

Key Terms

neural connections **p. 213**   deductive reasoning **p. 222**

formal operational thinking **p. 216**   scientific reasoning **p. 223**

egocentrism **p. 217**   analytical thinking **p. 229**

imaginary audience **p. 217**   figurative language **p. 230**

Apply What You Know

A. Apply What You Have Learned

Reread the brief developmental sketch about the Morena and Emilia at the beginning of the chapter and answer the following questions.

1. What social-emotional behaviors are characteristic of most typical thirteen- and fourteen-year-olds?
2. How do friendships and the nature of their importance differ for thirteen-year-olds and sixteen-year-olds? Would you consider Morena's and Emilia's relationship with friends to be typical for their age or not?
3. What factors may account for the differences in the girls' personalities?
4. What age-appropriate issues should Morena's and Emilia's parents be discussing with them to protect their safety and well-being?

B. Review Questions

1. What physical changes are thirteen- and fourteen-year-olds likely to experience?
2. What cognitive advantages does formal operational thinking give the adolescent?
3. Describe the nature of peer relationships and the role they play in the lives of fifteen- and sixteen-year-olds.
4. How would you respond to a parent who asks why their once well-behaved child is now acting impulsively and making questionable choices as an adolescent?
5. Why do adolescents prefer to stay up late at night? What are the consequences of sleep deprivation?
6. Explain, from a developmental standpoint, why adolescents seem to devote so much time to instant messaging and social networking.
7. What is egocentrism? What adolescent behaviors would illustrate this concept?

Helpful Websites

Elementary & Middle Schools Technical Assistance Center (cultural, linguistic, and ability differences)
http://www.emstac.org/resources/clad_resources.htm

National Center for Cultural Competence
http://nccc.georgetown.edu

Talk With Your Kids
http://www.talkwithkids.org
(about sex, violence, drugs, HIV, etc.)

Wired Safety (Internet)
http://www.wiredsafety.org

References

Bava, S. & Tapert, S. (2010). Adolescent brain development and the risk for alcohol and other drug problems, *Neuropsychology Review, 20*(4), 393–413.

Beebe, D., Rose, D., & Amin, R. (2010). Attention, learning, and arousal of experimentally sleep-restricted adolescents in a simulated classroom, *Journal of Adolescent Health, 47*(5), 523–525.

Best, J., & Miller, P. (2010). A developmental perspective on executive function, *Child Development 81*(6), 1641–1660.

Blakemore, S. (2010). The developing social brain: Implications for education, *Neuron, 65*(6), 744–747.

Brendgen, M., Lamarche, V., Wanner, B., & Vitaro, F. (2010). Links between friendship relations and early adolescents' trajectories of depressed mood, *Developmental Psychology, 46*(2), 491–501.

Cain, N., & Gradisar, M. (2010). Electronic media use and sleep in school-aged children and adolescents: A review, *Sleep Medicine, 11*(8), 735–742.

Giguère, B., Lalonde, R., & Lou, E. (2010). Living at the crossroads of cultural worlds: The experience of normative conflicts by second generation immigrant youth, *Social & Personality Psychology Compass, 4*(1), 14–29.

Haworth, C., Dale, P., & Plomin, R. (2010). Sex differences in school science performance from middle childhood to early adolescence, *International Journal of Educational Research, 49*(2-3), 92–101.

Heatherton, T., (2011). Neuroscience of self and self-regulation, *Annual Review of Psychology, 62,* 363–390.

Hirsch, A., Carlson, J., & Crowl, A. (2010). Promoting positive developmental outcomes in sexual minority youth through best practices in clinic-school consultation, *Journal of Child & Adolescent Psychiatric Nursing, 23*(1), 17–22.

Jackson, L., von Eye, A., Fitzgerald, H., Zhao, Y., & Witt, E. (2010) Self-concept, self-esteem, gender, race and information technology use, *Computers in Human Behavior, 26*(3), 323–328.

LaFontana, K., & Cillessen, A. (2010). Developmental changes in the priority of perceived status in childhood and adolescence, *Social Development, 19*(1), 130–147.

Leijenhorst, L., Moor, B., Op de Macks, Z., Rombouts, S., Westenberg, M., & Crone, E. (2010). Adolescent risky decision-making: Neurocognitive development of reward and control regions, *NeuroImage, 51*(1), 345–355.

Livingstone, S., & Brake, D. (2010). On the rapid rise of social networking sites: New findings and policy implications, *Children & Society, 24*(1), 75–83.

McCallum, C., & McLaren, S. (2011). Sense of belonging and depressive symptoms among GLB adolescents, *Journal of Homosexuality, 58*(1), 83–96.

Oh, J., & Fuligni, A. (2010). The role of heritage language development in the ethnic identity and family relationships of adolescents from immigrant backgrounds, *Social Development, 19*(1), 202–220.

Ojanen, T., Sijtsema, J., Hawley, P., & Little, T. (2010). Intrinsic and extrinsic motivation in early adolescents' friendship development: Friendship selection, influence, and prospective friendship quality, *Journal of Adolescence, 33*(6), 837–851.

Owens, J., Belon, K., & Moss, P. (2010). Impact of delaying school start time on adolescent sleep, mood, and behavior, *Archives of Pediatrics & Adolescent Medicine, 164*(7), 608–614.

Patchin, J., & Hinduja, S. (2010). Changes in adolescent online social networking behaviors from 2006 to 2009, *Computers in Human Behavior, 26*(6), 1818–1821.

Pieters, S., Van Der Vorst, H., Burk, W., Wiers, R., & Engels, R. (2010). Puberty-dependent sleep regulation and alcohol use in early adolescents, *Alcoholism: Clinical & Experimental Research, 34*(9), 1512–1518.

Rodgers, R., Paxton, S., & Chabrol, H. (2010). Depression as a moderator of sociocultural influences on eating disorder symptoms in adolescent females and males, *Journal of Youth & Adolescence, 39*(4), 393–402.

Root, A., & Denham, S. (2010). The role of gender in the socialization of emotion: Key concepts and critical issues, *New Directions for Child & Adolescent Development, 2010*(128), 1–9.

Ryan, C., Russell, S., Huebner, D., Diaz, R., & Sanchez, J. (2010). Family acceptance in adolescence and the health of LGBT young adults, *Journal of Child & Adolescent Psychiatric Nursing, 23*(4), 205–213.

Salvy, S., Elmo, A., Nitecki, L., Kluczynski, M., & Roemmich, J. (2011). Influence of parents and friends on children's and adolescents' food intake and food selection, *American Journal of Clinical Nutrition, 93*(1), 87−92.

Seiffge-Krenke, I., Bosma, H., Chau, C., Cok, F., Gillespie, C., Loncaric, D., Molinar, R., Cunha, M., Veisson, M., & Rohail, I. (2010). All they need is love? Placing romantic stress in the context of other stressors: A 17-nation study, *International Journal of Behavioral Development, 34*(2), 106−112.

Sleet, D., Ballesteros, M., & Borse, N. (2010). A review of unintentional injuries in adolescents, *Annual Review of Public Health, 31*, 195−212.

Smiga, S., & Elliott, G. (2011), Psychopharmacology of depression in children and adolescents, *Pediatric Clinics of North America, 58*(1), 155−171.

Sturman, D. & Moghaddam, B. (2011). Reduced neuronal inhibition and coordination of adolescent prefrontal cortex during motivated behavior, *Journal of Neuroscience, 31*(4), 1471−1478.

You are just a click away from a variety of interactive study tools and resources. Access the text's Education CourseMate website at **www.cengagebrain.com**, where you'll find a variety of enrichment materials, including videos, glossary flashcards, activities, tutorial quizzes, web links, and more.

CHAPTER 10
When and Where to Seek Help

Learning Objectives

After reading this chapter, you should be able to:

- Discuss five or more legislative acts passed on behalf of children with exceptionalities and their families.
- Describe several factors that can complicate the process of determining if a child is or is not developing typically.
- Defend this statement: Observing and recording a child's behavior is an essential first step in determining whether there is a developmental problem.
- Discuss the developmental team's role in the assessment and intervention process.

naeyc Standards Chapter Links:

1a and 1b: Promoting child development and learning
2a and 2b: Building family and community relationships
3a, 3b, 3c and 3d: Observing, documenting, and assessing to support young children and families
4a: Using developmentally effective approaches
6b and 6e: Becoming a professional

Meet Bhadra and Her Family

Bhadra's parents recently moved to the community where her father would begin working on a graduate degree at the local university. Her family's initial concern was to find a suitable child care program for four-year-old Bhadra, who was bilingual but spoke limited English. A neighbor suggested they contact the Head Start program located on campus to see if they had an opening. Fortunately for Bhadra's parents, the Head Start director was able to offer a space that had been vacated just days before.

The teachers' supportive attention helped ease Bhadra's transition into the program.

continued...

They quickly discovered that she understood more English words than she was able to speak. However, Bhadra's teachers became concerned about her overall development in the weeks and months that followed. She seemed to have difficulty acquiring additional words, frequently looked puzzled when spoken to, and often failed to respond appropriately when given directions. Bhadra seldom interacted with the other children despite their urgings, choosing instead to simply stand and observe. The teachers also expressed concern about her inability to stay engaged in an activity for more than two or three minutes at a time. There was one exception: Bhadra enjoyed painting and would remain at the easel until the teachers gently accompanied her to another activity.

When asked about Bhadra's health history, her mother spoke vaguely of earaches and "runny ears," "hot spells," and "twitches." Bhadra's mother, who recently celebrated her twenty-first birthday, is a thin, pale woman, midway into her second pregnancy. She works full-time in the university cafeteria and is the family's sole breadwinner while her husband attends school.

Bhadra's mother expressed warmth and concern for her daughter but apparently does not understand the importance of seeking medical care for herself or her family. The Head Start teachers have recommended that Bhadra be evaluated by a physician and have her hearing evaluated. However, Bhadra's parents do not have a family doctor or health insurance to help cover expenses. They also seem reluctant to accept that there may be anything wrong with Bhadra, believing instead that "she is only four and will eventually grow out of these problems."

Ask Yourself

1. What observations may have caused Bhadra's teachers to be concerned about her developmental progress?
2. In what ways may Bhadra's environment have contributed to her at-risk behaviors?

Is my child all right? Most parents, at one time or another, have asked this question during their child's early and growing-up years (Figure 10-1) (Restall & Borton, 2010). Many caregivers and teachers ask a similar question about a child who seems "different" from other children with whom they work. Such questions are a positive sign because they indicate awareness and concern. Children, as emphasized in Chapters 1 and 2, vary greatly in their development. Many factors, including genetics, culture, family structure and values, nutrition, health, and poverty can influence the rate and nature of children's

Figure 10-1
Families often wonder if their
child is developing "normally."

developmental progress. It is the rare child who is truly typical in every way. Some children with developmental irregularities of one kind or another do not experience any long-term negative effects. Other children with irregularities that do not appear significant may be at considerable developmental risk. In both instances, it is important that the child be seen by a health care professional or child development specialist and perhaps referred for evaluation and intervention services.

Public Policy and Social Attitudes

Supporting children's optimal development has become a major social and legislative focus. Much of the initial impetus came in the 1960s as part of the antipoverty movement (often referred to as the "war on poverty"). Many precedent-setting research studies provided conclusive evidence that developmental disabilities in infants and young children could be significantly reduced through early intervention. As a result, several major strategies have since evolved. One is based on the prevention of atypical development through improved prenatal care and maternal nutrition. Another is the early identification of children with, or at risk for, developmental problems. Both methods are associated with noteworthy improvements in reducing the incidence and long-term effects of childhood disabilities through a family systems approach (Ceballos & Bratton, 2010; Shulman et al., 2010).

Legislation Supporting Optimum Development

Beginning in the mid-1960s, several pieces of legislation led to the implementation of programs that supported child and family health and helped reduce developmental risks.

- **PL 88-452 Head Start (1965)** This act, part of the antipoverty movement, established the Head Start program and its supplemental services, including developmental screening, medical and dental care, nutrition, parent training, and early education for income-eligible children from three to five years of age. Amendments in 1972 and 1974 mandated Head Start to also serve children with disabilities. Reauthorization in 1994 created Early Head Start programs, which serve infants and toddlers from low-income families.

- **PL 101-239 Early and Periodic Screening, Diagnosis, and Treatment Act (EPSDT) (1967)** This national program was added to Medicaid and continues to serve the health and developmental needs (diagnosis and treatment) of income-eligible children at risk.

- **PL 94-105 Supplemental Nutrition Program for Women, Infants, and Children (WIC) (1975)** This act created a program aimed at improving maternal health during pregnancy, promoting full-term fetal development, and increasing newborn birth weight. Medical supervision, food vouchers, and nutrition education are provided to low-income pregnant and nursing women and their children under age five to ensure a healthy start.

Legislation that specifically addressed the needs of children with developmental differences has also been enacted, including:

- **PL 89-10 Elementary and Secondary Education Act (ESEA) (1965)** This act established federal requirements and funding for U.S. public schools (K–12). Additional funds and resources were authorized for schools and districts (preschool through high school) serving a high proportion of children from low-income families; these programs are designated as Title I programs.

- **PL 90-538 The Handicapped Children's Early Education and Assistance Act (HCEEAA) (1968)** This law provided funding for the establishment of model classrooms to serve preschool children with disabilities.

- **PL 94-142 (1975)** Originally called the **Education for All Handicapped Children Act (EHA)**, this law, now known as Part B, mandates states to provide comprehensive evaluation, "free and appropriate" education, and intervention services for all children ages three to five years who have, or are at-risk for, developmental problems. Amendments in 1990 and 1997 reauthorized the bill, renaming it the Individuals with Disabilities Education Act (IDEA) (PL 101-476).

- **PL 99-457 Education of the Handicapped Act Amendments (1986)** Because the original initiative (PL 94-142) had proven so successful, it was amended to extend early intervention services to infants, toddlers, and their families through the Individualized Family Service Plan (IFSP). This portion of

the bill (now known as Part C of IDEA) is not mandated or fully funded and, therefore, not available in all communities. Additional features of this act include an emphasis on multidisciplinary assessment, a designated service coordinator, a family-focused approach, and a system of service coordination

- **PL 101-336 Americans with Disabilities Act (ADA) (1990)** This national civil rights law protects against discrimination on the basis of a disability. The intent is to remove barriers that interfere with full inclusion in every aspect of society—education, employment, and public services. Implications for children and their families are clear: child care programs are required to adapt their settings and programs to accommodate children with disabilities.

- **PL 108-446 The Individuals with Disabilities Education Improvement Act of 2004 (2004)** This reauthorization of the original act (PL 94-142) increased accountability for children's educational outcomes, improved identification methods, enhanced family involvement, and reduced the amount of required paperwork. Guidelines for appropriate discipline of students with disabilities were also included.

- **PL 107-110 No Child Left Behind Act (NCLB) (2002)** This legislation, a reauthorization of the Elementary and Secondary Education Act (ESEA), addressed the problems of academic inequity and failure in this country. Its aim is to improve the quality of educational opportunities for all children and to increase academic success rates by making schools and teachers accountable. The current administration is preparing for the reauthorization of ESEA (including NCLB) and is considering reforms which would improve accountability, invest in educators, and focus more directly on students most at risk.

▶❚❚ TeachSource Video Connections

Including Children with Developmental Disabilities. Schools are experiencing many changes in their educational practices as a result of recent legislation—some are considered improvements while others continue to be debated. As you watch the learning video *Foundations: Aligning Instruction with Federal Legislation*, on the Education CourseMate website, consider the following questions:

1. What is the ultimate goal of No Child Left Behind?
2. Are these expectations reasonable for all students?
3. What limitations of this law were expressed by the experienced teachers?

Early Identification and Intervention Programs

Legislative and public policy changes have established several avenues for getting children with suspected developmental problems into appropriate evaluation and early-intervention programs.

Figure 10-2
Developmental delays
associated with certain
medical conditions and
syndromes are better
understood today.

Infants and Children at Medical Risk

Family physicians and pediatricians are becoming increasingly aware of the importance of evaluating infants and young children for developmental and behavioral problems (King et al., 2010) (Figure 10-2). Many pediatric practices today ask families to complete a developmental screening tool such as the Abbreviated Denver Developmental Screening Test, the Revised Parent Developmental Questionnaire, or the Ages and Stages Questionnaire during each office visit so that children's progress can be monitored more closely (Thompson et al., 2010; Schonwald et al., 2009). Physicians are also paying earlier attention to deviations in infants' neurological development that might indicate a potential irregularity and are referring families to genetic, neurological, and child development specialists for further evaluation. These trends have contributed to the earlier detection of high-risk conditions often associated with developmental delays.

Another group of children at medical risk for developmental problems includes infants discharged from premature nurseries and neonatal intensive care units. Many communities in urban areas now have follow-up clinics for this high-risk group. Continued monitoring of children born prematurely permits the early detection of any developmental irregularities or delays. Children with suspect development are typically referred to early childhood screening and intervention programs where they can receive needed services.

Older children's development can also be affected at any time by a variety of medical conditions such as diabetes, hearing loss, communicable diseases, or arthritis. Daily

observations become especially important in these situations so that any changes in a child's behavior or classroom performance are immediately noted. Intervention services can then be initiated in the early stages and, thus, lessen the negative effects a medical condition might otherwise have on children's learning and development.

Community Screening

The majority of young children who will benefit from early identification and intervention do not always come from medically high-risk groups. These children may be located most effectively through a variety of community screening services.

Screening programs are designed to identify children who have or might be at risk for developmental problems. The primary emphasis is on evaluating a child's hearing and vision, general health, speech and language, motor skills, and overall developmental progress. Most screening tests are easily administered locally to large numbers of children. Some procedures can be accessed through local public health departments, Head Start programs, community colleges and universities, clinics, public schools, and early education programs. Teachers and volunteers can also be trained to conduct certain types of screenings such as measurements of children's height, weight, and vision. More advanced training is usually required to administer other forms of assessment such as hearing, speech and language, and developmental progress. Early screening and detection of developmental disabilities permits children to receive intervention services before they reach school age. Delays in providing needed therapies and educational services can reduce the chances of successfully improving or overcoming some conditions.

Child Find is a nationwide system of screening programs mandated by IDEA and administered by individual states (Pizur-Bamekow et al., 2010; Bateman, 2009). Its purpose is twofold. One is to raise public awareness about developmental disabilities and to locate eligible infants and young children who have undiagnosed developmental problems or are at risk for the onset of such problems. The second purpose is to help families locate appropriate diagnostic screenings and intervention programs and services. The law (IDEA) requires all states to establish a Child Find system, identify eligibility criteria, and develop service guidelines.

 ## Is There a Problem?

Deciding whether a developmental delay or irregularity is of serious concern is not always easy. The signs can be so subtle, so hard to pinpoint, that it is often difficult to distinguish clearly between children who have a definite problem, the definite *yeses*, and those who definitely do not have a problem, the definite *nos*. Identifying the *maybes*—is there or is there not a problem—can be an even more complex issue.

Child Find—a screening program designed to locate children with developmental problems through improved public awareness.

In determining whether a delay or deviation is of real concern, several factors may complicate the matter. For example:

- Children who exhibit signs of developmental problems in certain areas often continue to develop like a typical child in every other way; such children present a confusing developmental profile. (See Developmental Checklists in Appendix A.)

- Great variation exists in the range of an individual child's achievements within developmental areas. The rate of maturation is uneven, and conditions in the child's environment are continually changing. Both maturation and environment interact to exert a strong influence on every aspect of development.

- Family beliefs, values, and cultural background exert a direct influence on child-rearing practices (Trawick-Smith, 2009). Developmental milestones are not universal; how they are perceived varies from culture to culture and from family to family. Thus, respect for diverse family and community lifestyles must always be taken into consideration when gathering and interpreting information about a child's development (Figure 10-3).

- Developmental delays or problems may not be immediately apparent. Many children learn to compensate for a deficiency. For example, children who have a mild to moderate hearing loss might position themselves closer to the teacher during story time so they can hear. Children who experience difficulty learning to read might depend on other cognitive strategies to overcome their disability. Sometimes deficiencies do not become apparent until the child is placed in structured and more demanding situations (as in a first-grade reading class) (Allen & Cowdery, 2012).

Figure 10-3
Diversity of family and community values, beliefs, and cultural differences must be considered and treated with respect and dignity.

- Intermittent health problems can affect children's performance. For example, a child may have severe and recurring bouts of **otitis media** that appear to clear up completely between episodes. A hearing test administered when the child is free of infection may reveal no hearing loss, although the same child might be quite deaf during an acute infection. Intermittent periods of hearing loss, sometimes lasting a week or more, can result in language and cognitive delays and severely challenging behaviors in some children (Stevenson et al., 2010). During these periods, children's perception of word and letter sounds may be distorted and result in learned mispronunciations over time. Children may also unknowingly misbehave or disregard requests and instructions simply because they cannot hear. Unfortunately, these behaviors may be misinterpreted as problematic instead of recognizing them as a sign of a medical problem that is interfering with a child's ability to learn.

When to Seek Help

At what point should a hunch or uncomfortable feeling about a child be a call for action? The answer is clear: whenever families or teachers are concerned about a child's development or behavior! Any such uneasiness needs to be discussed with a pediatrician, health care provider, or child development specialist.

Concern about a developmental irregularity also demands investigation anytime it interferes with a child's participation in everyday activities. The frequent occurrence or repetition of a troublesome behavior is often a reliable sign that professional help should be sought. However, seldom is a single incidence of a questionable behavior cause for concern. What is of concern is a child's *continuing* reluctance to attempt a new skill or to acquire a basic developmental skill fully. For example, a ten-month-old who tries to sit alone but still must use both hands for support might or might not have a problem. On the other hand, clusters of developmental differences are always significant—a ten-month-old who is not sitting without support, not smiling, and not babbling in response to others is likely to be at developmental risk.

What should teachers and caregivers do when a family fails to express concern or denies the possibility of a problem? Although it may be difficult, it is the teacher's responsibility to discuss any concerns in a conference with the family. In that setting, every effort must be made to be straightforward and objective. Teachers must report only what has been observed and what they would expect to see based on the child's developmental stage. Teachers must also refrain from making a diagnosis or labeling the child's behavior. For example, a teacher should say, "Danesha avoids eye contact and often responds inappropriately to questions," rather than "Danesha is probably autistic." Teachers should work closely with the family to help them understand and accept the child's need for further evaluation. Under no circumstances should a teacher or administrator bypass family members and make referrals without their permission. However, teachers can offer their support and willingness to assist families in making the necessary arrangements.

---

otitis media—an infection of the middle ear.

TeachSource Video Connections

Children with Developmental Disabilities in the Classroom. The importance of identifying children's developmental disabilities early and arranging appropriate intervention services has been stressed throughout the book. The lives of many children have benefitted as a result of the improved awareness, knowledge, and dedication of families and teachers. As you watch the learning video, *5–11 Years: Developmental Disabilities in Middle Childhood*, on the Education Course-Mate website, consider the following questions:

1. Why must first-person language always be used when referring to children with a disability?
2. How would you justify the importance of early identification, early intervention, and inclusionary practices after watching this video?
3. What social skills does each child in the video have that are similar to their typically developing counterparts? How do they differ?

 # Information Gathering

Multiple levels of information gathering must be included in a developmental evaluation: observation and recording, screening, and diagnostic assessment. Diagnostic assessment includes in-depth testing and clinical interpretation of results. Clinicians from various disciplines should participate in the diagnosis. It is their responsibility to provide detailed information about the specific nature of the child's problems. For example, a four-year-old's delayed speech might be observed by family members and noted during routine screening procedures. Subsequent diagnostic testing by clinicians may pinpoint several other conditions: a moderate, **bilateral** hearing loss, poor production of many letter sounds, and an expressive vocabulary typical of a three-year-old. These clinical findings can be translated into specific educational strategies and intervention procedures that will ultimately benefit the child's overall development.

Observing and Recording

The evaluation process always begins with systematic observation (see Chapter 1). Noting and recording various aspects of a child's behavior enables the evaluator—whether a family member, a teacher, or a clinician—to focus on what is actually occurring. In other words, observations yield objective information about what the child can and cannot do at the time of the observation.

---

bilateral—affecting both sides, as in loss of hearing in both ears.

An effective evaluation is also based on multiple observations, conducted over a period of days and in a variety of natural settings that are familiar to the child. Direct observation often confirms or rules out impressions or suspicions regarding a child's abilities (Keilty, LaRocca, & Casell, 2009). For example, a child might not count to five when asked to do so in a testing situation. That same child, however, may be observed counting seven or eight objects spontaneously and correctly while at play in the block area. A child thought to have attention deficit/hyperactivity disorder (ADHD) might be observed sitting quietly for five to ten minutes when given more interesting and challenging activities, thereby ruling out concerns about hyperactivity. *Note:* The term *hyperactive* is greatly overused and misused. A child should not be so labeled unless specifically diagnosed by a multidisciplinary team. Focusing on a child at play, alone or with other children, can be particularly revealing. Again, no evaluation is valid without direct and objective observations of a child in familiar surroundings.

A family's observations are an especially valuable component of the assessment process (Figure 10-4). Family members are often able to provide information that is not available from other sources. Their observations also give insight into unique family attitudes, perceptions, and expectations concerning the child. Involving families in the observation phase of evaluation also helps to reduce some of their anxieties. Furthermore, direct observation often points out unrecognized strengths and abilities. When family members have an opportunity to see their child engaged in appropriate activities, it may encourage them to focus more on the child's strengths and abilities rather than limitations.

Figure 10-4
Families contribute information that adds insight and meaning to the evaluation process.

Screening Tests

Screening tests are useful for gathering general information about children's developmental problems and determining whether more comprehensive evaluation is needed. They are designed to assess a child's current abilities as well as potential delays in fine and large motor skills, cognition, speech and language development, and personal and social responsiveness.

If problems or suspected problems are noted during an initial screening, further in-depth clinical assessment by a child development specialist is needed before a final diagnosis can be reached. *Note:* Results obtained from screening tests are neither conclusive nor diagnostic. They do not predict a child's future abilities or achievement potential and should not be used as a basis for planning intervention programs.

Several questions should be asked when choosing or interpreting a screening instrument:

- Is it appropriate for the child's age?
- Is it free of bias related to the child's economic, geographic, or cultural background (Erkut, 2010)?
- Can it be administered in the child's native language (Bornman et al., 2010)? If not, is a skilled interpreter available to assist the child and family?
- Is it reliable for identifying children who should be referred for further testing from those who do not require additional evaluation at this time?

A sample of widely used screening tests and assessment instruments is provided in Appendix B. Included are examples of ecological evaluations of home and school; information about the child's everyday surroundings is essential to gather and use in interpreting testing results and planning prevention and intervention programs.

Interpreting Screening Results

The widespread availability of community-based screening programs has contributed to the early detection of potential developmental problems among young children. However, the findings are always open to question. In some cases, the screening process itself may have a negative effect on the outcome. Children's attention spans, especially those of young children, are often short and inconsistent from day to day and from task to task. Illness, fatigue, anxiety, hunger, lack of cooperation, irritability, or distractions can also lead to unreliable results. Children may perform poorly when they are unaccustomed to being tested or unfamiliar with the person who is conducting the test. They are also more likely to cooperate and perform reliably when they are evaluated in familiar surroundings. Consequently, results derived from screening assessments must be regarded with caution. The following points are intended as reminders for both families and teachers.

- Avoid conclusions based on limited information or a single test score. The results may not be an accurate representation of the child's actual development or developmental potential. Only repeated and periodic observation will provide a comprehensive picture of the child's developing abilities (Salvia, Ysseldyke, & Bolt, 2010).

Figure 10-5
Labels are inappropriate
unless a disability has been
documented.

- Never underestimate the influence of home and family on a child's performance (Pang, 2010). Newer screening procedures make a greater effort to promote family participation and to evaluate family concerns, priorities, and resources. There also is increasing emphasis on screening in familiar or naturalistic environments and everyday situations where children feel more secure and at ease.

- Recognize the dangers of labeling a child as having a learning disability, mental retardation, speech impairment, or behavior disorder, especially on the basis of single test results. Labels can have a negative effect on expectations for both the child and the way in which adults respond to the child unless they have been validated through appropriate testing (Figure 10-5).

- Question test scores. Test results can easily be misinterpreted. One test might suggest that a child has a developmental delay when actually nothing is wrong. Such conclusions are called *false positives*. The opposite conclusion can also be reached. A child may have a developmental problem that does not show up in the screening process and so might be incorrectly identified as normal. This is a *false negative*. The first situation leads to unnecessary anxiety and disappointment and might change the way the family responds to their child. The latter situation, the false negative, can lull a family into not seeking further help, so the effect of the child's problem worsens. Both situations can be avoided through careful interpretation of test scores.

- Understand that results from screening tests *do not* constitute a diagnosis. Additional information must be collected and in-depth clinical testing completed before a diagnosis is given or confirmed (Roberts, Anderson, & Doyle, 2010). Even then, errors can occur. There are many reasons for misdiagnosis, such as inconsistent and rapid changes in a child's growth or changing environmental factors such as divorce or family relocation.

- Do not use failed items on a screening test as curriculum items or skills to be taught; a test item is simply one isolated example of a broad range of skills to be expected in a given developmental area at an approximate age. For example, a child who is unable to stand on one foot for five seconds will not overcome a developmental problem by being taught to stand on one foot for a given time period. *Screening test items are not a suitable basis for constructing curriculum activities.*

- Recognize that test results do not predict the child's developmental future, nor do they necessarily correlate with subsequent testing. There is always the need for *ongoing* observation, assessment, and in-depth clinical diagnosis when screening tests indicate potential problems and delays.

IQ Tests: Are They Appropriate for Young Children?

Intelligence tests, such as the Wechsler Intelligence Scale for Children (WISC) and the Stanford Binet Intelligence Scales, were not designed or intended to be used as screening instruments (Mindes, 2010). Neither are they regarded by most developmental specialists as appropriate to use with young children for any purpose. IQ tests administered during the early years are not valid predictors of future or even current intellectual performance. Nor do they predict subsequent academic performance. IQ tests do not take into account the opportunities a child has had to learn, the quality of those learning experiences, or what the *dominant culture* says a child should know at a given age. Children raised in poverty or in non-English-speaking homes often do not have the same opportunities to acquire specific kinds of information represented by the test items. For example, studies have identified maternal education as an important predictor of children's academic achievement, especially among ethnically diverse and low-income families (Hanson et al., 2011). Therefore, an IQ test score used as the sole determinant of a child's cognitive or intellectual development must be challenged.

Achievement Tests

The administration of formal **achievement tests** in elementary and secondary schools has become a widespread practice since the passage of No Child Left Behind (Figure 10-6). These tests are designed to measure how much the child has learned in school about specific subject areas (Wiliam, 2010). Depending on the results, each child is assigned a percentile ranking, based on a comparison with other children of the same grade level. For example, a child in the 50th percentile in mathematics is doing as well as 50 percent of the

---

achievement tests—tests used to measure a child's academic progress (what the child has learned).

Figure 10-6
Achievement tests are often administered to assess student learning.

children in the same grade. Test results are increasingly being used to determine children's placement, assess teacher performance, and evaluate a school's overall academic effectiveness (Mumane & Papay, 2010). Again, test scores should be backed up by observations of children and collected samples (portfolios) of their work to have valid meaning.

Diagnosis and Referral

Information obtained from authentic assessment, including direct observations and samples of children's products, combined with screening test results, provides the basis for the next question: Are comprehensive diagnostic procedures required? Not all children will require an in-depth clinical assessment, but many will if they and their family are to receive the best possible referral for intervention services. Families can be directed to early childhood intervention programs (Child Find) in their community for evaluation and services offered under Part B for preschool-age children and Part C for infants and toddlers. Evaluation and assessment services are available to school-age children through their local school system. An interdisciplinary team approach that combines the input of clinicians, child development specialists, and the child's family is always essential for achieving effective and meaningful diagnoses and referrals.

The Developmental Team

Federal law (PL 105-17, IDEA) requires families to be involved in all phases of the assessment and intervention process. They become important members of the child's **developmental team** when they work collaboratively with educators and multidisciplinary

---

developmental team—a team of qualified professionals such as special educators, speech pathologists, occupational therapists, social workers, audiologists, nurses, and physical therapists who evaluate a child's developmental progress and together prepare an intervention plan that addresses the child's special needs.

professionals. A family-centered approach improves information sharing and enables family members to learn and implement therapy recommendations at home (Swanson, Raab, & Dunst, 2011;Trivette, Dunst, & Hamby, 2010). Sustained interest and participation in the child's intervention program can be achieved when the developmental team:

- Keeps families informed.
- Explains rationales for treatment procedures.
- Uses terms that families can understand and takes time to explain those that may not be familiar.
- Emphasizes the child's progress.
- Teaches family members how to work with their child at home.
- Provides families with positive feedback and supports their continued efforts and advocacy on the child's behalf.

Best practice suggests that the pooling of knowledge and multidisciplinary expertise is required to manage children's developmental disabilities effectively—in other words, a team approach. For example, a team effort provides the most accurate picture of how a delay in one area can affect development in other areas, just as progress in one area supports progress in others. A two-year-old with a hearing loss could potentially experience delays in language as well as in the areas of cognitive and social-emotional development. Thus, appropriate intervention strategies for this child might require the services of an audiologist, speech and language therapist, early childhood teacher, nurse, and, perhaps, social worker. If a team approach is to benefit the child's overall development, effective communication and cooperation among specialists, service providers, and the family is essential. This process is facilitated by the inclusion of an Individual Family Service Plan (IFSP for infants and toddlers) or an Individualized Educational Plan (IEP for preschool through school-age children).

Family Service Coordinator

Many families are overwhelmed by the process of approaching multiple agencies and dealing with bureaucratic red tape. As a result, they often fail or are unable to complete the necessary arrangements unless they receive assistance. This supportive role was viewed as so crucial to successful intervention that the position of **Family Service Coordinator** was written into federal legislation (PL 99-457, Part C) to help families address their infants' and toddlers' developmental problems. A Family Service Coordinator works closely with families, matching their needs and their child's needs with appropriate community

---

Family Service Coordinator—an individual who serves as a family's advocate and assists them with identifying, locating, and making final arrangements with community services.

services and educational programs. The coordinator also assists the family in establishing initial contacts and provides continued support.

Referral

The referral process involves a multiple-step approach. As described earlier, the child's strengths, weaknesses, and developmental skills are evaluated. The family's needs and resources (such as financial, psychological, physical, and transportation capabilities) must also be taken into consideration. For example, if a family cannot afford special services, has no knowledge of financial assistance programs, and does not own a car, it is unlikely they will be able to follow through on professional recommendations. However, such problems are seldom insurmountable. Most communities have individuals and social service agencies available to assist families in meeting these needs and arranging for intervention services.

Placement in an appropriate educational setting is frequently recommended as part of the intervention plan. In these settings, classroom teachers, child development specialists, and other members of the developmental team conduct ongoing assessments of the child's progress (Figure 10-7). In addition, the developmental team reviews the appropriateness of the placement and special services provided on a regular basis to determine whether the child's and family's needs are being met. This step is especially critical with infants and toddlers because their development progresses so quickly. Throughout, there must be effective communication and support among teachers, practitioners, and families to ensure that the child is receiving individually appropriate services and benefiting from the prescribed program.

Figure 10-7
Collaboration among teachers, families, and service providers is essential to an effective intervention plan.

SUMMARY

Beginning in the mid-1960s, a series of federal laws changed public attitudes and policies related to persons with developmental disabilities. Several laws focus on infants and children with, or who are at risk for, developmental problems. Mandated specifically are programs concerned with prevention, early identification, and intervention where there is an obvious or potential problem. The role of the family is formally recognized as essential to meeting the child's needs, as is the clinical expertise from an interdisciplinary team. Integral to the family–team collaboration approach is a designated Family Service Coordinator who orchestrates the needs, concerns, and recommendations of the child, family, and team members.

Any concern about a child's development demands immediate evaluation. The starting point is firsthand observation of the child in a familiar, everyday (natural) environment. If warranted, several screening tests appropriate to the child's age, language, and culture should be administered and all results interpreted with caution. *Remember:* The findings of a single test are likely to yield a misleading outcome. In-depth clinical diagnosis should follow if observation and screening results identify a developmental problem. Therapeutic intervention for infants, toddlers, and preschoolers often includes placement in an early education program. A Family Service Coordinator works closely with the child, family, and early intervention program to assure a successful plan. An IEP is developed for school-age children identified as having a disability and appropriate services provided in the least restrictive environment (usually the school).

Key Terms

Child Find **p. 247**

otitis media **p. 249**

bilateral **p. 250**

achievement tests **p. 254**

developmental team **p. 255**

Family Service Coordinator **p. 256**

Apply What You Know

A. Apply What You Have Learned

Reread the brief developmental sketch about Bhadra and her family at the beginning of the chapter and answer the following questions.

1. Prior to holding a first conference with Bhadra's mother, what observations and information should her teachers gather and prepare?
2. Why is it imperative that the teachers' initial evaluation of Bhadra's development include a series of firsthand observations (and recorded notes) conducted in a familiar setting such as the classroom and play yard?
3. Describe three pieces of legislation discussed in this chapter that could be of benefit to a high-risk family such as Bhadra's.
4. What role and what forms of assistance might a Family Service Coordinator provide for Bhadra's family?

B. Review Questions

1. Identify and discuss three concerns that might prevent families from seeking help for their child.
2. What three features must be considered when determining if a screening test is appropriate for a given child.
3. Identify and discuss three reasons why it is important to encourage family involvement in a child's intervention program.
4. Describe three factors that may complicate the early identification of a developmental problem.
5. Describe three reasons why screening test results should be interpreted with caution.

Helpful Websites

Center for the Study of Autism
http://www.autism.org

Family and Advocates Partnership for Education (FAPE)
http://www.fape.org

National Center on Secondary Education and Transition (NCSET)
http://www.ncset.org

The Iris Center
http://iris.peabody.vanderbilt.edu/index.html

References

Allen, K., & Cowdery, G. (2012). *The exceptional child: Inclusion in early childhood education.* (7th ed.). Belmont, CA: Wadsworth Cengage Learning.

Bateman, D. (2009). Due process hearing case study, *Teaching Exceptional Children, 42*(2), 73–75.

Bornman, J., Sevcik, R., Romski, M., & Pae, H. (2010). Successfully translating language and culture when adapting assessment measures, *Journal of Policy and Practice in Intellectual Disabilities, 7*(2), 111–118.

Ceballos, P., & Bratton, S. (2010). Empowering Latino families: Effects of a culturally responsive intervention for low-income immigrant Latino parents on children's behaviors and parental stress, *Psychology in the Schools, 47*(8), 761–775.

Erkut, S. (2010). Developing multiple language versions of instruments for intercultural research, *Child Development Perspectives, 4*(1), 19–24.

Hanson, M., Miller, A., Diamond, K., Odom, S., Lieber, J., Butera, G., Horn, E., Palmer, S., & Fleming, K. (2011). Neighborhood community risk influences on preschool children's development and school readiness, *Infants & Young Children, 24*(1), 87–100.

Keilty, B., LaRocco, D., & Casell, F. (2009). Early interventionists' reports of authentic assessment methods through focus group research, *Topics in Early Childhood Special Education, 28*(4), 244–256.

King, T., Tandon, D., Macias, M., Healy, J., Duncan, P., Swigonski, N., Skipper, S., & Lipkin, P. (2010). Implementing developmental screening and referrals: Lessons learned from a national project, *Pediatrics, 125*(2), 350–360.

Mindes, G. (2010). *Assessing young children.* (4th ed.). Upper Saddle River, NJ: Prentice Hall.

Mumane, R., & Papay, J. (2010). Teachers' views on No Child Left Behind: Support for the principles, concerns about the practices, *Journal of Economic Perspectives*, *24*(3), 151–166.

Pang, Y. (2010). Selecting appropriate assessment instruments to ensure quality transition services, *Early Childhood Education Journal*, *38*(1), 43–48.

Pizur-Bamekow, K., Erickson, S., Johnston, M., Bass, T., Lucinski, L., & Bleuel, D. (2010). Early identification of developmental delays through surveillance, screening, and diagnostic evaluation, *Infants & Young Children*, *23*(4), 323–330.

Restall, G., & Borton, B. (2010). Parents' concerns about their children's development at school entry, *Child: Care, Health & Development*, *36*(2), 208–215.

Roberts, G., Anderson, P., & Doyle, L. (2010). The stability of the diagnosis of developmental disability between ages 2 and 8 in a geographic cohort of very preterm children born in 1997, *Archives of Disease in Childhood*, *95*(10), 786–790.

Salvia, J., Ysseldyke, J., & Bolt, S. (2010). *Assessment: In special and inclusive education*. (11th ed.). Belmont, CA: Wadsworth Cengage Learning.

Schonwald, A., Huntington, N., Chan, E., Risko, W., & Bridgemohan, C. (2009). Routine developmental screening implemented in urban primary care settings: More evidence of feasibility and effectiveness, *Pediatrics*, *123*(2), 660–668.

Shulman, S., Besculides, M., Saltzman, A., Ireys, H., White, K., & Forsman, I. (2010). Evaluation of the Universal Newborn Hearing Screening and Intervention Program, *Pediatrics*, *126*, S19–S27.

Stevenson, J., McCann, D., Watkin, P., Worsfold, S., & Kennedy, C. (2010). The relationship between language development and behaviour problems in children with hearing loss, *Journal of Child Psychology & Psychiatry*, *51*(1), 77–83.

Swanson, J., Raab, M., & Dunst, C. (2011). Strengthening family capacity to provide young children with everyday natural learning opportunities, *Journal of Early Childhood Research*, *9*(1), 66–80.

Thompson, L., Tuli, S., Saliba, H., DiPietro, M., & Nackashi, J. (2010). Improving developmental screening in pediatric resident education, *Clinical Pediatrics*, *49*(8), 737–742.

Trawick-Smith, J. (2009). *Early childhood development: A multicultural perspective*. (5th ed.). Upper Saddle River, NJ: Prentice Hall.

Trivette, C., Dunst, C., & Hamby, D. (2010). Influences of family-systems intervention practices on parent-child interactions and child development, *Topics in Early Childhood Special Education*, *30*(1), 3–19.

Wiliam, D. (2010). What counts as evidence of educational achievement? The role of constructs in the pursuit of equity in assessment, *Review of Research in Education*, *34*(1), 254–284.

 You are just a click away from a variety of interactive study tools and helpful resources. Access the text's Education CourseMate website at **http://www.cengagebrain.com**, where you'll find a variety of enrichment materials, including videos, glossary flashcards, activities, tutorial quizzes, web links, and more.

Developmental Checklists

A simple checklist, one for each child, can be a useful tool for observing young children and adolescents. Questions on the checklists that follow can be answered during the course of a child's everyday activities and over a period of one week or more. "No" answers signal that further investigation may be in order. Several "No" answers indicate that additional investigation is a necessity.

The "Sometimes" category is also an important one. It suggests what the child can do at least part of the time or under some circumstances. The "Sometimes" category includes space where brief notes and comments about how and when a behavior occurs can be recorded. In many instances, a child may simply need more practice, incentive, or adult encouragement. Hunches often provide an effective starting point for working with the child. Again, if "Sometimes" is checked a number of times, additional evaluation is recommended.

The observation checklists may be duplicated and used as part of the assessment process. They are based on detailed information provided in each of the preceding chapters. The items represent a sampling of developmental milestones associated with each approximate age. When completed, a checklist contains information that members of a developmental team will find useful in evaluating a child's progress and determining appropriate intervention strategies. However, it is important to interpret these findings cautiously and consider cultural, linguistic, and family background variations that may influence children's development.

Child's Name _____   **Age** _____

Observer _____   **Date** _____

DEVELOPMENTAL CHECKLIST

BY SIX MONTHS *Does the child . . .*	Yes	No	Sometimes
Show continued gains in height, weight, and head circumference?			
Reach for toys or objects when they are presented?			
Begin to roll from stomach to back?			
Sit with minimal support?			
Transfer objects from one hand to the other?			
Rise up on arms, lifting head and chest, when placed on stomach?			
Babble, coo, and imitate sounds?			
Turn to locate the source of a sound?			
Focus on an object and follow its movement vertically and horizontally?			
Exhibit a blink reflex?			
Stop crying and relax when held and cuddled?			
Recognize and respond to familiar faces?			
Begin sleeping six to eight hours through the night?			
Suck vigorously when it is time to eat?			
Enjoy (splash, coo) playing in water during bath time?			

Child's Name _____ Age _____

Observer _____ Date _____

DEVELOPMENTAL CHECKLIST

BY TWELVE MONTHS	Yes	No	Sometimes
Does the child . . .			
Walk with assistance?			
Roll a ball in imitation of an adult?			
Pick objects up with thumb and forefinger?			
Transfer objects from one hand to the other?			
Pick up dropped toys?			
Look directly at an adult's face?			
Imitate gestures: peek-a-boo, bye-bye, pat-a-cake?			
Find object hidden under a cup?			
Feed oneself crackers (munching, not sucking on them)?			
Hold cup with two hands; drink with assistance?			
Smile spontaneously?			
Turn head or come when name is called?			
Respond to "no" and "come"?			
Show hesitation with strangers; want to be picked up only by familiar persons?			
Respond differently to sounds: vacuum, phone, door?			
Look at person who speaks to him or her?			
Respond to simple directions accompanied by gestures?			
Make several consonant–vowel combination sounds?			
Vocalize back to person who has talked to him or her?			
Use intonation patterns that sound like scolding, asking, exclaiming?			
Say "da-da" or "ma-ma"?			

Child's Name _____   **Age** _____

Observer _____   **Date** _____

DEVELOPMENTAL CHECKLIST

BY TWO YEARS	Yes	No	Sometimes
Does the child . . .			
Walk alone?			
Bend over and pick up a toy without falling over?			
Climb up and sit in a child-size chair?			
Walk up and down stairs with assistance?			
Place several rings on a stick?			
Place five pegs in a pegboard?			
Turn pages two or three at a time?			
Scribble?			
Follow one-step direction involving something familiar:			
"Give me _____,"			
"Show me _____,"			
"Get a _____"?			
Match familiar objects?			
Use a spoon with some spilling?			
Drink from cup, holding it with one hand unassisted?			
Take off coat, shoe, sock?			
Zip and unzip large zipper?			
Name and point to self in a mirror?			
Refer to self by name?			
Imitate adult behavior in play—for example, feeds "baby?"			
Help put things away?			
Respond to specific words by showing what was named: toy, pet, family member?			
Ask for desired items by name: "cookie"?			
Name an object when asked "What's that?"			
Make and maintain eye contact when asking or responding to questions?			
Utter some two-word statements: "Daddy bye-bye?"			

Child's Name _____ Age _____

Observer _____ Date _____

DEVELOPMENTAL CHECKLIST

BY THREE YEARS	Yes	No	Sometimes
Does the child . . .			
Run with coordination in a forward direction; avoid running into objects or people?			
Jump in place, two feet together?			
Walk heel to toe (not on tiptoe)?			
Throw a ball (but without direction or aim)? Kick ball forward?			
String four large beads?			
Turn pages in book singly?			
Hold crayon: imitate circular, vertical, horizontal strokes?			
Match shapes?			
Demonstrate number concepts of 1 and 2? (Can select 1 or 2; can tell if one or two objects.)			
Use a spoon without spilling?			
Drink from a straw?			
Put on and take off coat?			
Wash and dry hands with some assistance?			
Watch other children; play near them; sometimes join in their play?			
Defend own possessions?			
Use symbols in play (basket placed on head becomes a helmet, crate turns into a spaceship)?			
Respond to "Put _____ in the box," "Take the _____ out of the box"?			
Select correct item on request (big versus little; one versus two)?			
Identify objects by their use (show their own shoe when asked "What do you wear on your feet?")?			
Ask questions and make eye contact?			
Tell about something with functional phrases that carry meaning ("Daddy go airplane," "Me hungry now")?			

Child's Name _____ Age _____

Observer _____ Date _____

DEVELOPMENTAL CHECKLIST

BY FOUR YEARS *Does the child . . .*	Yes	No	Sometimes
Walk on a line?			
Balance on one foot briefly? Hop on one foot?			
Jump over an object six inches high and land on both feet together?			
Throw a ball with direction?			
Copy circles and Xs?			
Match six colors?			
Count to 5?			
Pour well from a pitcher?			
Spread butter, jam with a knife?			
Button, unbutton large buttons?			
State own gender, age, last name?			
Use toilet independently and when needed?			
Wash and dry hands unassisted?			
Listen to stories for at least five minutes?			
Draw head of a person and at least one other body part?			
Play with other children?			
Share, take turns (with some assistance)?			
Engage in dramatic and pretend play?			
Respond appropriately to "Put it beside," "Put it under"?			
Respond to two-step directions: "Give me the sweater and put the shoe on the floor"?			
Respond by selecting the correct object (hard versus soft object)?			
Answer "if," "what," and "when" questions?			
Answer questions about function: "What are books for?"			
Make and maintain eye contact?			

Child's Name _____ Age _____

Observer _____ Date _____

DEVELOPMENTAL CHECKLIST

BY FIVE YEARS	Yes	No	Sometimes
Does the child . . .			
Walk backward, toe to heel?			
Walk up and down stairs, alternating feet?			
Cut on line?			
Print some letters?			
Point to and name three shapes?			
Group common related objects: shoe, sock, and foot; apple, orange, and plum?			
Demonstrate number concepts to 4 or 5?			
Cut food with a knife: celery, sandwich?			
Lace shoes?			
Read from story picture book (tell story by looking at pictures)?			
Draw a person with three to six body parts?			
Play and interact with other children; engage in dramatic play that is close to reality?			
Build complex structures with blocks or other building materials?			
Respond to simple three-step directions: "Give me the pencil, put the book on the table, and put your feet on the floor"?			
Respond correctly when asked to show penny, nickel, and dime?			
Ask "How" questions?			
Respond verbally to "Hi" and "How are you?"			
Describe an event using past and future tenses?			
Use conjunctions to string words and phrases together ("I saw a bear and a zebra and a giraffe at the zoo")?			

Child's Name _____ **Age** _____

Observer _____ **Date** _____

DEVELOPMENTAL CHECKLIST

BY SIX YEARS	Yes	No	Sometimes
Does the child . . .			
Walk across a balance beam?			
Skip with alternating feet?			
Hop for several seconds on one foot?			
Cut out simple shapes?			
Copy his or her own first name?			
Show well-established handedness; demonstrate consistent right- or left-handedness?			
Sort objects on one or more dimensions (color, shape, or function)?			
Name most letters and numerals?			
Count by rote to 10; know what number comes next?			
Dress self completely; tie bows?			
Brush teeth unassisted?			
Have some concept of clock time in relation to daily schedule?			
Cross street safely, holding an adult's hand?			
Draw a person with head, trunk, legs, arms, and features; often add clothing details?			
Play simple board games?			
Engage in cooperative play with other children; participate in group decisions, role assignments, and rule observance?			
Use construction toys such as Legos and blocks to make recognizable structures?			
Do fifteen-piece puzzles?			
Use all grammatical structures: pronouns, plurals, verb tenses, conjunctions?			
Carry on conversations using complex sentences?			

Child's Name _____ Age _____

Observer _____ Date _____

DEVELOPMENTAL CHECKLIST

BY SEVEN YEARS	Yes	No	Sometimes
Does the child . . .			
Continue to grow in height and weight?			
Concentrate on completing puzzles and board games?			
Ask many questions?			
Use correct verb tenses, word order, and sentence structure in conversation?			
Correctly identify right and left hands?			
Make friends easily?			
Show some control of anger, using words instead of physical aggression?			
Participate in play that requires teamwork and rule observance?			
Seek adult approval for efforts?			
Enjoy reading and being read to?			
Use a pencil to write words and numbers?			
Sleep undisturbed through the night?			
Catch a tennis ball, walk across a balance beam, hit a ball with a bat?			
Plan and carry out simple projects with minimal adult help?			
Tie his or her own shoes?			
Draw pictures with greater detail and sense of proportion?			
Care for own personal needs with some adult supervision? Wash hands? Brush teeth? Use toilet? Dress self?			
Show some understanding of cause-and-effect concepts?			

Child's Name _____ **Age** _____

Observer _____ **Date** _____

DEVELOPMENTAL CHECKLIST

BY EIGHT YEARS *Does the child . . .*	Yes	No	Sometimes
Have energy to play?			
Continue to grow and experience few illnesses?			
Use a pencil in a deliberate and controlled manner?			
Express relatively complex thoughts in a clear and logical fashion?			
Carry out multiple four- or five-step instructions?			
Become less easily frustrated with his or her own performance?			
Interact and play cooperatively with other children?			
Show interest in creative expression (telling stories, jokes, writing, drawing, singing)?			
Use eating utensils with ease?			
Have a good appetite? Show interest in trying new foods?			
Know how to tell time?			
Read and comprehend the story?			
Participate in some group activities (games, sports, plays)?			
Want to go to school? Seem disappointed if he or she must miss a day?			
Demonstrate beginning skills in reading, writing, and mathematics?			
Accept responsibility and complete work independently?			
Handle stressful situations without becoming overly upset or aggressive?			

Child's Name _____ Age _____

Observer _____ Date _____

DEVELOPMENTAL CHECKLIST

BY NINE AND TEN YEARS	Yes	No	Sometimes
Does the child . . .			
Continue to gain in height and weight?			
Exhibit improving coordination (running, climbing, riding a bike, writing)?			
Handle stressful situations without losing control or becoming overly upset or violent?			
Construct sentences using reasonably correct grammar (nouns, adverbs, verbs, adjectives)?			
Understand concepts of time, distance, space, volume?			
Express thoughts clearly?			
Understand simple abstract concepts?			
Have one or two "best friends"?			
Maintain friendships over time?			
Approach challenges with a reasonable degree of self-confidence?			
Play cooperatively and follow group instructions?			
Begin to show an understanding of moral standards (right from wrong, fairness, honesty, good from bad)?			
Look forward to and enjoy school most days?			
Appear to hear well, listen attentively, respond appropriately?			
Enjoy reasonably good health with few episodes of illness or health-related complaints?			
Have a good appetite and enjoy mealtimes?			
Take care of own personal hygiene without assistance?			
Sleep through the night, waking up refreshed and energetic?			

Child's Name _____   **Age** _____

Observer _____   **Date** _____

DEVELOPMENTAL CHECKLIST

BY ELEVEN AND TWELVE YEARS	Yes	No	Sometimes
Does the child . . .			
Continue to grow (gain in height and maintain a healthy weight, not too thin or too heavy)?			
Understand changes associated with puberty or have an opportunity to learn and ask questions?			
Have good vision or wear glasses; not complain of headaches or blurred vision?			
Have straight posture (no curving of the spine or other abnormality)?			
Seem energetic and not chronically fatigued?			
Remain focused on tasks and complete assignments?			
Remember and carry out complex instructions?			
Sequence, order, and classify objects?			
Use longer and more complex sentence structure?			
Engage in conversation; tell jokes and riddles?			
Enjoy playing organized games and team sports?			
Respond to anger-invoking situations without resorting to violence or physical aggression?			
Begin to understand and solve complex mathematical problems?			
Accept blame for actions on most occasions?			
Participate in and enjoy competitive activities?			
Accept and carry out responsibility in a dependable manner?			
Go to bed willingly and wake up refreshed?			
Take pride in personal appearance and hygiene?			

Child's Name _____ Age _____

Observer _____ Date _____

DEVELOPMENTAL CHECKLIST

BY THIRTEEN AND FOURTEEN YEARS	Yes	No	Sometimes
Does the child…			
Continue to experience growth and changes associated with puberty?			
Have sufficient energy to participate in school and extracurricular activities?			
Demonstrate improved handeye coordination?			
Think through situations and anticipate the potential outcomes and/or consequences?			
Like school and show interest in learning new material?			
Plan and manage time wisely; complete homework and projects on time?			
Understand right from wrong and accept responsibility for own behaviors?			
Begin to develop empathy and consider others' viewpoints and perspectives?			
Read and comprehend material?			
Express thoughts and ideas clearly?			
Work cooperatively with classmates on projects?			
Have friends and do things with them outside of school?			
Understand and engage in humorous antics and interactions?			
Approach daily activities and unfamiliar tasks with reasonable self-confidence?			
Get adequate sleep (8–9 hours) and appear well-rested?			
Take pride in personal cleanliness and appearance most times?			
Maintain a healthy weight and consume a nutritious diet?			

Child's Name _____   **Age** _____

Observer _____   **Date** _____

DEVELOPMENTAL CHECKLIST

BY FIFTEEN AND SIXTEEN YEARS	Yes	No	Sometimes
Does the child...			
Continue to gain and exhibit self-confidence?			
Make and keep friends who have a positive influence on behavior?			
Set and achieve established goals?			
Understand complex problems and cause–effect relationships?			
Communicate and express ideas logically?			
Take pride in personal accomplishments?			
Make independent decisions and follow through?			
Express emotions and resolve conflicts in a healthy manner?			
Develop improved emotional control and stability? Limit impulsivity and aggression?			
Show interest in school and extracurricular activities?			
Experience relatively good health (infrequent illness, energetic, appropriate weight)?			
Respect limits and rules set by adults (on most occasions)?			
Have a trusted and supportive adult with whom to talk?			
Avoid peer pressure to engage in drugs and alcohol?			
Use appropriate protective gear when participating in sports, outdoor activities, or work?			

Child's Name _____ Age _____

Observer _____ Date _____

DEVELOPMENTAL CHECKLIST

BY SEVENTEEN AND EIGHTEEN YEARS	Yes	No	Sometimes
Does the child...			
Make independent decisions and assume personal responsibility for outcomes?			
Set realistic goals and take steps to achieve them?			
Have and acknowledge a clear sexual identity?			
Demonstrate effective work and study habits?			
Use analytical thinking to solve complex problems?			
Express ideas with clarity and logical thought? Answer questions appropriately?			
Have a positive outlook on life?			
Exhibit emotional stability and decreased conflict with family?			
Seek advice appropriately?			
Show initiative in achieving independence from family?			
Maintain a healthy lifestyle (diet, activity, sleep, safety)?			
Demonstrate moral maturity in social behaviors?			
Possess problem-solving, communication, and intellectual skills and use them when confronted with adversity?			

APPENDIX B

Selected Screening and Assessment Instruments

EXAMPLES OF SCREENING TESTS

Ages and Stages Questionnaires (ASQ) is a monitoring system for assessing children's development in five areas: communication, personal-social, problem-solving, fine motor, and gross motor. Questionnaires are available for children 4, 6, 8, 10, 12, 14, 16, 18, 20, 22, 24, 27, 30, 33, 36, 42, 48, 54, and 60 months of age. Families complete the questionnaires based on their observations. Forms require two to three minutes to score. Spanish, French, Korean, and other language versions of the questionnaires are available.

GS Early Screening Profiles test children two to seven years of age for cognitive, language, social, self-help, and motor skills; includes information provided by families, teachers, and child care providers.

Battelle Developmental Screening Test is a screening tool that includes 96 items from the Battelle Developmental Inventory that can be used to assess children, birth to eight years, in five domains: communication, cognitive, personal-social, motor, and adaptive. This instrument is effective for assessing typical development, school readiness, and identification of children with disabilities.

Beck Depression Inventory-Second Edition (BDI-II) provides a quick screening test for identifying depression and rating its severity (number values are assigned to the adolescent's responses).

Denver Developmental Screening Test (Denver II) is appropriate for testing children from birth to six years of age in four developmental areas: personal-social, language, fine motor, and gross motor. Ratings of the child's behavior during testing can be recorded.

Developmental Activities Screening Inventory (DASI II) screens children one month to five years; a nonverbal test especially useful for children with hearing or language disorders; adaptations for children with vision problems are also offered.

Developmental Indicators for the Assessment of Learning, 3rd Edition (DIAL-3) is designed to screen children ages three to six years, eleven months, in five developmental domains: motor, concepts, communication, self-help, and social. A Spanish-language version is available. *Speed DIAL-3* is an abbreviated version of the test that includes items for motor, language, and concepts development and can be administered in less than 15 minutes. New versions of these tests are currently being tested.

First Steps: Screening Test for Evaluating Preschoolers can be used with children two years, nine months to six years, two months on cognitive, communication, and motor skills; an Adaptive Behavior Checklist and a Social-Emotional Scale are included as well as a Parent–Teacher Scale related to the child's behavior at home and at school.

EXAMPLES OF ASSESSMENT INSTRUMENTS

APGAR Scoring System is administered at one minute and again at five minutes after birth; the APGAR assesses muscle tone, respiration, color, heartbeat, and reflexes for a maximum score of 10. The information is used to determine which infants may require special care.

Assessment, Evaluation, and Programming Systems (AEPS) for Infants and Children, 2nd Edition (volume 2, birth to three, three to six; volumes 3 and 4, curriculum interventions for birth to three, three to six) is an authentic, family-friendly system for assessing very young children. It ties together assessment outcomes with early intervention strategies that are activity based and family centered. Test results can be used to determine a child's eligibility for services, establish IEP/IFSP goals, and evaluate intervention effectiveness.

Audiology, that is, hearing assessment of infants and children, requires clinical testing by a trained technician. It is *imperative*, however, in terms of early identification, for teachers and families to record and report their observations whenever they suspect a child is not hearing well. Warning signs include:

- Pulling or banging on an ear.
- Drainage from the ear canal.
- Failing to respond or looking puzzled when spoken to.
- Requesting frequent repetitions—What? Huh?
- Speaking in too loud or too soft of a voice.
- Articulating or discriminating sounds poorly.

Bayley Scales of Infant Development II Assessment evaluates both motor and cognitive development. The age range has been expanded to cover children from one month to three years, six months. The Mental Scales and the Motor Scales are separate instruments.

Brigance Diagnostic Inventory of Early Development II (IED-II) is a criterion-referenced instrument for assessing children, birth through six years, in multiple

developmental domains: fine and gross motor, speech and language, knowledge and comprehension, self-help, and pre-academic skills (basic reading, mathematics, and writing readiness). Test results can be used for goal-setting and curriculum planning but are not intended for determining a child's eligibility for special services.

Child Behavior Checklist (CBCL) is a standardized rating scale commonly used to assess children for emotional, social, and behavioral problems (e.g., aggression, defiance, attention deficit, anxious-depressed, withdrawn). Two versions of the test are available—one for two- to three-year-olds, another for four- to eighteen-year-olds. Parents rate the child on a hundred items which are then scored and used to develop a behavioral profile. A *Teacher's Report Form* and *Youth Self-Report Form* are also available.

Early Childhood Environmental Rating Scale-Revised (ECERS-R) is a well-respected, culturally sensitive assessment tool for evaluating classroom environments, including space, materials, activities, language, personal care routines, communication, program structure, and family/staff interaction. Additional versions are available for assessing infant/toddler (ITERS-R), family home child care (FDCRS), and school-age care environments (SACERS).

Hawaii Early Learning Profile (HELP) is a user- and family-friendly assessment instrument designed for monitoring children's (birth through age three) developmental progress and developing play-based interventions. Developmental milestones for each of the six domains are outlined on an easy-to-read chart. HELP fosters an interdisciplinary and family-centered approach.

Home Observation for Measurement of the Environment (HOME) is the best known and most widely used in-home inventory. Scales range from infancy to middle childhood; each version assesses the physical environment as well as the social, emotional, and cognitive support available to the child. A modified version, *Supplement to the HOME for Impoverished Families (SHIF)*, is available for assessing the home environment of children who live in poverty.

Kaufman Assessment Battery for Children, 2nd Edition (KABC-II) is a "culturally fair" test developed to assess the cognitive abilities of children ages three to eighteen years. Test items are designed to minimize the effects of verbal, gender, and ethnic bias.

Kaufman Survey of Early Academic and Language Skills (K-SEALS) assesses three- to seven-year-olds' reception and expressive language skills as well as concepts related to numbers, counting, letters, and words; includes an articulation survey.

Learning Accomplishment Profile—Diagnostic Edition (LAP-D) can be used to assess children aged two years, six months to six years on fine motor (writing and manipulative skills), gross motor (body and object movement), matching and counting (viewed as cognitive tasks), and language skills (comprehension and object naming).

Learning Accomplishment Profile—Revised (LAP-R) is a criterion-referenced instrument designed to assess children's development across seven domains.

A modified version, the *Early Learning Accomplishment Profile (Early LAP)*, is available for use with children whose functional development ranges from birth to three years.

Minnesota Multiphasic Personality Inventory—Adolescent (MMPI-A) is used to evaluate adolescents for a variety of mental health disorders, including family conflict, substance abuse, defiant behavior, and depression.

Neonatal Behavioral Assessment Scale (NBAS—often referred to as the Brazelton) assesses behavioral responses in full-term infants up to 28 days of age. A significant modification of the NBAS is the *Kansas Supplement (NBAS-K)*. It adds a number of critical parameters as well as assessing the infant's typical behavior (state) and optimal behavior (the only focus of the original NBAS).

Peabody Developmental Motor Scales (PDMS-2) are used to evaluate children from birth through five years of age in fine motor (grasping, eye–hand coordination, and manual dexterity) and gross motor development (reflexes, balance, locomotion, throwing, and catching). Strategies for remediation are also included.

Peabody Picture Vocabulary Test, 4th Edition (PPVT-IV) is a norm-referenced test that can be administered in 10 to 15 minutes to assess receptive language and verbal ability; appropriate for use with children thirty months and older. A Spanish version is also available.

Preschool Language Scale-4 (PLS-4) can be used to assess children, birth through six years, on auditory comprehension, articulation, grammatical forms, and basic concept development. A Spanish version based on cultural variations is also available.

The Snellen E or *Illiterate E* eye test is an instrument commonly used for assessing young children's visual acuity (knowing the alphabet is not required). Observation of behavioral indicators also plays an important role in identifying children who may have a vision problem:

- Rubbing eyes frequently or closing or covering one eye.
- Constantly stumbling over or running into things.
- Complaining of frequent headaches.
- Blinking excessively when looking at books or reading.
- Brushing hand over eyes as if trying to get rid of a blur.

Healthy eye development has important long-term implications. A nationwide public health program called InfantSEE® was initiated in 2005 to promote early detection and treatment of vision problems. Infants can receive free screening and eye care provided by participating optometrists. Observations are also useful for noting early signs of potential vision problems:

- Observing the infant's ability to focus on an object.
- Watching for uncoordinated eye movements such as crossed or wandering eyes.

- Checking for a blink reflex.
- Seeing if the infant can visually follow (track) an object, such as a toy, as it is moved in a 180-degree arc.

Woodcock-Johnson III (COG) can be used to assess adolescent cognitive abilities and to identify learning disabilities.

Work Sampling System (WSS) is a unique approach for documenting authentic and ongoing evaluation of children's developmental progress; it uses a combination of portfolio development (with samples of child's work) and checklists for data collection. Assessments are conducted three times during the course of one year and provide teachers with feedback on effective instructional strategies as well as on how children are responding; appropriate for children preschool to fifth grade.

APPENDIX C

Resources for Families and Professionals

Many resources are available to families, teachers, and service providers who work with children. These resources are provided at the community, state, and national levels and fall into two major categories: direct services and information sources.

DIRECT SERVICES

Developmental screenings are available through a number of local agencies and organizations. In addition, most communities offer an array of services and programs designed to help families cope with and meet the special needs and challenges of caring for a child with developmental disabilities. Some agencies also provide technical assistance to educators and other professionals who are working with these children. Often, the agencies themselves serve as a valuable networking resource because they are familiar with other community-based services, assistance programs, and trained specialists.

Examples of Community Services and Resources for Families

- Child Find screening programs
- Interagency Coordinating Councils (ICCs)
- Early childhood centers and therapeutic programs for exceptional children
- Public health departments at city, county, and state levels
- Local public school districts, especially the special services divisions
- Hospitals, medical centers, and well-child clinics
- University-Affiliated Programs (UAPs)
- Head Start and Even Start programs
- Mental health centers
- State-supported low-cost health insurance for children
- Parent support groups

- Service groups that provide respite care, transportation, or financial assistance
- Marriage counseling programs
- Philanthropic organizations such as the Lion's Club (glasses), Shriners, and Make a Wish Foundation
- Professional practitioners: pediatricians, nurses, psychologists, audiologists, ophthalmologists, early childhood specialists, educators, speech-language therapists, occupational and physical therapists, and social workers

Examples of National and Professional Organizations

There are also many national organizations that offer extensive information as well as direct assistance to children and families with specific needs. Contact information can usually be found in local telephone directories, the *Encyclopedia of Associations* (at the library), or on the Internet. For example:

- Allergy and Asthma Foundation *www.aafa.org*
- American Council of the Blind *www.acb.org*
- American Diabetes Association *www.diabetes.org*
- The American Foundation of the Blind *www.afb.org*
- American Heart Association *www.americanheart.org*
- American Society for Deaf Children *www.deafchildren.org*
- The Autism Society of America *www.autism-society.org*
- Children's Craniofacial Association *www.ccakids.org*
- Cleft Palate Foundation *www.cleftline.org*
- Council for Exceptional Children *www.cec.sped.org*
- Epilepsy Foundation of America *www.epilepsyfoundation.org*
- Learning Disabilities Association *www.ldanatl.org*
- National Association for Down Syndrome *www.nads.org*
- National Easter Seals *www.easter-seals.org*
- The United States Cerebral Palsy Athletic Association *www.uscpaa.org*

Examples of Technical Assistance Programs

There are also a number of programs and organizations whose purpose is to provide direct technical assistance to educational programs and agencies serving children with developmental disabilities. Many of these groups also offer instructional material. A sample of such agencies includes:

- American Printing House for the Blind at *www.aph.org*. This group produces materials and services for children with visual impairments, including talking

books, magazines in Braille, and large-type books as well as materials intended for educators of blind or visually impaired children.

- Head Start Resource Access Projects (RAPs). Their purpose is to assist Head Start programs in providing comprehensive services to children with developmental problems.
- National Early Childhood Technical Assistance Center (NECTAC) at *www. nectac.org*. This agency provides many forms of assistance to federally funded early-childhood programs and projects (IDEA) serving children with disabilities.
- National Dissemination Center for Children with Disabilities at *http://nichcy.org*. This organization serves as a central source for information about disabilities, early intervention, research, law, and parent materials. A bilingual site is also provided.
- National Technical Assistance Center for Children's Mental Health at *http://gucchdtacenter.georgetown.edu*. Information, training, and technical assistance are available to programs serving children and youth. The Center's goal is to assist programs in improving mental health outcomes for children and their families.

INFORMATION SOURCES

Extensive information is also published for families, teachers, and professionals who work with children who have developmental problems. Many professional journals, government publications, CD-ROMs, and reference books are available in public and university libraries. Special-interest groups and professional organizations also offer printed and online material focused on high-risk children and youth who have developmental delays.

Selected Examples of Information Resources

- Professional journals and periodicals such as the *Journal of the Division for Early Childhood, Topics in Early Childhood Special Education, Young Exceptional Children, Teaching Exceptional Children, Child Development, Developmental Psychology, Early Childhood Research Quarterly, Early Childhood Digest, Journal of Adolescent Research, Journal of Learning Disabilities,* and *Young Children*.
- Trade magazines for families, such as *Parents of Exceptional Children, Parenting,* and *Parents Magazine*.
- Government documents, reports, and pamphlets. These cover almost any topic related to child development, child care, early intervention, nutrition, parenting, and specific developmental problems. Publications can be obtained through the Superintendent of Documents, U.S. Government Printing Office, Washington, DC, 20401; many are available in local government buildings, including public libraries, and on the Internet.

- Bibliographic indexes and abstracts usually located in university, college, and large public libraries. These are particularly useful to students and practitioners who need to locate information quickly on a specific topic. Examples of several include:
  - *The Review of Child Development*
  - *Current Topics in Early Childhood Education*
  - Electronic journals and serials such as *Early Childhood Research & Practice, Networks* (online journal for teacher research), *Parent News, Contemporary Issues in Early Childhood, Future of Children, Health Child Care,* and *Bulletin of the World Association of Early Childhood Educators*

Examples of Professional Organizations that Focus on Child and Adolescent Issues

- American Academy of Pediatrics *www.aap.org*
- American Association on Intellectual and Developmental Disabilities *www.aaidd.org*
- American Public Health Association *www.apha.org*
- American Speech, Language, Hearing Association (ASHA) *www.asha.org*
- Association for Childhood Education International *www.acei.org*
- Association for Retarded Citizens (ARC) *www.thearc.org*
- Center for Effective Collaboration and Practice *http://cecp.air.org*
- Center for Mental Health in Schools *http://smhp.psych.ucla.edu*
- Children's Defense Fund *www.childrensdefense.org*
- Council for Exceptional Children (CEC) *www.cec.sped.org*
- Early Childhood Resource Center *www.rti.org*
- Early Head Start National Resource Center *www.ehsnrc.org*
- March of Dimes *www.modimes.org*
- National Association for the Education of Young Children (NAEYC) *www.naeyc.org*
- National Association for Family Child Care *http://nafcc.net*
- National Association of Child Care Resource & Referral Agencies *www.naccrra.org*
- National Center for Cultural Competence *http://nccc.georgetown.edu*
- The National Dissemination Center for Children with Disabilities *www.nichcy.org*
- National Head Start Association *www.nhsa.org*
- National Parent Information Network (NPIN) *www.npin.org*

- Positive Behavioral Interventions & Supports *www.pbis.org*
- Special Olympics International *www.specialolympics.org*

CONCLUSION

Finding help for children with developmental delays and disabilities is not a simple matter. The issues are often complex; some children present tangles of interrelated developmental problems that tend to become more complex when not addressed during the crucial first five years of life. Therefore, effective intervention must begin early and be comprehensive, integrated, ongoing, and family-centered. It must also take into account multiple developmental areas at the same time. This effort requires teamwork on the part of specialists from many disciplines, service providers, and agencies working cooperatively with the child and family. It also requires an awareness of legislative acts and public policies that affect services for children with developmental problems and their families, as well as available resources and effective means of collaboration. Only then will children and families fully benefit from an early intervention team approach.

GLOSSARY

A

abstract   The ability to think and use concepts; an idea or theory.

achievement tests   Tests used to measure a child's academic progress (what the child has learned).

acquisition   The process of learning or achieving objectives (e.g., walking, counting, reading).

amniocentesis   Genetic-screening procedure in which a needle is inserted through the mother's abdomen into the sac of fluid surrounding the fetus to detect abnormalities such as Down syndrome or spina bifida; usually performed between the twelfth and sixteenth weeks.

analytical thinking   A cognitive process used when attempting to solve problems or make plans; identifying and evaluating the pros/cons of alternative solutions.

anencephaly   A birth defect resulting in malformation of the skull and brain; portions of these structures might be missing at birth.

at risk   Term describing children who might be more likely to have developmental problems due to certain predisposing factors such as low birth weight, neglect, or maternal drug addiction.

authentic assessment   A process of collecting and documenting information about children's developmental progress; data is gathered in children's naturalistic settings and from multiple sources.

autonomy   A sense of self as separate from others.

B

bilateral   Affecting both sides, as in loss of hearing in both ears.

binocular vision   Both eyes working together, sending a single visual image to the brain.

bonding   The establishment of a close, loving relationship between an infant and an adult, usually the mother and father; also called *attachment*.

bullying   Verbal and physical behavior that is hurtful, intentional, and repeatedly directed toward a person or child who is viewed as weaker.

C

cephalocaudal   Bone and muscular development that proceeds from head to toe.

cervix   The lower portion of the uterus that opens into the vagina.

cesarean section   The delivery of a baby through an incision in the mother's abdomen and uterus.

Child Find   A screening program designed to locate children with developmental problems through improved public awareness.

chronological   Events or dates in sequence in the passage of time.

cleft lip/cleft palate   Incomplete closure of the lip, palate (roof of the mouth), or both, resulting in a disfiguring deformity.

conception   The joining of a single egg or ovum from the female and a single sperm from the male.

concrete operational thought   Piaget's third stage of cognitive development; period when concepts of conservation and classification are understood.

conservation   The stage in children's cognitive development when they begin to understand that an object's physical qualities (e.g., weight, mass) remain the same despite changes in its appearance; for example, flattening a ball of Play-Doh does not affect its weight.

constructivism   A learning approach in which a child forms his or her own meaning through active participation.

continuity   Developmental progress that gradually becomes increasingly refined and complex.

cumulative   An add-on process, bit by bit or step by step.

CVS   Chorionic villus sampling; a genetic-screening procedure in which a needle is inserted and cells are removed from the outer layer of the placenta; performed between the eighth and twelfth weeks to detect some genetic disorders, such as Down syndrome.

cyber-bullying   Sending hurtful, threatening, or harassing messages via the Internet or cell phone.

D

deciduous teeth   Initial set of teeth that eventually fall out; often referred to as baby teeth.

deductive reasoning   A process of considering hypothetical alternatives before reaching a conclusion.

depth perception   Ability to determine the relative distance of objects from the observer.

descriptive praise   Words or actions that describe to a child specifically what she or he is doing correctly or well.

development   Refers to an increase in complexity, from simple to more complicated and detailed.

developmental sequence   A continuum of predictable steps along a developmental pathway of skill achievement.

developmental team   A team of qualified professionals, such as special educators, speech pathologists, occupational therapists, social workers, audiologists, nurses, and physical therapists, who evaluate a child's developmental progress and together prepare an intervention plan that addresses the child's special needs.

developmentally appropriate   A term used to describe learning experiences that are individualized based on a child's level of skills, abilities, and interests.

discrete behaviors   Behaviors that can clearly be observed and described: hitting, pulling hair, spitting.

domains   A term describing an area of development, such as physical, motor, social-emotional, or speech and language.

dysfluency   Repetition of whole words or phrases uttered without frustration and often at the beginning of a statement such as, "Let's go, let's go get some cookies."

E

ecology   In terms of children's development, refers to interactive effects between children and their family, child care situation, school, and everything in the wider community that affects their lives.

egocentricity   Believing that everything and everyone is there for your purpose.

egocentrism   An adolescent's belief in their own importance.

embryo   The cell mass from the time of implantation through the eighth week of pregnancy.

emerging literacy   Early experiences, such as being read and talked to, naming objects, and indentifying letters, that prepare a child for later reading, writing, and language development.

essential needs   Basic physical needs such as food, shelter, and safety as well as psychological needs such as love, security, and trust, required for survival and healthy development.

expressive language   Words used to verbalize thoughts and feelings.

F

Family Service Coordinator   An individual who serves as a family's advocate and assists them with identifying, locating, and making final arrangements with community services.

figurative language   Words or statements that have meaning other than their literal definition.

fine motor   Also referred to as manipulative skills; includes stacking blocks, buttoning and zipping, and toothbrushing.

fontanels   Small openings (sometimes called soft spots) in the infant's skull bones, covered with soft tissue. Eventually, they close.

food jag   A period when only certain foods are preferred or accepted.

formal operational thinking   Piaget's fourth stage of cognitive development; period when children are capable of using abstract thought to predict, test, and reason to arrive at a logical conclusion.

functional language   Language that enables children to get what they need or want.

G

gender   Reference to being either male or female.

genes   Genetic material that carries codes, or information, for all inherited characteristics.

gross motor   Large muscle movements such as locomotor skills (walking, skipping, swimming) and nonlocomotive movements (sitting, pushing, pulling, squatting).

growth   Physical changes leading to an increase in size.

H

hand dominance   Preference for using one hand over the other; most individuals are said to be either right- or left-handed.

hands-on learning   A curriculum approach that involves children as active participants, encouraging them to manipulate, investigate, experiment, and solve problems.

head circumference   Measurement of the head taken at its largest point (across forehead, around back of head, returning to the starting point).

holophrastic speech   Using a single word to express a complete thought.

I

imaginary audience   A component of egocentrism whereby an adolescent believes that others care about and notice their behavior and appearance.

implantation   The attachment of the blastocyst to the wall of the mother's uterus; occurs around the twelfth day.

in utero   Latin term for "in the mother's uterus."

inclusion programs   Community child care, school, and recreational facilities in which all children from the most gifted to the most disabled participate in the same activities. Inclusion is a federal law mandated by the Congress of the United States. Originally, it was referred to as *mainstreaming*.

intelligible   Language that can be understood by others.

interdependent   Affecting or influencing development in other domains.

intuition   Thoughts or ideas based on feelings or a hunch.

J

jargon   Unintelligible speech; in young children, it usually includes sounds and inflections of the native language.

L

linguistic code   Verbal expression that has meaning to the child.

logic   Process of reasoning based on a series of facts or events.

logical consequence   A planned response that is implemented if the child misbehaves.

low birth weight (LBW)   An infant who weighs less than 5.5 pounds (2500 grams) at birth regardless of age.

N

natural consequence   An outcome that occurs as a result of the behavior.

naturalistic settings   Environments that are familiar and part of children's everyday experiences, such as classrooms, care arrangements, and home.

nature vs. nurture   Refers to whether development is primarily due to biological and genetic forces (heredity/nature) or to external forces (environment/nurture).

neural connections   Organized linkages formed between brain cells as a result of learning.

neurological   Refers to the brain and nervous system.

norms   Age-level expectancies associated with the achievement of developmental skills.

normal (typical) development   Achievement of certain skills according to a fairly predictable sequence, although with many individual variations.

nurturing   Includes qualities of warmth, loving, caring, and attention to physical needs.

O

obesity   Although no uniform definition exists, experts usually consider a child whose height–weight ratio (BMI) exceeds the 85th percentile for age to be overweight, and obese if it is greater than the 95th percentile.

object permanence   Piaget's sensorimotor stage when infants understand that an object exists even when it is not in sight.

otitis media   An infection of the middle ear.

P

parallel play   Playing alongside or near another person but not involved in their activity.

placenta   A specialized lining that forms inside the uterus during pregnancy to support and nourish the developing fetus.

premature infant   An infant born before 37 weeks following conception.

proximodistal   Bone and muscular development that begins closest to the trunk, gradually moving outward to the extremities.

pruning   Elimination of neurons and neural connections that are not being used; this process strengthens developing connections the child is using.

pupil   The small, dark, central portion of the eye.

R

receptive language   Ability to understand words that are heard.

reciprocal   Exchanges between individuals or groups that are mutually beneficial (or hindering).

refinement   Progressive improvement in ability to perform fine and gross motor skills.

reflexive   Movements resulting from impulses of the nervous system that cannot be controlled by the individual.

respite care   Child care assistance given to families to allow them temporary relief from the demands of caring for a child with disabilities.

S

scientific reasoning   Critical thinking skills (identify, analyze, conclude) used to achieve a solution.

self-esteem   Feelings about one's self-worth.

sensory   Refers to the five senses: hearing, seeing, touching, smelling, and tasting.

sensory information   Information received through the senses: eyes, ears, nose, mouth, and touch.

sexting   Sending sexually explicit pictures or messages via cell phone.

solitary play   Playing alone.

sonogram   Visual image of the developing fetus created by directing high-frequency sound waves (ultrasound) at the mother's uterus; used to determine fetal age and physical abnormalities.

sphincter   The muscles necessary to accomplish bowel and bladder control.

spina bifida   A birth defect caused by a malformation of the baby's spinal column.

stammering   To speak in an interrupted or repetitive pattern; not to be confused with stuttering.

strabismus   Condition in which one or both eyes appear to be turned inward (crossed) or outward.

stranger anxiety   A cross-cultural phenomenon in which infants begin to show distress or fear when approached by persons other than their primary caregivers.

T

telegraphic speech   Uttering two-word phrases to convey a complete thought.

temperament   An individual's characteristic manner or style of response to everyday events, including degree of interest, activity level, and regulation of her or his own behavior.

teratogens   Harmful agents that can cause fetal damage (e.g, malformations, neurological, and behavioral problems) during the prenatal period.

transactional process   The give-and-take relationship between children, their primary caregivers, and daily events that influences behavior and developmental outcomes.

tripod grasp   Hand position whereby an object, such as a pencil, is held between the thumb and first and second fingers.

typical   Achievement of certain skills according to a fairly predictable sequence, although with many individual variations.

V

voluntary   Movements that can be willed and deliberately controlled and initiated by the individual.

Z

Zone of Proximal Development   Vygotsky's term for tasks that prove too difficult for children to master by themselves, but are able to do so with guidance or assistance.

zygote   The cell formed as a result of conception; called a zygote for the first 14 days.

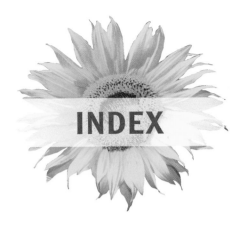

INDEX

NAEYC Standards and Outcomes	Chapter and Topical Location
STANDARD 4. Using Developmentally Effective Approaches	
4a. Understanding positive relationships and supportive interactions as the foundation of their work with young children. 4b. Knowing and understanding effective strategies and tools for early education, including appropriate uses of technology. 4c. Using a broad repertoire of developmentally appropriate teaching/learning approaches. 4d. Reflecting on own practice to promote positive outcomes for each child.	**Chapter 2:** Age-level Expectancies or Norms, pp. 27–28; Brain Growth and Development, pp. 28–30; TeachSource Video Connections: Brain Development in Infancy, p. 30; Typical Growth and Development, pp. 30–31; Developmental Domains, pp. 34–42. **Chapter 4:** Learning Activities, pp. 77, 84, 91, 98; Safety Concerns, pp. 78, 85, 92, 99; TeachSource Video Connections: Attachment in Infants and Toddlers, p. 88; Positive Behavior Guidance, p. 100. **Chapter 5:** Learning Activities, pp. 113–114, 122; Safety Concerns, pp. 114–115, 123; Positive Behavior Guidance, p. 124. **Chapter 6:** Learning Activities, pp. 137–138, 144–145, 152; Safety Concerns, pp. 139, 146, 153; Positive Behavior Guidance, p. 154. **Chapter 7:** Learning Activities, pp. 168, 175–176, 182–183; Safety Concerns, pp. 169–170, 177, 183–184; Positive Behavior Guidance, p. 184. **Chapter 8:** Learning Activities, pp. 197, 205; Safety Concerns, pp. 198, 206; Positive Behavior Guidance, p. 207. **Chapter 9:** Learning Activities, pp. 219, 226, 231; Safety Concerns, pp. 220–221, 227, 233–234; Positive Behavior Guidance, pp. 234–235. **Chapter 10:** TeachSource Video Connections: Children with Developmental Disabilities in the Classroom, p. 245; Is There a Problem?, pp. 247–249; When to Seek Help, p. 249; Screening Tests, pp. 252–254; IQ Tests, p. 254.
STANDARD 5. Using Content Knowledge to Build Meaningful Curriculum	
5a. Understanding content knowledge and resources in academic disciplines: language and literacy; the arts – music, creative movement, dance, drama, visual arts; mathematics; science, physical activity, physical education, health and safety; and social studies. 5b. Knowing and using the central concepts, inquiry tools, and structures of content areas or academic disciplines. 5c. Using own knowledge, appropriate early learning standards, and other resources to design, implement, and evaluate developmentally meaningful and challenging curriculum for each child.	**Chapter 4:** TeachSource Video Connections: Early Infant Language, p. 83, Fine Motor Development, p. 95; Developmental Applications for Families and Teachers, pp. 77, 84, 91, 98. **Chapter 5:** TeachSource Video Connections: Toddlers Cognitive Development, p. 120; Developmental Applications for Families and Teachers, p. 113–114, 122. **Chapter 6:** Developmental Applications for Families and Teachers, pp. 137–138, 144–145, 152; TeachSource Video Connections: Preschooler's Motor Development, p. 133, Social Skill Development, p. 150. **Chapter 7:** Developmental Applications for Families and Teachers, pp. 168, 175–176, 182–183; TeachSource Video Connections: Cognitive Development and Concrete Operations, p. 174. **Chapter 8:** Developmental Applications for Families and Teachers, pp. 197, 205; TeachSource Video Connections: Middle Childhood and Cognitive Development, p. 203. **Chapter 9:** TeachSource Video Connections: Technology and Learning, p. 223; Developmental Applications for Families and Teachers, pp. 219, 226, 231.

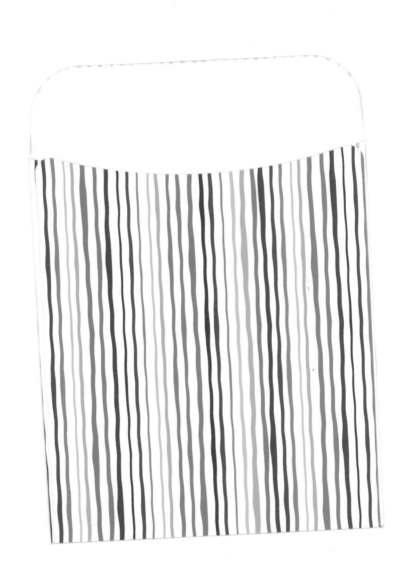

P9-BIK-044

STANDARD 2. Building Family and Community Relationships

2a. Knowing about and understanding diverse family and community characteristics. 2b. Supporting and engaging families and communities through respectful, reciprocal relationships. 2c. Involving families and communities in young children's development and learning.	**Chapter 1:** Families as Observers, pp. 14–15; Bioecological Theory, p. 9. **Chapter 2:** Growth, p. 24; Development, pp. 25–27; Gender Roles, pp. 31–32; Ecological Factors, pp. 32–33; Developmental Domains, pp. 34–42. **Chapter 3:** Threats to Optimum Fetal Development, pp. 57–61; Maternal Depression, pp. 63–64. **Chapter 4:** Developmental Applications for Families and Teachers, pp. 77, 84, 91, 98; Positive Behavior Guidance, p. 100. **Chapter 5:** Developmental Applications for Families and Teachers, pp. 113–114, 122; Positive Behavior Guidance, p. 124. **Chapter 6:** Developmental Applications for Families and Teachers, pp. 137–138, 144–145, 152; TeachSource Video Connections: Preschooler's Motor Development, p. 133, Preschoolars and Language Development, p. 142, Social Skill Development, p. 150; Positive Behavior Guidance, p. 154. **Chapter 7:** Developmental Applications for Families and Teachers, pp. 168, 175–176, 182-183. **Chapter 8:** Developmental Applications for Families and Teachers, pp. 197, 205. **Chapter 9:** Developmental Applications for Families and Teachers, pp. 219, 226, 232. **Chapter 10:** When to Seek Help, p. 249; Observing and Recording, pp. 250–251; Screening Tests, p. 252–254.

STANDARD 3. Observing, Documenting, and Assessing To Support Young Children and Families

3a. Understanding the goals, benefits, and uses of assessment – including its use in development of appropriate goals, curriculum, and teaching strategies for young children. 3b. Knowing about assessment partnerships with families and with professional colleagues to build effective learning environments. 3c. Knowing about and using observation, documentation, and other appropriate assessment tools and approaches, including the use of technology in documentation, assessment, and data collection. 3d. Understanding and practicing responsible assessment to promote positive outcomes for each child, including the use of assistive technology for children with disabilities.	**Chapter 1:** Data Gathering, pp. 13–15; Families as Observers, pp. 14–15; TeachSource Video Connections: Portfolio Assessment, p. 19. **Chapter 3:** TeachSource Video Connections: Prenatal Assessment, p. 57; Newborn Assessment, p. 63. **Chapter 4:** Developmental Alerts, pp. 77, 85, 92, 99. **Chapter 5:** Developmental Alerts, pp. 114, 122–123. **Chapter 6:** Developmental Alerts, pp. 138–139, 145, 153. **Chapter 7:** Developmental Alerts, pp. 169, 176–177, 183. **Chapter 8:** Developmental Alerts, pp. 198, 205. **Chapter 9:** Developmental Alerts, pp. 220, 226–227, 232–233. **Chapter 10:** Case Study, pp. 241–242; TeachSource Video Connection: Including Children with Developmental Disabilities, p. 245; Is There a Problem?, pp. 247–249; When to Seek Help, p. 249; Information Gathering, pp. 250–255; Diagnosis and Referral, pp. 255–257.

(Continued on back cover)